MAKE MONEY

IN

REAL ESTATE
TAX LIENS

How to Guarantee
Returns Up to 50%

CHANTAL HOWELL CAREY
BILL CAREY

WILEY

John Wiley & Sons, Inc.

Library of Congress Cataloging-in-Publication Data:
Howell Carey, Chantal.
   Make money in real estate tax liens : how to guarantee returns up to 50% / Chantal Howell Carey, Bill Carey.
      p. cm.
   Includes index.
   ISBN 0-471-69286-7 (cloth)
      1. Real estate investment--United States. 2. Tax liens--United States. 3. Foreclosure--United States. 4. Real property--Purchasing--United States. I. Carey, Bill, 1951- II. Title.

HD255.H658   2005
332.63'24-dc22   2004063704

Printed in the United States of America.

10 9 8 7 6 5 4 3

With love to all our family, friends, and dedicated students!
May you always have more blessings than you need!

CONTENTS

PREFACE

Real estate tax liens are very powerful and safe investments. In a comprehensive step-by-step method we will show you how to obtain the maximum financial yield with a minimum of risk in a time of historically low interest rates by investing in real estate tax liens.

Real estate tax liens are liens placed against the title to real property by an entity of the government for unpaid taxes. Federal tax liens are placed against the title to real estate by the Internal Revenue Service for unpaid federal income taxes. State tax liens are placed against the title to real estate by a state income taxing authority for unpaid state income taxes. Local tax liens are placed against the title to real estate by the county or city property taxing authority for unpaid property taxes.

Whatever the source of the tax lien, there is a huge opportunity to make tons of money. The taxpayer cannot sell their property and give clear title to a buyer unless the tax lien is paid off. This is the key to how this investment works.

In the event the taxpayer does not pay the tax, after a period of time the taxing authority will foreclose on the property. The taxing authority sells the property to the highest bidder at the tax lien sale.

As the winning bidder, you receive either the title to the property or a tax lien certificate from the taxing authority. The taxpayer does not automatically lose the property. They have a statutory time period to come up with the back taxes and penalties and interest to redeem their property. As the holder of the tax lien certificate you are entitled to receive all of these payments.

Number of States

Of the 50 states, 27 or 28 (depending on how you categorize them), the District of Columbia, most U.S. territories, and the provinces of Canada issue tax lien certificates. More than 1,400 local governments in these states, territories, and provinces issue tax lien certificates. This is what creates the investment opportunity for you.

Florida is a state that issues tax lien certificates. Within six months of the property taxes being unpaid, they conduct a tax lien sale. The winning bidder pays the unpaid property taxes, plus penalties and interest. The winning bidder is issued a tax lien certificate. The county owed the property tax receives its money immediately.

California is a state that by law can issue tax lien certificates in all of its 58 counties, but it does not issue tax lien certificates. Local governments wait for five years of unpaid property taxes to accumulate before a foreclosure sale occurs. At the foreclosure sale the winning bidder must pay a minimum of the five years of unpaid property taxes, plus penalties and interest. The county owed the tax receives nothing for five years. Too bad if they needed the money to provide county services. (And which state has money problems?)

Two Ways to Make Money

As a holder of the tax lien certificate you have two ways to make money. The first is the interest and penalties on the tax lien certificate. In Florida this interest you receive may be as high as 18 percent. In Texas the penalties you receive for the second year are 50 percent!

The interest rate on the tax lien certificate is set by the taxing authority. This interest must be paid by the taxpayer in addition to the tax lien itself for the lien to be paid off. In some states, and for some tax lien certificates, this interest rate can be quite hefty. In Iowa the tax lien certificate interest rate is 24 percent per annum or 2 percent per month.

Real Estate Tax Lien Certificates Interest Rates

Alabama	6%	Montana	10%
Arizona	16%	Nebraska	14%
Colorado	10%	New Hampshire	18%
Florida	18%	New Jersey	20%–24%
Georgia	10%	New York	10%
Illinois	18%	North Dakota	9%–12%
Indiana	Varies	Oklahoma	8%
Iowa	24%	Rhode Island	6%–18%
Kentucky	12%	South Carolina	8%
Louisiana	17%	South Dakota	12%
Maryland	Varies	Tennessee	10%
Massachusetts	14%–16%	Vermont	6%–12%
Mississippi	17%	West Virginia	12%
Missouri	10%	District of Columbia	18%

The second way you as the holder of the tax lien certificate can make money is in the event the taxpayer does not redeem or pay off the tax lien certificate. Then, as its holder, you can convert the tax lien certificate into a tax deed for title to the property.

Receive Super-High Rewards with Super-Low Risks

When you invest in real estate tax lien certificates, as you can see from the Real Estate Tax Lien Certificates Interest Rates table, you receive super-high rewards. You also invest with super-low risks.

All of the tax lien certificates are secured by real property. Every property has been appraised by a government agency at 10 to 100 times the amount of the tax lien certificate. Some states insure the tax lien certificates. If the taxpayer does not pay the tax lien certificate holder, the government entity will.

In Arizona, if the tax lien certificate holder is not paid back all their principal and interest, after three years the tax lien certificate holder automatically receives a treasurer's deed for the property. All mortgage liens are wiped out by the treasurer's deed. This means the investor gets title to the property free and clear!

Let us look at some numbers. Say you bought a tax lien certificate in Sedona, Arizona. You paid $4,000 for the certificate. Let us say the property is vacant land worth $100,000. There is a first mortgage loan on the property for $40,000. This loan is held by a private party. By the way, it would make no difference if the first mortgage was held by an institutional lender.

Sedona, Arizona

Property Value	$100,000
First Mortgage	$40,000
Tax Lien Certificate	$4,000

One of two things is going to happen for you. The taxpayer will pay you 16 percent annual interest on your $4,000 tax lien certificate for up to three years plus pay you back your principal.

Tax Lien Certificate	$4,000
Interest Rate	×16%
Annual Interest	$640
For Three Years	×3
Total Interest	$1,920
Plus Principal	$4,000
Total Return	$5,920

Or, after neither the taxpayer nor the holder of the first mortgage steps in to pay you, you automatically receive a treasurer's deed to the property. You have now paid $4,000 for a property that is worth more than $100,000. And, you own it free and clear. The first mortgage of $40,000 held by the private party is wiped out!

Sedona, Arizona

Property Value	$100,000
First Mortgage	0
Your Equity in Property	$100,000

In Maryland, if the tax lien certificate holder is not paid back, the taxpayer's property must be foreclosed after two years and title given to the investor. State law allows for foreclosure after only 60 days if that is what the tax lien certificate holder wants.

Who Buys Real Estate Tax Lien Certificates?

Real estate tax lien certificates are held in the investment portfolios of major banks, brokerage houses, and institutional investors. We feel that with the continuing paltry interest rates being offered around the country for certificates of deposit and money market accounts, plus a risk-filled stock market, there is a broader market for tax lien certificates.

This book, *Make Money in Real Estate Tax Liens: How to Guarantee Returns Up to 50%,* is designed to fill an important niche for the small to midsize investor who wants super-high rewards with super-low risks. You can invest in tax lien certificates with very small amounts of cash.

You could fund your Roth IRA or other retirement vehicles with an investment in tax lien certificates. Or, you could make a more substantial investment and still feel comfortable about the safety of your money.

Best Places to Buy Real Estate Tax Lien Certificates

We show investors who live in areas that issue real estate tax lien certificates where the best places to buy those tax lien certificates are. We show investors who live in areas that do not issue tax lien certificates how to travel to areas like Colorado, Florida, or Arizona for fun in the snow or sun and purchase real estate tax lien certificates as part of a working vacation.

With the traditional investment climate still uncertain, this book gives you the insider information necessary to make a successful entrance into this exciting new investment opportunity. Good reading and successful investing!

INTRODUCTION

O ver the years we have traveled throughout the country teaching real estate, financial, motivational, and interpersonal skills seminars. We are always striving to be on the leading edge.

Regarding real estate, we have taught everything from buying and selling it creatively as an individual or an investor to core classes for licensing and passing real estate broker's exams. Just about anything you can think of related to real estate, we have taught to someone somewhere!

With a new millennium come new ideas. We have distilled the knowledge and experience we have gained from buying and selling real estate for ourselves and our clients and helping our students over the last three decades.

Make Money in Real Estate Tax Liens: How to Guarantee Returns Up to 50% is the eighth real estate book we have written. Our first book, *How to Sell Your Home Without a Broker* (1990), is in its fourth edition. Robert J. Bruss, a nationally syndicated real estate columnist, wrote: "On a scale of 1 to 10 this book rates a 10." Bruss picked this book as a Top Ten book for 2004.

Our fifth book, *Going Going Gone! Auctioning Your Home for Top Dollar* (1996), was also written to benefit the homeowner in the selling of a home. Like *How to Sell Your Home Without a Broker,* our auctioning book was designed to show you how to sell your home successfully without paying a real estate commission.

Our sixth book, *The New Path to Real Estate Wealth: Earning Without Owning* (2004), was the first book in our new series designed specifically for active real estate investors. The Win Going In! series is designed to take you from being a novice real estate investor to being an expert real estate investor.

The New Path to Real Estate Wealth: Earning Without Owning takes you from the real estate basics through the four best ways to make money in real estate. From flipping property to assigning contracts to controlling property using options to buying discount mortgage paper, it teaches you everything you need to know to become a successful real estate investor. In all four areas we train you how to make money without buying or owning property!

Our premise for the Win Going In! series is that no matter what kind of real estate investment you are going to make, you have to win going in. It is no longer enough to make money on the back end of a deal or make a profit when you get out of a deal. The deal must have a profit built in on the front end or else you should not do it at all.

Our seventh book, *Quick Cash in Foreclosures* (2005) was the second book in the Win Going In! series. In it we show you how to make money going into to a foreclosure deal. It is a hands-on book that teaches you how to enter the real estate foreclosure market and make deals happen. What is unique about the book is that we show you how to have a Quick Cash investment strategy that you can successfully implement with little or no investment capital. This book was also picked by Robert J. Bruss as a Top Ten book for 2004.

Our philosophy is that you need to be in control of your investments. Counting on a stock broker, investment adviser, accountant, general partner, or real estate investment fund leaves you completely out of control. When you are an active real estate investor, you are the one calling the shots. You are the one responsible for your successes and failures.

Make Money in Real Estate Tax Liens: How to Guarantee Returns Up to 50% is the third book in the Win Going In! series. In this book we teach you how to make money investing in real estate tax liens. We build on the foreclosure strategies from *Quick Cash in Foreclosures.*

Once a real estate tax lien is placed against real property one of two things will happen. Either the lien will be paid off by the owner of the property or an investor will buy the lien from the taxing agency that filed it. If the owner of the property does not redeem the lien from the investor, the investor can foreclose on the property and gain an ownership interest.

By investing in real estate tax liens, you can control a property for pennies on the dollar. Your guarantee is you have the power of foreclosure in the event you are not paid back your original tax lien investment plus hefty interest and penalties. Investing in real estate tax liens is definitely a win going in!

We recommend you read this book in a particular way. Bring a lot of energy to your reading. This does not mean that you must necessarily read the book quickly, though that is fine with us. We want you to be excited about the material. We want you to win going in as you read.

If you find yourself bogging down, stop reading. The material is designed to be comprehended in bursts. See if you can go from one light bulb turning on in your mind to the next. As it gets brighter and brighter you will find yourself energized.

Our purpose for the Win Going In! series is to teach you all our real estate knowledge and expertise. We want to be the Brain Trust for your successful real estate investments and your lucrative financial investments. You will know you are being a successful investor after you make money on your first deal.

We would love to hear from you about your successes. Also, we want to hear what is working and what is not working for you. Please email us at thetrustee@hotmail.com or contact us through our publisher, John Wiley & Sons.

We are available to partner deals. We are available to help you put your deals together for a fee. Good luck and good deals!

Chantal & Bill Carey

CHAPTER 1

What Are Real Estate Tax Liens?

Government claims against property for unpaid taxes are called liens. The federal government can place a lien against your property for unpaid federal income taxes. If you live in a state where there is a state income tax, your state government can place a lien against your property for unpaid state income taxes.

In every state, U.S. territory (Guam, Puerto Rico, the U.S. Virgin Islands), and Canadian province or territory, the local government (city, county, or parish) sets and levies a real property tax. Property taxes are secured by the real property itself. This means that if they are not paid when due, the local taxing authority has the right to place a lien on the property. It could be said that property taxes are always a lien against the title to a property—even if they are current. Technically, property taxes are a lien that is due, but not yet payable.

Once a tax lien is placed against the title to a property, ownership rights are impacted. Lenders will not accept the property as collateral for a loan until the tax lien is paid. Tax liens also have priority over other liens. If there is to be a change of ownership, the tax lien must be paid off before clear title can be given to the new owner. If a property is foreclosed on, the tax lien will have priority over other existing liens. (This is an important point for successful tax lien investing to which we will return.)

Real Estate Tax Lien Investing

Real estate tax lien investing is a real estate arena most people have no idea even exists. Of the few people who have heard of real estate tax lien investing fewer still know anything about how to succesfully make an investment.

The biggest reason for this is each state, territory, or province has different laws and procedures. In fact the laws and procedures can vary county by county! Some states do not even sell tax liens.

Investors who do not know about real estate tax lien investing will continue to invest in an uncertain stock or bond market, put money into certificates of deposit, buy annuities from insurance companies, or, worse, make no investments at all. The sooner you start to invest in real estate tax liens, the more money you are going to make.

There is a simple method to use to make successful real estate tax lien investments. We are going to give you the knowledge and information so you can earn super-high returns with super-low risks.

Number of Properties

There are literally tens of thousands of properties with unpaid and delinquent property taxes. Any of these properties can be available to you as a potential real estate tax lien investment. Some of these properties are quite valuable. Most of these properties are remarkably average.

Investment Strategies

You can choose an investment strategy to buy the real estate tax lien on a property. This can earn you an annual return on your investment from 6 percent to 24 percent in interest alone. When you factor in how quickly your investment may be paid back and the penalties you are allowed to collect as the holder of the tax lien, you easily can have a guaranteed return of up to 50 percent!

Say you buy a real estate tax lien at a county tax lien auction for $4,000. The property owner redeems your tax lien within 30 days after you buy it. How much money will you make? You will receive your $4,000 back plus 1 percent interest for the 30 days if the property is in Kentucky, South Dakota, or West Virginia. This is $40. You will also receive a $125 penalty for the late fee for a total return of $165.

Real Estate Tax Lien	$4,000
Interest	$\times$ 1%
	$40
Penalty	+$125
Total Return	$165

What does a $165 return on a $4,000 investment in 30 days represent when computed as an annual return? Of the initial $4,000 investment, $165 is more than a 4 percent return. That return of 4 percent or more in 30 days computes to a 49.5 percent return annually!

$$\$165 / \$4,000 = 4.125\%$$
$$4.125\% \times 12 \text{ Months} = 49.5\%$$

Buy the Real Estate

You can choose an investment strategy to buy the real estate itself. You buy real estate tax liens as a way to control real estate with very small amounts of money. This is called leverage.

You may be able to obtain the deed to the property for the cost of the real estate tax lien and any legal fees involved. You may then rent these properties for monthly income and long-term wealth building. You could sell these properties for huge profits.

We are going to focus on the investment strategy of buying the real estate tax liens for maximum yield and profit. Because our strategy in real estate investing is Quick Cash, we want to make money quickly and with a minimum of problems.

We will talk about the benefits of acquiring the title to property by foreclosing on real estate tax liens. If that is your investment strategy, the material we present will give you the information you need to get involved in real estate tax liens and how to foreclose on them.

You may apply the Quick Cash strategy here as well. Once you complete the foreclosure process on your tax lien, you will acquire the deed to the property. You can then immediately sell the property, that is flip it, for quick cash.

We are going to take a deeper look into answering the question "What are real estate tax liens?" We will give you access to the material by presenting different facets or layers for you to digest. See how you do with the next batch of material.

Real Estate Tax Liens

A real estate tax lien is a monetary charge placed on real property resulting from nonpayment of debt or other unperformed duty. There are many types of real estate liens. They can be created by different events. We will be focusing on real estate liens arising from the nonpayment of property taxes.

A real estate property tax lien gives the taxing authority the power to enforce the payment of property taxes. The taxing authority also has the ability to charge interest and assess extra fees on the past due taxes.

The real estate tax liens, interest, and past due fees do not create cash for the taxing authority. They only place more pressure on the property owner to make the payments as soon as possible. If the taxes remain unpaid after a certain period of time, the taxing authority has the legal right to foreclose on the property.

Taxing Authority

The most common form of a taxing authority in the United States is the county government. County and other local government entities derive the majority of their revenues from property taxes. Property taxes are used to fund every type of local government service. These include police protection, fire protection, county court systems, public improvements, public hospitals, and—the big one—public schools. Property taxes that are collected provide the vast majority of funding for these services. Counties set their property tax rates based on their annual budgets. The amount of property taxes assessed equals the amount needed to cover all county expenses for the year.

If property owners do not pay their property taxes, this decreases a county's revenue. In fact a county has increased expenses to pay for enforcement actions to collect delinquent tax payments. It is for these reasons that these taxing authorities have such strong means of enforcement.

Real Estate Tax Lien Certificates

Some states provide a quick cash solution so that needed tax dollars can flow into the local government coffers. This is where your investment opportunity arises. These states allow taxing authorities to sell real estate tax lien certificates at a public auction. The real estate tax lien is sold to an investor. The investor pays off all the property taxes and fees that are due and payable. The investor receives a real estate tax lien certificate from the taxing authority as the paperwork that documents the real estate tax lien sale.

The purchase of a real estate tax lien certificate is not the same as purchasing title to the property. You are purchasing the rights associated with the real estate tax lien and not the rights of property ownership. You may eventually have a right to obtain the deed to the property, but, as we have said, this is another process and involves further action on your part.

After the sale of the tax lien you, the investor, are entitled to any additional interest, penalties, and fees associated with owning the tax lien. The taxing authority has received more of the funding it needs. The tax lien certificate is secured by the property. If the owner never pays up, the investor has a legal right to foreclose on the property, obtaining a deed and all rights of ownership.

Tax Lien Sales

Real estate tax liens are sold at auctions held by the taxing authority. These auctions are usually held once a year. There are several types of auction bidding, depending on your local procedures. We will talk about the different types of bids in Chapter 7.

Tax liens that are not sold at the auction, either through a lack of bidding or because there were no acceptable bids, will be sold by the county over the counter. This means that you can purchase these tax liens at a later date.

Being at the auction is not a condition for being able to make over the counter real estate tax lien purchases. You will even find that some taxing authorities allow you to purchase real estate tax liens by mail!

We recommend, however, that you buy them in person over the counter. There is less room for error when you are dealing face to face than trying to make an investment through the mail.

The Property Owner's Right of Redemption

After you have purchased a real estate tax lien certificate, each state allows the property owner a time period to pay the amount owed to the tax lien holder. Once the property owner pays off the principal, interest, penalties, and fees attached to the tax lien certificate, the tax lien certificate is considered extinguished. This payoff is called redeeming or redemption.

When the tax lien certificate is redeemed, this eliminates any right you may have to obtain the deed to the property. The right of redemption gives the property owner some time to repay the debt before their rights of ownership are lost forever. Each state specifies to its counties how long this period should last.

The Paperwork

As we have said, when you pay the delinquent real property taxes on behalf of a property owner, you receive as evidence of such payment a document called a tax lien certificate. Depending on your area the tax lien certificate may be called a tax certificate, a certificate of purchase, a certificate of sale, or four or five other names.

No matter what the tax lien certificate is called, real estate tax lien certificates are a real estate paper investment similar to buying discounted mortgages. They are also a real estate foreclosure investment.

When you pay the delinquent real property taxes on behalf of the property owner in Indiana you receive a tax certificate. You also receive with the tax certificate an assignment of the real property tax lien. Indiana law states:

> When a certificate of sale is issued under this section, the purchaser acquires a lien against the real property for the entire amount that he paid.

When you pay the delinquent real property taxes on behalf of the property owner in Iowa, Iowa law states:

> The delinquent tax lien transfers with the tax sale certificate.

To attract investors to pay delinquent property taxes, many states offer very high interest rates. For example, the 99 counties in Iowa offer returns of 24 percent annually or 2 percent per month or any fraction of a month. The District of Columbia, Florida, and New Hampshire pay 18 percent annual interest.

This high interest paid on tax lien certificates makes it look similar to real estate discounted mortgages. A real estate discount mortgage investor buys mortgages at a discount from a mortgage holder. This gives the mortgage holder immediate cash. (See our book *The New Path to Real Estate Wealth: Earning without Owning* for information on investing in discounted mortgages.)

In return the investor receives paperwork for their cash. The mortgage holder assigns the promissory note, which is the evidence of the debt, and the mortgage or trust deed, which is the lien against the property title, as the security for the debt to the investor.

After you pay a property owner's delinquent property taxes, you receive paperwork for your cash. The taxing authority gives you a tax certificate, which is the evidence of the property tax payment, and assigns the real estate tax lien, which is the lien against the property title, as the security for the payment to you.

First Lien

The real estate tax lien is always the first lien on property with very few exceptions. Indiana law states:

> When a certificate of sale is issued under this section, the purchaser acquires a lien against the real property for the entire amount that he paid. The lien of the purchaser is superior to all liens against the real property which exist at the time the certificate is issued.

Tax lien certificates are virtually unknown, high-yield, local government issued paper. They would be regarded as junk bonds if the tax lien certificates were issued by a private company. Unlike junk bonds, tax lien certificates are backed by a government agency. Better still, tax lien certificates are secured by real estate.

Super-High Returns

Compare what happens if you invest $25,000 in a bank certificate of deposit for 20 years and if you invest $25,000 in tax lien certificates over 20 years. Suppose you receive 4 percent interest with the bank certificate of deposit. How much money would you have after 20 years?

Certificate of Deposit

Investment	$25,000
Interest Rate	4%
Term	20 Years
Return	$54,778

Your $25,000 investment in the certificate of deposit will more than double. That seems okay, especially because there is no risk in your investment. A bank certificate of deposit is insured by a government agency, the Federal Deposit Insurance Corporation (FDIC) up to $100,000.

Suppose you receive 12 percent interest with Kentucky tax lien certificates. How much money would you have after 20 years?

Tax Lien Certificate

Investment	$25,000
Interest Rate	12%
Term	20 Years
Return	$241,157

Your $25,000 investment in the tax lien certificate will go up in value almost 10 times! Talk about a great return. What about the risk to your investment?

What risk? Your investment is guaranteed by a government agency, the local taxing authority, and is secured by real estate.

Retirement Programs

Consider the difference this would make to your retirement program. Open a self-directed Roth IRA, a SEP IRA, or a Keogh at age 35 and invest in tax lien certificates. At age 70, by investing $3,000 a year with an 18 percent annual return, you would have $5.5 million!

Tax Lien Certificate

Roth IRA

Investment	$3,000 Yearly
Interest Rate	18%
Term	35 Years
Return	$5,500,000

What would happen if you opened a Roth IRA at age 25? We will use the same numbers: $3,000 yearly, 18 percent interest rate, but for 45 years. You better stand up for this.

Tax Lien Certificate

Roth IRA

Investment	$3,000 Yearly
Interest Rate	18%
Term	45 Years
Return	$28,500,000

Too Good to Be True?

Yes, you won the lottery! We know what some of you are thinking. If these tax lien certificates are such good investments, then how come we have never heard about them? The bottom line is it is hard to get information on tax lien certificates. We are going to give you that information.

Banks, thrifts, finance companies, and credit unions do not sell tax lien certificates. In fact, no financial institution sells them. Stockbrokers, mortgage loan brokers, real estate brokers, or any other kind of brokers do not broker tax lien certificates. How come? They do not make a profit on them. You are the one who will make the profit!

Tax lien certificates are available in amounts ranging of less than $10 each to amounts of more than $100,000. Even if you have limited funds to invest, you could buy many small certificates in several different counties in the same state or even in different states.

In Chapter 2 we will show you the areas and entities that are involved in this investment opportunity. You are the one who will profit immensely by investing in tax lien certificates. Are you getting excited?

Who Files Real Estate Tax Liens?

Every state, territory, and province has laws and statutes that allow local governments to file real estate tax liens. Roughly half the states, most of the U.S. territories, and all of the Canadian provinces sell real estate tax liens to investors; however, many states do not sell real estate tax liens to investors.

How the states that do not sell real estate tax liens to investors handle delinquent tax liens varies. Once a tax lien is placed on a home in California, for example, the owner has five years to pay the delinquent taxes and associated interest, penalties, and fees. After that time period has passed, the taxing entity has the right to foreclose and sell the property.

Many of the states that do not sell tax liens can foreclose on a property only after a court order has authorized a foreclosure sale. Some of these states accept bids at the foreclosure sale based on the value of the property.

The states that sell real estate tax liens accept bids for the amount of the outstanding taxes. This can be a huge difference in the amount of money you, as an investor, have to invest. Your investment dollars go a lot further paying off a $5,000 property tax lien than having to pay the entire $100,000 value of the property.

This is not to say that the states that sell real estate tax liens all do it the same way. We may lump them together for discussion purposes because these states have similar procedures. But there are differences between these states. In some states that sell real estate tax liens, you can obtain a tax deed immediately. In others you must wait for a redemption period to expire.

If your investment goal is to obtain title to property rather than collect the interest and penalties by purchasing real estate tax liens, your course of action would be to check the procedures for tax sales for the states that do not sell real estate tax liens. In some of these states, once an order of foreclosure has been issued by the court, the process to obtain the title may be streamlined.

States That Sell Tax Liens	States That Do Not Sell Tax Liens
Alabama	Alaska
Arizona	Arkansas
Colorado	California
Florida	Connecticut
Illinois	Delaware
Indiana	Georgia
Iowa	Hawaii
Kentucky	Idaho
Louisiana	Kansas
Maryland	Maine
Massachusetts	Michigan
Mississippi	Minnesota
Missouri	Nevada
Montana	New Mexico
Nebraska	New York
New Hampshire	North Carolina
New Jersey	Ohio
North Dakota	Oklahoma
Rhode Island	Oregon
South Carolina	Pennsylvania
South Dakota	Texas
Tennessee	Utah
Vermont	Virginia
West Virginia	Washington
Wyoming	Wisconsin
District of Columbia	

Tax Lien Jurisdictions

The following jurisdictions might be characterized as pure real estate tax lien certificate jurisdictions: Alabama, Arizona, Colorado, District of Columbia, Florida, Illinois, Indiana, Iowa, Kentucky, Maryland, Mississippi, Missouri, Nebraska, New Hampshire, New Jersey, North Dakota, Oklahoma, Puerto Rico, South Carolina, South Dakota, Vermont, West Virginia, and Wyoming.

Different states and territories refer to tax lien certificates by different names. These names include tax lien, tax certificate, tax lien certificate, certificate of purchase, certificate of sale, tax claims, certificate of delinquency, receipt showing the amount paid, receipt for the purchase money, tax sale receipt, and tax sale certificate.

Tax Lien Names

Alabama: tax lien, tax certificate, or certificate of purchase.

Arizona: tax lien or certificate of purchase.

Colorado: tax sale certificate, certificate of purchase, tax certificate, or tax lien.

District of Columbia: tax lien or certificate of sale.

Florida: tax certificate.

Illinois: certificate of purchase or tax sale certificate.

Indiana: tax sale certificate or certificate of sale.

Iowa: certificate of purchase or tax sale certificate.

Kentucky: tax claims or certificate of delinquency.

Maryland: certificate of sale.

Mississippi: receipt showing the amount paid.

Missouri: certificate of purchase.

Nebraska: certificate of purchase, tax certificate, or certificate of sale.

New Hampshire: tax lien.

New Jersey: certificate of tax sale or certificates of tax sale.

North Dakota: certificate of sale or tax sale certificate.

Oklahoma: tax sale certificate or certificate of purchase.

Puerto Rico: certificate of purchase.

South Carolina: receipt for the purchase money or tax sale receipt.

South Dakota: tax certificate, certificate of sale, or tax sale certificate.

Vermont: the form of the document you receive at the tax lien sale is not provided for in Vermont law; however, the document is clearly not a deed.

West Virginia: certificate of sale, tax certificate of sale, certificate of purchase, or tax certificate.

Wyoming: certificate of purchase.

Three Additional States

There are three additional states where tax lien certificates are authorized by law to be sold. However, the tax lien certificate system is not the preferred delinquent tax sale system used. The following states fit this category. As you can see by the information following the name of the states, it looks like they would sell tax lien certificates.

California: tax certificate.

Ohio: tax certificate or certificate.

New York City: tax lien or tax lien certificate.

Deed with Right of Redemption Jurisdictions

There are jurisdictions where the buyer at a tax lien sale does not receive a tax certificate, tax lien, or tax lien certificate. Many of these jurisdictions seem to imply that the investor will receive a deed to the property. However, when examined more closely, that deed does not really convey marketable title to the property. Often it does not even convey the right of possession of the real estate.

In these jurisdictions the deed you receive comes with a right of redemption for the former owner. The defaulting taxpayer can buy back the real estate that was sold at the tax lien sale for a certain period of time after the sale.

When the deed does not convey the right of possession and the former owner has a right of redemption, some writers in their discussion of tax lien certificates classify the state as a tax lien certificate state. They take the position that the deed given by the taxing jurisdiction is nothing more than a tax certificate.

Joel S. Moskowitz, in his book *The 16% Solution* (Andrews and McNeel: Kansas City, MO, 1992), classifies the states of Georgia, Louisiana, Massachusetts, and Rhode Island as tax lien certificate states. The following taxing jurisdictions refer to the winning bidder at a tax lien sale as receiving a deed. We will call these jurisdictions tax deed jurisdictions.

Tax Deed Jurisdictions

Connecticut: collector's deed.
Delaware: deed (as to Kent and Sussex Counties).
Georgia: deed or sheriff's deed.
Guam: deed or tax sold property.
Hawaii: conveyance deed or tax deed.
Louisiana: deed of sale or tax deed.
Massachusetts: deed of the land, deed, or collector's
     deed.
Rhode Island: collector's deed or deed.
Tennessee: tax deed.
Texas: deed.

If you add the taxing jurisdictions classified as pure lien certificate jurisdictions to the jurisdictions classified as deed with right of redemption jurisdictions, you have 31 states, the District of Columbia, Guam, Puerto Rico, and the Virgin Islands.

We next will examine where to find real estate tax lien opportunities. With a little work and the right place to look, you can find literally thousands of real estate tax lien investment opportunities.

Finding Real Estate Tax Lien Investment Opportunities

In nearly all counties, tax sales must be published and advertised to the public. The only exceptions would be counties that are very small and have no local newspaper. For the most part, counties have one sale per year. Some counties have more than this for special circumstances.

Some states' statutes specify a specific date for all their counties to hold real estate tax lien sales. Please see Chapter 14 for this information. Some states do not specify the dates so you will have to contact the specific county in which you are interested.

Publication

The properties scheduled for tax lien sales are published in either a newspaper or a county publication from one to six weeks before the date of the tax sale. If you know when the tax sale is in a given county, you will need to look for this publication during that period prior to the sale. This will give you enough time to do the appropriate research. Property tax lien sales are typically conducted by the county treasurer. Call the county treasurer's office to verify the publication and sale dates. More and more counties publish this information on the Internet. Enter the county's name and key words "treasurer's sale" to conduct your search.

The newspaper notices will be in the legal section with the other public notices. These should contain at least the parcel number of the property, the legal description, and the amount of the delinquent taxes.

Sometimes the notices also will contain the address and the name of the property owner. If they do not, you can obtain this information from the local assessor's office or the office of the county recorder. Once you locate the publication of available properties, you will need to focus on those that are really worth your time.

Decision Time

The first decision you need to make is whether you are interested in buying the tax lien or owning the property. If you want to buy the tax lien, your investment process will be more streamlined. If you want to own the property, you may need to repair the property before you can resell it to make your profit or rent it.

Even if you are interested in buying the tax lien, you still have to consider what could happen if the property owner does not redeem your tax lien and you are forced to foreclose the tax lien and take ownership of the property. You must consider this possibility to keep your investment risk minimized.

If you want to wind up owning the property, you will have to decide whether you want to sell it immediately or rent it. The profit potential calculation will be different for each option because the expenses involved in selling versus renting are different.

Also, as part of your decision-making process, you must also choose where you would like to invest. There are several factors that go into this decision, including whether or not you want to obtain the deed to the property. You must decide where to invest so that you will know where to look!

Target Area

If you live in a state or area that has tax lien sales, we suggest you make this your initial target area. If you live in a place that does not offer tax lien sales, or the investment return does not meet your parameters (e.g., Alabama, 6 percent), then we suggest you choose a target area closer to where you live rather than farther away.

Evaluation

Once you have located the properties you are interested in you need to do some preliminary research. How much is the tax lien amount? What is the interest rate on the tax lien? When is the tax lien sale date? With this general information, you can determine if the property fits your investment budget, your required investment return, and your investment timing parameters.

If the property does not fit all three of your investment criteria, then do not spend any more time on it. If it looks good at this point, you will make a more detailed analysis of the value of the tax lien and of the property. This will help you determine what your maximum investment in the tax lien will be.

We recommend you make a file for each property you are considering. Start with a Tax Lien Property Evaluation Worksheet to keep the information you collect organized. We have provided a Tax Lien Property Evaluation Worksheet on the next page.

We recommend you use this worksheet to evaluate every property. You will find it impossible to keep the information in your head. By using the worksheet you will save time and keep yourself organized.

We will give you instructions on how to use the worksheet in the pages that follow the worksheet page. By all means make multiple copies of this worksheet to use in your tax lien investing.

At this point, we need to spend some time explaining some of the terms listed in the above worksheet. In most cases everything appears to be self-explanatory.

You may find that the tax lien amount and the property taxes are different figures. This is because the tax lien amount may include fees and penalties already incurred before the tax lien sale date.

We point out to you that the interest rate, tax lien sale date, bidding type, payment requirements, redemption period, and procedures for obtaining deed lines in the property evaluation worksheet correspond to the six pieces of information we provide you in Chapter 14.

The tax parcel number will be given in the tax lien sale announcement. With the tax parcel number you can look up information about the property on the local tax assessor's or tax appraiser's Web sites.

Property Tax Exemptions

By looking at these Web sites, you can find out if there are any homestead or agricultural exemptions. This is important be-

Tax Lien Property Evaluation Worksheet

State Where Property Is Located _____

Tax Lien Amount _____ Property Taxes _____

Interest Rate _____ Tax Lien Sale Date _____

Bidding Type _____

Payment Requirements _____

Redemption Period _____

Procedures For Obtaining Deed _____

Tax Parcel Number _____ Owner _____

Property Address _____

_____

_____

Property Type _____ Zoning _____ Year Built _____

Number of Bedrooms/Bathrooms _____ Square Footage _____

Mortgages _____

_____

_____

Appraised Value _____ Type of Valuation _____

Bid Amount _____ Buy Tax Lien _____ Buy Property _____

cause these types of exemptions extend the redemption period of the property owner. You cannot get the property deed until the redemption period is over.

In Texas the standard redemption period for the property owner is six months. If there is a homestead exemption or an agricultural exemption on the property, the redemption period is extended to two years!

If your investment strategy is to buy the tax lien to foreclose on the property, no foreclosure can take place until the redemption period afforded to the property owner expires. Obviously, two years is a much longer time period than six months to wait to see if the property owner is going to redeem the property.

The tax assessor's or tax appraiser's Web sites may also give you the year the property was built, zoning information, and square footage. There also will be an appraised value given by the tax assessor. This appraised value may or may not reflect market value.

Finally, the buy tax lien and buy property lines are for you to have a quick reference point. This is literally the bottom line of the tax lien evaluation worksheet. Are you buying the tax lien only? Are you buying the tax lien to be in a position to buy the property? Are you buying the property and are not interested in buying the tax lien? (We will come back to this last question in Chapter 6.)

Most of you will be buying the tax lien only. There are fewer steps and less time involved until you make a profit. So how do you make sure the property owner redeems your tax lien? Obviously, you cannot force the property owner to redeem your tax lien. However, you do have leverage when you own the tax lien. You own the highest priority lien. This may also be the first priority lien.

Three Key Elements

When evaluating properties look for three key elements. These three key elements are owner-occupied, one to four units (single family, duplex, triplex, fourplex) that are less than

10 years old, and mortgaged (the more mortgages on the property the better).

A homeowner will redeem the tax lien of a few thousand dollars rather than lose their home. Newer homes have higher assessed values and higher property taxes. A higher property tax bill is more likely to be delinquent than a lower property tax bill. And, as we have just said, the homeowner will redeem the tax lien rather than lose the home to foreclosure.

Mortgages on a home will work in your favor as well. The bank has accepted the property as collateral for the bank loan. The bank or mortgage lender has the legal right to foreclose on the property. The home will be sold and used to pay off the debt if the owner defaults. A tax lien has higher priority than a mortgage.

This means that you as the owner of the tax lien have the first right to foreclose on the property. This is the case even though there may be $150,000 owed on the mortgage and only $4,000 due in taxes. As a tax lien holder, you are between the lender and its collateral.

Mortgage Lenders Are Your Friends

Once the loan is in default, it is in the lender's best interest to pay off the tax lien. By paying you off, the bank extinguishes your tax lien and the mortgage lien will move to first priority. This means you will receive the delinquent taxes, plus interest, penalties, and fees. The lender can then foreclose on the property and sell it to pay off the outstanding debt. They will simply add the amount they paid you to the foreclosure proceeding.

Now you know why we said the more mortgages the better. How great would it be if there were a property with two or even three mortgages? Then you would have an additional three possible sources to pay off your tax lien besides the property owner!

You can check if there is a mortgage or mortgages by checking the property title. This information is a matter of public record. You can find it at the local county recorder, city clerk, or whichever office records official documents in the region.

Profit Potential

After you have determined what the tax lien and the property are worth, you will estimate all expenses involved with the tax lien purchase. Calculate the expenses involved with ownership even if you do not intend to own the property. The purpose of this is to insure your investment return no matter what happens.

When you determine your profit potential, you will also be calculating the maximum amount you are willing to invest in the tax lien itself. As we have mentioned, never exceed your maximum purchase price when bidding on the tax lien.

In the next chapter we will show you how to get super-high returns with super-low risks investing in real estate tax liens. We suggest as a learning tip that you go back and reread this chapter beginning at the "Target Area" section. Have in mind what your target area is before beginning Chapter 3.

Super-High Returns with Super-Low Risks

How high is high when you are talking about the potential annualized yields you can receive investing in real estate tax liens? You can receive yields from 10 percent to 300 percent and higher by investing in real estate tax liens, tax lien certificates, and tax deeds with rights of redemption.

Super-High Returns

If you had purchased a tax lien at the Cochise County, Arizona, sale held on February 25, 2005, at the maximum potential annual interest (16 percent) and that certificate was redeemed four days later on March 1, 2005, you would have been entitled to 2.67 percent worth of interest. (The maximum return in Arizona is 1.33 percent per month or fraction thereof.) In four days you would have earned more interest than you could have earned in a year from a bank money market account!

If you purchase a tax lien in Wyoming, you get a 15 percent annual interest rate or 1.25 percent per month plus a 3 percent penalty upon payoff. This penalty is an amount that you receive no matter when the tax lien is paid off. When you combine both the annual return of 15 percent together with the penalty of 3 percent, you would get a minimum combined annual return of 18 percent, assuming the tax lien was paid off after one year. When there is a penalty feature to the tax lien, you get the entire penalty amount whenever the tax lien is redeemed. Even if the tax lien were paid off the same day you bought it, in Wyoming you would still receive a 3 percent return.

Let us see. Which would be better? Do you want to receive 3 percent in one day? Or, do you want to receive less than that amount if you left your money for one year in a bank checking, savings, or money market account or certificate of deposit?

If you purchase a tax lien in Iowa, you get a 24 percent annual interest rate, or 2 percent per month or fraction thereof! Buy an Iowa tax lien on June 15 and if it gets redeemed on July 6, you receive 4 percent interest! Let us see. Do you want to receive 4 percent in three weeks? Or, do you want to wait two years to receive 4 percent on an annuity?

We live in Texas. Technically, Texas does not sell tax liens. If you are the successful bidder at a sheriff's tax sale you receive a sheriff's deed. The former property owner retains a right of redemption. They can buy the property back from you for a period of time that, for most properties, is six months from the date the sheriff's deed is recorded at the county recorder's office.

For homestead properties and agriculturally appraised properties, the redemption period is two years. If the former property owner redeems the property during the first year, the investor receives a 25 percent penalty return on their investment. If the former owner redeems during the second year, the investor receives a 50 percent penalty return.

Say you purchase a sheriff's deed on a homesteaded property in Texas for $10,000. You would receive $12,500 if the former owner redeems the property in the first year. You would receive $15,000 if the former owner redeems the property in the second year.

Texas Sheriff's Deed Purchase

Purchase Price	$10,000
First Year Penalty	$2,500
First Year Return	$12,500
Second Year Penalty	$2,500
Second Year Return	$15,000

If your sheriff's deed is redeemed 13 months after you buy it, you have received a $5,000 return on a $10,000 investment, or a yield of 46 percent annually.

10 Percent or Higher Returns

We now present the areas that have maximum potential yields of 10 percent or more ranked from the lowest to the highest potential yields. Some of these areas have assessments, penalties, fees, and costs in addition to an annual interest rate. This can affect the yield available.

South Carolina

The state sets an 8 percent to 12 percent annual return depending upon whether real estate is redeemed during the first six months of the redemption period or thereafter. South Carolina law states:

> The defaulting taxpayer, any grantee from the owner, or any mortgage or judgment creditor may within twelve months from the date of the delinquent tax sale redeem each item of real estate by paying to the person officially charged with the collection of delinquent taxes, assessments, penalties, and costs, together with eight percent interest on the whole amount of the delinquent tax sale bid.
>
> In the case of a redemption in the last six months of the redemption period, for all real property except that classified as the legal residence of the owner of real estate being sold at the tax sale, the applicable rate of interest is twelve percent.

Tennessee

The state sets 10 percent simple interest annually. Tennessee law states:

> In order to redeem property which has been sold, any person entitled to redeem the property shall pay to the clerk of the court who sold the property the amount

paid for the delinquent taxes, interest and penalties, court costs and any court ordered charges, and interest at the rate of ten percent (10%) per annum computed from the date of the sale on the entire purchase price paid at the tax sale.

Frederick County, Maryland

The county sets 12 percent simple interest annually. Maryland law states:

The rate of redemption is 6 percent a year except in Frederick County the rate is 6 percent a year or as fixed by the County Commissioners.

The Frederick County Code states:

The interest rate to redeem property sold for taxes is hereby fixed at twelve (12) percent per annum, provided that the interest rate established herein shall be applicable beginning with the redemption of properties sold at the November, 1980 tax sale and thereafter, unless changed by the board of county commissioners.

Worcester County, Maryland

The county sets 10 percent simple interest annually computed per month or fraction thereof.

Missouri

The state sets 10 percent simple interest annually and 8 percent simple interest annually for subsequent real property taxes paid. Missouri law contains a significant restriction on who may bid. Tax lien sales in Missouri typically occur annually on the fourth Monday in August.

A nonresident may not bid unless and until that person has properly appointed a resident agent for service of process. And, according to the Boone County Collector of Revenue, the nonresident cannot even bid at the annual tax certificate sale. The bidding must be done by the appointed resident agent! Additionally, that appointed resident agent must be a resident of the county in which the nonresident bidder wishes to buy! If the appointed resident agent dies or becomes incapacitated, Missouri law says the county clerk would become the nonresident certificate holder's new agent for service of summons.

Nova Scotia, Canada

The province sets 10 percent simple interest annually.

Quebec, Canada

The province sets 10 percent simple interest annually.

Alabama

The state sets 12 percent simple interest annually.

U.S. Territory of Guam

The territory sets 12 percent simple interest annually.

Hawaii

The state sets 12 percent simple interest annually.

Kentucky

The state sets 12 percent simple interest annually.

Baltimore County, Maryland

The county sets 12 percent simple interest annually computed at 1 percent per month or fraction thereof.

Cecil County, Maryland

The county sets 12 percent simple interest annually computed at 1 percent per month or fraction thereof.

Charles County, Maryland

The county sets 12 percent simple interest annually.

Harford County, Maryland

The county sets 12 percent simple interest annually.

Queen Anne's County, Maryland

The county sets 12 percent simple interest annually computed per month or fraction thereof.

Somerset County, Maryland

The county sets 12 percent simple interest annually.

South Dakota

The state sets 12 percent simple interest annually.

Vermont

The state sets 12 percent simple interest annually computed at 1 percent per month or fraction thereof.

United States Virgin Islands

The territory sets 12 percent simple interest annually.

West Virginia

The state sets 12 percent simple interest annually.

Georgia

The state sets 12 percent simple interest annually computed at 1 percent per month or fraction thereof.

Montana

The state sets 12 percent (or more) simple interest annually depending upon the date of redemption.

Carroll County, Maryland

The county sets 14 percent simple interest annually.

Nebraska

The state sets 14 percent simple interest annually.

Allegany County, Maryland

The county sets 15 percent simple interest annually.

Indiana

The state sets 15 percent simple interest annually.

Arizona

The state sets 16 percent simple interest annually computed monthly for each full month or fraction thereof.

Massachusetts

The state sets 16 percent simple interest annually.

Rhode Island

The state sets 16 percent simple interest annually.

Louisiana

The state sets 17 percent annual yield depending upon the date of redemption. A Louisiana tax sale investor receives 12 percent simple interest annually. If redemption occurs during the first year the investor receives the interest plus a penalty return. If the tax certificate were redeemed one month from the date of sale, the annualized return would be 72 percent. If it were redeemed after six months, then the annualized return would be 22 percent. If it were to be redeemed after 12 months the rate would be 17 percent. After two years, the annualized return would drop to 14.5 percent.

Mississippi

The state sets 17 percent annual yield depending upon the date of redemption. A Mississippi tax sale investor receives 12 percent simple interest annually. There is a 5 percent damages fee paid by the property owner added on to the amount of all taxes.

Wyoming

The state sets 18 percent annual yield depending upon the date of redemption.

Connecticut

The state sets 18 percent simple interest annually.

Anne Arundel County, Maryland

The county sets 18 percent simple interest annually.

Howard County, Maryland

The county sets 18 percent simple interest annually.

Kent County, Maryland

The county sets 18 percent simple interest annually or 1.5 percent per month or portion of a month from the date of sale.

New Hampshire

The state sets 18 percent simple interest annually from the date of sale. However, very few tax sales are held in New Hampshire. This is because many areas have chosen a real estate tax lien procedure under which only a municipality or county where the property is located, or the state, may acquire a tax lien against land and buildings for unpaid taxes.

New Jersey

The state sets 18 percent simple interest annually.

Ohio

The state sets 18 percent simple interest annually from the date of sale. Historically, Ohio has been a tax deed state. Ohio tax sales have been public oral bid foreclosure auction tax sales of the real estate itself. However, the tax sale law was amended allowing counties having a population of over 200,000 to sell certificates at public auction or by negotiated sale.

District of Columbia

The district sets 18 percent simple interest annually or 1.5 percent thereon for each month or part thereof.

Florida

The state sets 18 percent simple interest annually from the date of sale.

Kent and Sussex County, Delaware

The county sets 20 percent simple interest annually.

Montgomery County, Maryland

The county sets 20 percent simple interest annually computed on a daily basis from date of sale to date of redemption.

Prince George's County, Maryland

The county sets 20 percent simple interest annually from the date of sale.

Commonwealth of Puerto Rico

The commonwealth sets 20 percent penalty interest. Puerto Rico has a unique system of computing annualized interest rate returns. Under Puerto Rican law, tax liens, called certificates of purchase, can be redeemed within one year from the date of issue of the certificate of purchase. This can be done by paying to the certificate purchaser the full amount of the purchase money, plus the improvements and expenses incurred by the purchaser, together with the fees accrued and taxes due to the date of redemption. Added to this will be 20 percent of all of the above as compensation to the purchaser.

Georgia

The state sets 20 percent penalty interest. As we have said, Georgia is not a tax lien certificate state. Georgia is a tax deed with right of redemption state. However, if the property is redeemed, the tax deed operates in a manner similar to a tax certificate.

Baltimore, Maryland

The city sets 24 percent simple interest annually from the date of sale.

Iowa

The state sets 24 percent simple interest annually or 2 percent per month, counting each fraction of a month as an entire month, from the month of sale.

Super-Low Risks

There are super-low risks associated with buying real estate tax liens. The best way to reduce investment risk is to know what you are buying. Many of the obviously risky properties will be eliminated from your list of potential investments during your evaluation process.

Real estate tax lien investing is a low-risk investment because it is secured by the property. The biggest risk you take in real estate tax lien investing is purchasing a tax lien on a property that is worth less than the tax lien.

This will never happen to you when you make a real estate tax lien investment using the knowledge we give you. A far more likely possibility, and a risk that has its rewards, is the property owner will not redeem the tax lien.

Taxes Never Paid

What if the taxes never get paid on the property? Does that mean you will lose your investment? If you buy a tax lien that is not paid off, you may find that you have made an even better investment.

You will not get back your cash investment. You will not receive your high interest rate return. You may get something better! You will get to foreclose on your tax lien. In Arizona, Wyoming, Iowa, and most other tax lien certificate states, you are the only person allowed to bid at the foreclosure sale! You either will have your tax lien or tax certificate paid back, with a high annual interest rate return, or you will end up owning the property for the back real estate taxes, penalties, interest, and foreclosure costs.

Price You Pay for the Property

Consider the price you will end up paying for the property. There are potentially huge profits to be made. The tax lien securing your tax certificate is a priority lien. You may end up owning the property free and clear!

In practically every tax lien and tax certificate state all private party deeds of trust and mortgages are wiped out. That means they are removed from the property title. You take the property free and clear. There are no mortgage payments to be made. You would end up buying a free and clear property for literally pennies on the dollar!

The statistics say only a very small percentage of property owners will let their good properties slip through their hands and into yours through foreclosure of the tax lien. Typically, 95 percent to 98 percent of real estate tax liens will be redeemed by the owner.

Investors will take title to 2 percent to 5 percent of these properties. There are hundreds of thousands of these tax liens and tax certificates being sold each year. This means there are tens of thousands of properties that will end up in investor real estate portfolios. How many of these properties do you want in your portfolio?

Three Risks

We will touch on three situations that can cause you risk in real estate tax lien investing. These three risks are the bankruptcy of the property owner, the destruction of the property, and environmental problems that are discovered after you buy the tax lien. We will discuss these three issues in Chapter 13. At this point we just want to make you aware of them.

We have already said that we feel the biggest risk in real estate tax lien investing is purchasing a tax lien on a property that is worth less than the tax lien. In order to minimize this risk, you have to know value.

In the next chapter we will thoroughly train you on how to know value in real estate. Because the real estate is the security for the tax lien, you have something of value that is your safety net for your investment. By knowing the value of the safety net, your investment risk is minimized if not effectively eliminated.

CHAPTER 4

Why Buy Real Estate Tax Liens?

Why buy real estate tax liens? Buy real estate tax liens to make money! Buy real estate tax liens to earn super-high investment returns. Buy real estate tax liens to have super-low risks.

In this chapter we are going to train you in two important areas. We are going to give you the top 10 reasons to invest in real estate tax liens. We are also going to give you all the tools you need to know value in real estate.

Once you understand the reasons for investing in real estate tax liens you will feel more comfortable making a real estate tax lien investment. Once you have the tools you need to know value in real estate you will have the confidence to make a real estate tax lien investment.

Top 10 Reasons for Investing in Real Estate Tax Liens

10. Diversification

Any investment program requires diversification. Tax lien investing can be a part of your overall investment strategy. How much of your investment capital you put in real estate tax lien investing is up to you.

Because you are reading this book you are most likely looking for a way to diversify either your investment portfolio or the type of real estate investments you are making. Real estate tax lien investing is your answer.

9. Viable Investment Opportunity

Real estate tax lien investing is a viable investment opportunity. When we say "viable" we mean workable and practical. Once you have completed reading and studying this book you will understand how workable and practical real estate tax lien investing can be.

Then it will be up to you to put what is only a theory for you into reality. You will actually have to do the work and make a real estate tax lien investment. Once you have done your first real estate tax lien investment you will have turned this viable investment opportunity into a part of your investment reality.

8. Super-Low Risk

Tax lien investing is a super-low risk investment. Your return will come in the form of the repayment of your investment plus interest or in the receipt of the deed to the property. You are guaranteed to receive one or the other.

You will receive repayment of your investment plus interest 95 percent to 98 percent of the time. Two to 5 percent of the time you will receive a deed to a property that may be worth 10 to 20 times what you invested in the tax lien.

7. Less Competition

Face it. Is there competition in real estate tax lien investing? Yes, there is always competition in every investment area. Our previous book, *Quick Cash in Foreclosures,* explored a real estate investment area where there is a ton of competition.

How many of you had heard about real estate tax lien investing before you saw this book? Be truthful. Most of you bought this book because you were attracted with the part of the title that said how to guarantee returns up to 50 percent!

Compared to investing in real estate foreclosures, investing in real estate tax liens is the white space on old maps. It is unexplored territory.

6. Simple to Understand

Real estate tax lien investing is simple to understand. While there is a lot of information in this book, the process itself is not difficult to grasp once you know how it works. It is far less complicated than trying to choose stocks, bonds, or mutual funds.

Once you understand real estate tax lien investing you do not have to relearn the investment because something changes in the economy. While procedures may change, or interest rates may change, your investment strategy never changes. Your investment outcome is guaranteed.

5. Tax Liens Have Priority

The government, whether federal, state, or local, by law gives its own liens priority over all other liens on a property. The real estate tax lien takes priority over mortgages, mechanics liens, or any other lien.

When you buy the tax lien, you receive this right of priority. If there is a mortgage on the property, the lender must decide whether it wants to pay off the tax lien or lose its collateral. If the mortgage lender wants to foreclose on the property, it has to pay off the tax lien first.

4. Little Up-Front Cash to Get Started

How much money do you need in order to begin real estate tax lien investing? You will need to start with some cash. If you start with smaller deals in the $1,000 to $5,000 range, you can use your subsequent profits to grow your investment capital substantially in a short period of time.

If you have no money of your own to invest, we will teach you how to find a money partner in Chapter 11. Finding a good real estate tax lien investment opportunity is the hard part of the equation. The easy part is finding someone who will partner with you and put up the money. Contact us!

3. Investment Secured by Real Estate

Real estate lenders routinely loan 80 percent of a property's value. They have the borrower sign a promissory note for the amount of the loan. They also have the borrower sign a mortgage or trust deed. This gives the lender a lien on the owner's property title.

A real estate tax lien is typically 3 percent or less of a property's value. No signatures on the part of the property owner are required to make the tax lien valid. There is no better security for an investment than real estate.

2. Earning without Owning

A real estate tax lien is an investment secured by property without the responsibilities of property ownership. There are no repairs to make and no maintenance to deal with. There are no tenants who are destroying the property while not paying the rent. You do not have to have good credit.

You do not have to qualify for and procure a real estate loan. You do not have to worry about interest rates going up. You do not have to be concerned if your property is appreciating. A real estate tax lien investment earns you money without owning property.

1. Super-High Returns

The number one reason to invest in real estate tax liens is to make super-high returns on your investment dollars. Receiving an 18 percent return on your investment is almost unheard of in today's economic times. You can do this routinely with real estate tax liens.

When you calculate the time value of money, real estate tax liens blow away the competition. Yields of 30 percent, 40 percent, 50 percent and higher are possible. These super-high returns are worth your best efforts.

Knowing Value

Are you ready to become an expert in valuing real estate? We are going to take you step by step through the knowledge we have gained in our combined 50-plus years as real estate investors valuing real estate. We will define the six values that every real estate investor needs to know about the property in which they are investing.

We will show you the three ways to value real estate that are used by real estate appraisers. We will explain the four elements of real estate value that are unique to the real estate market. We will reveal the four great forces that influence real estate value. Then we will teach you the seven ways to know value in your target area.

The Six Values Every Real Estate Investor Needs to Know

There are six values every real estate investor needs to know about the property they are investing in. These six values are the retail value, the wholesale value, the replacement value, the property tax value, the loan value, and the appraised value.

1. Retail Value
The retail value is the value an end user, like a homeowner, places on a piece of real estate. The retail value tends to be the highest value of all the values placed on real estate.

2. Wholesale Value
The wholesale value is the value a real estate investor, like you, places on a piece of real estate. The wholesale value tends to be the lowest value of all the values placed on real estate.

3. Replacement Value

The replacement value is the value insurance companies place on the improvements on a piece of real estate. The replacement value is determined by the cost approach.

4. Property Tax Value

The property tax value is the value the local property tax assessor in your area places on a piece of real estate. The property tax value could be higher or lower than the retail value.

5. Loan Value

The loan value is the value a real estate lender, like a bank or mortgage company, places on a piece of real estate. The loan value tends to vary as a percentage of the appraised value.

6. Appraised Value

The appraised value is the value a real estate appraiser places on a piece of property. The appraised value is typically at or near the retail value.

Three Ways to Value Real Estate

There are three ways to value real estate. The three ways are the cost approach, the income approach, and the market comparison approach. When a real estate appraiser makes an appraisal, the appraiser will use one, two, or possibly all three of these valuation approaches.

1. Cost Approach

The cost approach consists of three parts. First, value the land. Second, value the improvements on the land, such as buildings, and add the value of the improvements to the value of the land. Third, determine the accrued depreciation of the improvements and subtract the accrued depreciation from the combined value of the land and improvements.

Cost Approach Example

Let us look at an example. If the land is valued at $100,000, the improvements are valued at $250,000, and the accrued depreciation is $25,000, what is the value of the property according to the cost approach?

Land value	$100,000
Improvements	$250,000
Total	$350,000
Accrued Depreciation	-$25,000
Property value	$325,000

We added the value of the improvements, $250,000, to the value of the land, $100,000, and got $350,000. We then subtracted the accrued depreciation, $25,000, and came up with a property value of $325,000.

2. Income Approach
The income approach uses the income a property produces to determine its value. We say it this way: The value of an income property is in direct relationship to the income the property produces.

Gross Rent Multiplier
Let us look at an example. The gross rent multiplier says the value of an income-producing property is determined by the gross annual rent the property receives multiplied by the gross rent multiplier.

You can find out the gross rent multiplier for your area by calling a commercial real estate company and asking them what the gross rent multiplier is for your city. If the gross annual rent is $120,000 and the gross rent multiplier for the area is eight, then we multiply $120,000 times eight and come up with a value of $960,000.

Gross Rent	$120,000
Gross Rent Multiplier	× 8
Value	$960,000

Another way to determine value using the income approach is with the formula value = income/capitalization rate. In this case the income is the net operating income (NOI), which is the gross income minus the operating expenses. The capitalization rate is determined by the market in the area the property is located.

Capitalization Rate

For example, in Dallas, Texas, real estate investors might require an 8 percent capitalization rate, and in Phoenix, Arizona, real estate investors might require a 9 percent capitalization rate. You can find out the capitalization rate for your area by calling a commercial real estate company and asking them what the capitalization rate is in your city.

If the net operating income is $80,000 and the capitalization rate is 8 percent (Dallas, Texas) then the value of the property is $1,000,000 ($80,000/0.08 = $1,000,000). However, if the property was located in Phoenix, Arizona, with the same $80,000 net operating income then the value of the property is only $888,888 ($80,000/0.09 = $888,888).

Dallas, Texas		Phoenix, Arizona
$80,000	Net Operating Income	$80,000
0.08	Capitalization Rate	0.09
$1,000,000	Property Value	$888,888

3. Market Comparison Approach

The market comparison approach uses the value of similar properties to determine the value of a particular property. How many of you have heard the term "comps"? "Comps" is short for "comparable properties." You compare properties that are similar to the property you are interested in to determine its value. We say it this way: "No comps, no contract."

Market Comparison Example

Let us look at an example. If you are trying to determine the value of a three bedroom, two bathroom, 1,600 square feet, attached two-car garage home, you compare it to as many similar properties as you can find that have sold within the last 180 days in the neighborhood.

Similar property 1 is a three bedroom, two bathroom, 1,625 square feet, attached two-car garage home that sold for $195,000 45 days ago. Property 2 is a three bedroom, two bathroom, 1,575 square feet, attached two-car garage home that sold for $190,000 60 days ago. Property 3 is a three bedroom, two bathroom, 1,700 square feet, attached two-car garage home that sold for $205,000 30 days ago.

The price per square foot for each of these similar properties is $120 ($195,000/1,625 square feet is $120.00; $190,000/1,575 square feet is $120.63; $205,000/1,700 square feet is $120.59). If we multiply our 1,600 square feet by $120 we get a value of $192,000 for the value of the property we are looking at.

Property 1	Property 2	Property 3
$195,000	$190,000	$205,000
1,625 Square Feet	1,575 Square Feet	1,700 Square Feet
$120.00	$120.63	$120.59

Subject Property
1,600 Square Feet
×$120.00
$192,000

This, of course, is a summary chart of the market comparison example information. To help you determine the most accurate values of properties you are analyzing you may want to use a form to organize the information you gather. On the next page we provide a sample Comparative Market Analysis form like we use.

Four Elements of Value

There are four elements of value in real estate. They are demand, utility, scarcity, and transferability. These four elements of value constitute the value of a piece of real estate. We use the acronym DUST as a memory aid to keep the four elements of value in mind. Other people prefer STUD, but we will not get into that.

Demand
Demand is the first element of value. Demand is the number of people that want the property. The more people that want the property, the more valuable the property becomes.

Utility
Utility is the second element of value. Utility is the use to which a property can be put or of which it can be made. The

COMPARATIVE MARKET ANALYSIS

Date _____

Subject Property Address _____

_____

	BDRS	BATHS	SQFT	PRICE	TERMS

For Sale Now

1. _____ ____ ____ ____ ____ ____

   _____

2. _____ ____ ____ ____ ____ ____

   _____

3. _____ ____ ____ ____ ____ ____

   _____

Pending Sales

1. _____ ____ ____ ____ ____ ____

   _____

2. _____ ____ ____ ____ ____ ____

   _____

3. _____ ____ ____ ____ ____ ____

   _____

Sold Past 6 Months

1. _____ ____ ____ ____ ____ ____

   _____

2. _____ ____ ____ ____ ____ ____

   _____

3. _____ ____ ____ ____ ____ ____

   _____

Expired Past 6 Months

1. _____ ____ ____ ____ ____ ____

   _____

2. _____ ____ ____ ____ ____ ____

   _____

3. _____ ____ ____ ____ ____ ____

   _____

Notes and Comments _____

_____

_____

more uses that a property can be put to or made of, the more valuable the property.

Scarcity

Scarcity is the third element of value. Scarcity has to do with the supply of real estate available. This supply could be what is on the market or the total possible number of properties in an area. The scarcer the supply of real estate available, the more valuable the property.

Transferability

Transferability is the fourth element of value. Transferability is the key element of value in real estate. You can have the best property in the world, worth millions of dollars, and if you cannot transfer the title to your property to a buyer, then you have no sale. Likewise if you are a real estate buyer and have written a great wholesale offer that has been accepted by the seller, your deal is worthless unless you can get the seller to transfer clear property title to you.

Four Great Forces Influencing Value

There are four great forces that influence the value of real estate. They are physical forces, economic forces, political forces, and social forces. These four great forces are present in every real estate market in the country. How they influence your target area is up to you to determine. We use the acronym PEPS as a memory aid to keep the four great forces that influence value in mind.

Physical Forces

Physical forces are the first of the great forces that influence the value of real estate. The availability of schools, shopping, churches, transportation, and parks are physical forces that influence real estate value. If these physical amenities are present in your target area, they influence the value of the area in an upward manner. If these physical amenities are not present or are minimally present in your target area, they influence the value of the area in a downward manner.

Economic Forces

Economic forces are the second of the great forces that influence the value of real estate. The number and types of jobs available, the wages being paid, where in the economic cycle the economy is nationally, and the interest rates for real estate loans are economic forces that influence real estate value. The economic cycle is a repeating expansion-prosperity-recession-depression cycle. Real estate value is greatly influenced by the economic cycle. Typically, real estate is said to do well in the expansion and prosperity phases of the economic cycle and do poorly in the recession and depression phases of the economic cycle.

Political Forces

Political forces are the third of the great forces that influence the value of real estate. The types of zoning, pro-growth or no-growth policies, and environmental regulations are political forces that influence the value of real estate. It is important for you to know the political forces that influence the value of real estate in your area, both for the present investment climate and for the future investment climate.

Social Forces

Social forces are the fourth of the great forces that influence the value of real estate. The quality and the number of schools in the area, blighted neighborhoods or well-kept neighborhoods, racial or ethnic strife, and social amenities are the social forces that influence the value of real estate.

Seven Ways to Know Value in Your Target Area

There are seven ways to know value in your target area. They are sold comparables, pending comparables, listed comparables, expired comparables, appreciation rates, new or planned development, and vacancy rates.

Sold Comparables

Sold comparables are the first way to know value in your target area. Sold comparables set the floor of retail value for real estate. This means that if a sold comparable sold for $125,000, a similar property should sell for no less than $125,000 in a normal real estate market. Sold comparables as the name implies are properties that have been sold and have actually closed escrow. Sold comparables are useful for properties that have sold in the last six months. Anything beyond six months is not considered a good comparable.

Pending Comparables

Pending comparables are the second way to know value in your target area. Pending comparables indicate the direction of real estate value. A pending comparable is a property that has sold but has not closed escrow. When the pending comparable closes escrow it will become a sold comparable. If the sold comparables are indicating a value of $125,000 and the pending comparables are indicating a value of $127,000, then you are getting an indication that the direction of real estate values is going up.

Listed Comparables

Listed comparables are the third way to know value in your target area. Listed comparables set the ceiling of retail value for real estate. Listed comparables are properties that are currently on the market and are similar to property in which you are considering investing. Listed comparables set the ceiling of value because they have neither sold nor closed escrow. They are merely an indicator of what sellers would like to get for their properties.

Expired Comparables

Expired comparables are the fourth way to know value in your target area. Expired listings indicate the value that is beyond the present market in terms of what retail real estate buyers are willing to pay for property. Retail buyers will buy the lower-priced comparable properties first, all things being equal. Expired comparables are properties that never sold, let alone closed escrow.

Appreciation Rates

Appreciation rates are the fifth way to know value in your target area. Appreciation rates give you a sense of how hot or cold the real estate market is. Double-digit appreciation rates indicate a hot real estate market. Single-digit appreciation rates indicate a good real estate market. Zero or negative appreciation rates indicate a cold real estate market.

New or Planned Developments

New or planned developments are the sixth way to know value in your target area. By studying the path of new development and buying property in the path of that development, you can insure that you are buying property that is going to appreciate in value.

Vacancy Rates

Vacancy rates are the seventh way to know value in your target area. High vacancy rates indicate an area that may have problem properties. Low vacancy rates indicate an area that may have profitable properties.

The Final Four

We are going to conclude this training on real estate value with the final four pieces of the value puzzle. We are going to teach you about the principle of progression, average price, median price, and the principle of regression.

The Principle of Progression

The economic principle of progression as it relates to real estate investing says that if you buy a property below the median price for the area there will be a positive impact on the future value of that property just because of the area itself. Another way to say this is that when you buy a property that is priced below the median price, there are more properties priced at a higher level than are priced at a lower level relative to the property you are buying.

First of all, let us figure out what the median price means. The median price is the price where half of the property in the area is more expensive than the median price and half of the property is less expensive than the median price.

The median price is different than the average price. The average price is higher than the median price and is skewed that way because of the expensive property in an area.

Average Price versus Median Price

As we have already said, the median price is the price where half of the properties in an area are more expensive and half of the properties in an area are less expensive. We know that the market comparison approach to value places the most emphasis on sold comparable properties. The median price takes all properties, not just comparable properties, into account. Let us look at five properties in the same neighborhood that have sold and closed escrow in the last six months.

Five Properties

Property 1 is a three bedroom, two bathroom, 1,200 square feet starter home that sold for $105,000. Property 2 is a four bedroom, two bathroom, 1,500 square feet older home that sold for $120,000. Property 3 is a four bedroom, two bathroom, 2,000 square feet newer home that sold for $155,000. Property 4 is a three bedroom, two bathroom, 1,800 square feet upgraded home that sold for $180,000. Property 5 is a five bedroom, four bathroom, 3,500 square feet executive home that sold for $290,000.

Median Price

What is the median price for these five properties? The answer may surprise you. The median price is $155,000, which is the price for which property 3 sold. Remember the median price is the price where half of the properties sell for a higher price (properties 4 and 5) and half of the properties sell for a lower price (properties 1 and 2).

Average Price

What is the average price for these five properties? Again, the answer may surprise you. The average price for these five properties is $170,000! You can see that the average price is $15,000 higher than the median price ($170,000 versus $155,000). Property 4 and especially property 5 with their higher sales prices of $180,000 and $290,000, respectively, skew the average price higher. As a real estate investor you are much more interested in the median price.

Average Price versus Median Price

Average Price		Median Price	
Property 1	$105,000	Property 1	$105,000
Property 2	$120,000	Property 2	$120,000
Property 3	$155,000	Property 3	$155,000
Property 4	$180,000	Property 4	$180,000
Property 5	$290,000	Property 5	$290,000
Average Price = $170,000		Median Price = $155,000	

The Principle of Regression

The economic principle of regression as it relates to real estate investing says that if you buy a property above the median price for the area there will be a negative impact on the future value of that property just because of the area itself. Another way to say this is that when you buy a property that is priced above the median, there are more properties priced at a lower level than are priced at a higher level relative to the property you are buying.

Using our property examples from above, if you had purchased property 4 for $180,000, the value of that property for investment purposes would be negatively impacted by the principle of regression. Properties 1, 2, and 3 would all be pulling down the value of your property. Only property 5 would be pulling up the value of your property.

It is now time to turn our attention to how to buy real estate tax liens. You may choose to make your investment before the tax lien auction. You may choose to make your investment during the tax lien auction. You may choose to make your investment after the tax lien auction. Your course of action depends on your investment goals and the opportunities available.

CHAPTER 5

How to Buy Real Estate Tax Liens

I n this chapter we are going to teach you how to buy real estate tax liens. Some of you have an investment strategy of buying a tax lien for a super-high return. Others of you have an investment strategy of buying a tax lien and turning it into a deed for the property if the lien is not redeemed by the property owner.

Real Estate Paperwork

The first thing you have to figure out is the real estate paperwork involved in tax lien investing. There are three sides to real estate paperwork. There is the paperwork involved on the title side, such as grant deeds and warranty deeds. These deeds convey title to real estate from the seller to the buyer. Check Appendix A for which kind of deed your state uses.

Then there is the paperwork involved on the financing side. This is the evidence of debt, such as promissory notes and mortgage notes. This paperwork is used by lenders and borrowers to create a written agreement about the terms and conditions for the real estate loan.

Finally, there is the paperwork that bridges the financing side and the title side. These are trust deeds and mortgages, which are regarded as security devices for the promissory notes and mortgage notes respectively.

They become liens against the property title to real estate when they are officially recorded at the county recorder's office in the county where the property that is the security for the lien is located. Check Appendix B for which kind of security device your state uses.

Title	Security Devices	Finance
Grant Deed Warranty Deed	Trust Deed	Promissory Note
Grantor/Seller Grantee/Buyer	Trustee	Trustor
	Beneficiary	
	Mortgage	Mortgage Note
	Mortgagor/Mortgagee	
	Real Estate Tax Liens	

Real Estate Tax Liens

Real estate tax liens are the third kind of real estate paperwork. A tax lien becomes a security device for the taxing authority to assure the payment of property taxes.

If the property taxes are not paid, then the taxing authority sells the tax lien or forecloses on the property. When you buy a real estate tax lien you are buying a security interest in the property. All the taxing authority's rights and privileges are assigned to you.

The assurance you have as the tax lien holder is the same as the taxing authority. If the property owner does not pay the delinquent property taxes, interest, fees, costs, and penalties to you, then you foreclose on the property.

Three Investment Time Periods

There are actually three time periods when you can become involved in real estate tax lien investing. You can choose to buy before the tax lien sale, during the tax lien sale, or after the tax lien sale.

Three Investment Time periods

Before the Auction	At the Auction	After the Auction

Buying before the Tax Lien Sale

If your investment strategy is buying the tax lien and turning it into a deed for the property, buying before the tax lien sale may be the most efficient method to use. After you have received the published notice of the impending tax lien sale, you will contact the owner directly as soon as possible thereafter and before the tax lien sale.

You will use the impending tax lien sale as leverage. The property owner may be in a financial crisis and in need of cash. You and the property owner may be able to reach a mutually beneficial agreement. You will buy the property at a wholesale price and the owner will avoid the tax lien sale and subsequent fees, costs, penalties, and interest.

We recommend you send the property owner of record a letter. Let them know you have seen a public notice in the newspaper about the tax lien sale. Tell the owner you are prepared to help the owner keep some of their equity in the property and avoid the tax sale.

We suggest you send a letter first before you phone the owner. When you do phone, you are following up on your letter. Do not expect to get a response to your letter. We have re-

---

Letter To Property Owner

June 15, 2005

To the Owners of 711 Lucky Street

We have become aware that your property has been scheduled for a property tax lien sale on July 22. We are bringing this to your attention so you may avoid this happening. We are real estate investors who can provide you with alternatives.

One alternative is for you to consider the sale of your home. This will avoid the tax lien sale. This will also save some of your hard earned equity. Please contact us immediately. We look forward to your response. With the impending tax lien sale, you will need to respond quickly.

Sincerely,
Chantal & Bill Carey
Phone number
E-mail

ceived responses to our letters 1 to 2 percent of the time. See page 53 for a letter we use.

Setting an Appointment with the Property Owner

When setting the appointment with the owner for the tax lien sale alternatives presentation, you should plan on only one presentation per evening. This is important because some owners will take longer to make a decision than others. In circumstances where you have planned appointments too close together, each one will be rushed and opportunities to acquire properties may be missed.

No appointment should be set unless all owners will be present. If you get to the appointment and one of the owners cannot be present, then reschedule for another time. Otherwise, you are wasting your time.

It is important that the owner feels relaxed and is able to discuss their situation with you at the stated time. Accordingly, as with any real estate contract presentation, the time for the appointment should be at an hour when distractions, such as kids and favorite TV shows, are not competition.

Let us turn our attention to your initial phone conversation with the owner. The purpose of the conversation is to set an appointment with the owner. At this appointment you will make the tax lien alternatives presentation.

Phone Appointment Script

Hello, my name is _____ and I am calling because I may have an interest in buying your property. Are you the owner? What is your name?

Wait for their response. If they are not the owner, ask to speak to the owner.

According to public records, I understand that your property is scheduled for a tax lien sale, and that you might be able to use some help. Did you get my letter?

Whatever their response ask: *Is this a convenient time to talk?*

Wait for their response. If they say no, ask when would be a good time for you to call back?

As I said, my name is _____ and I am a private real estate investor who makes it my practice to understand the tax lien sale process and how to avoid it. My interest in your property stems from the fact that I can often find a good investment by talking to people who have a tax lien problem.

I sometimes find that they have a desire to sell their property at a price that will save some of their equity, help them protect their credit, and, at the same time, I may find a property to acquire.

I have developed a presentation that will show you the alternatives to having a tax lien sale. I recognize that nearly 9 out of 10 owners will be able to save their property with this information.

I am willing to share this information with you without cost or obligation. The properties I do buy have made it worth my time to help many property owners such as yourself avoid a tax lien sale. Do you have an interest in finding out about the alternatives you have with regard to your impending tax lien sale?

At this point you have aroused the curiosity of the property owner, and setting the time for an appointment should almost be automatic.

I have time on my schedule tonight or tomorrow night. Because time is of the essence for some of these tax lien sale alternatives, would tonight or tomorrow night be better for you?

Wait for their response.

Would seven o'clock or eight o'clock be better for you?

Wait for their response.

After you have set a time ask this last question:

Do you have younger children at home?

Wait for their response. If the say they have younger children say:

I recognize that it is important that parents spend quality time with their children, and I do not wish to disturb that. Is there a time, perhaps after your children have gone to bed, that we can talk?

Such consideration will make an impression on the owner, show great respect for their family, and insure you of an uninterrupted appointment.

At the Appointment

Your purpose at the appointment is to create a mutually beneficial solution to the tax lien sale for you and the property owner. After no more than five minutes of chitchat during which you build rapport with the owner, you should begin your tax lien sale alternatives presentation at the owner's kitchen table.

We recommend you sit with your back to an outside wall. That way the owner or owners are giving you their full attention and will not be distracted by what is going on in the rest of the house. Ask that TV or loud music that can be heard in the kitchen please be turned off or down.

Ask questions first. Expand on your knowledge of the owner's situation. Make sure you understand the owner's situation completely before you propose any solutions to their tax lien sale problem. Then make your tax lien sale alternatives presentation.

Tax Lien Sale Alternatives

The tax lien sale alternatives are: Pay the back taxes, penalties, fees, interest, and costs; legal delay; bankruptcy; sell the property; redeem the tax lien after the sale; or do nothing. Some of these tax lien sale alternatives are time sensitive. Others require an expenditure of money that the owner probably does not have.

By analyzing the owner's situation you can determine the best solution. If they have the ability to get their hands on some money, the owner may be able to pay the back taxes or redeem the tax lien after the sale. If they want to go the legal route, they may seek a legal delay or file bankruptcy, both of which cost money.

If they have enough time, the owner may be able to sell the property. That way they can possibly save some of their equity. If the owner does nothing, they could lose their property at the tax lien sale. If they continue to do nothing, they will actually lose their property once the redemption period ends.

You Are the Solution

You are the solution to the owner's tax lien sale problem. Let us assume the owner has neither the money nor the time to make something positive happen on their own with the information you have shared with them. This is where you step in and propose some very creative solutions.

The simplest solution is for you to "buy" the owner's equity. The owner would give you a quit claim deed to the property. You would pay the back taxes and own the property. Or, you could flip the property for Quick Cash and let the new buyer work things out with the taxing authority.

Buy the Owner's Equity

Say the property is worth $210,000. The loan balance is $150,000. The owner is behind $8,000 in property taxes. Their equity position is $52,000.

Owner's Equity

Property Value	$210,000
Loan Balance	$150,000
Behind in Taxes	$8,000
Owner's Remaining Equity	$52,000

You offer the owner $11,000 for their remaining equity. You, or the new buyer, will have to come up with an additional $8,000 to pay the back taxes. You would be paying $169,000 for the property. If the property has a value of $210,000, this looks like you have $41,000 in equity.

Purchase Price

Loan Balance	$150,000
Behind in Taxes	$8,000
Equity Offer	$11,000
Purchase Price	$169,000

Equity Sharing

Let us get more creative. We have the same owner with the same numbers. They really want to keep their property. They have had a temporary financial setback. They feel that if they can buy some time and get some financial help they will be able to keep their property.

You propose paying the $8,000 they are behind in their property taxes in return for a 75 percent equity position in the property. Remember, the equity in the property will be $60,000 after the property taxes are paid off ($210,000 property value minus $150,000 loan balance).

You will pay 25 percent of the future monthly loan payments and the owner will pay 75 percent of the future monthly loan payments. You will pay $8,000 cash and have a $45,000 equity position in the property. The property owner will retain a $15,000 equity position in the property.

This deal is a win for you and a win for the property owner. Plus, instead of having just a renter living in the property that may tear the property up, you have a co-owner who has a stake in the property. We have found property owners who have a stake in the property almost never destroy or damage a property.

Equity Sharing

Your Equity		Owner's Equity	
Property Equity	$60,000	Property Equity	$60,000
Equity Percentage	×75%	Equity Percentage	×25%
Equity Position	$45,000	Equity Position	$15,000

Equity Sharing Redux

Equity sharing is a way in which two or more parties, one being an owner occupant and the other being a real estate investor, pool their funds to buy or hold a property. There are many ways that equity sharing can work. In the usual equity sharing agreement, a real estate investor puts up the down payment and the owner occupant in effect becomes the tenant.

The owner occupant will pay the fair market rent, and both the owner occupant and the real estate investor split all the expenses of the property based on their ownership percentage. It does not have to be 50-50 (see previous example).

From a tax point of view, the owner occupant will usually get the write-off of their share of the interest on the loan and the property taxes. The real estate investor will include half of the rent as income and deduct their share of the interest, property taxes, all expenses on the property, and depreciation on their ownership interest.

Reverse Lease Option (Sale Leaseback with Option to Purchase)

As a final creative solution we give you the reverse lease option. When we think of lease options, we think of leasing the property with an option to purchase the property at some point in the future at some agreed-upon price.

A tax lien sale twist on this technique is to purchase the property and lease it back to the owner. You also give them an option to purchase the property at some point in the future at some agreed-upon price.

The agreed-upon future price should include any cash you put into paying the delinquent property taxes plus any negative cash flow (if applicable) and an acceptable return on your investment. As with the equity sharing arrangement, consult with your attorney for assistance in structuring the transaction.

Buying during the Tax Lien Sale

One of the advantages of trying to buy the property before the tax lien sale is that you will be able to walk through the property and assess its condition at the appointment with the owner. If any repairs are needed, you can estimate the costs of these repairs and use those estimates to negotiate a lower purchase price with the owner.

A second advantage of seeing the interior of the property before the tax lien sale is that you will know the condition of the property when you are buying the tax lien at the tax lien sale. Then, whether your strategy is to buy the tax lien for super-high returns or foreclose on the tax lien to get title to the property, you will know how good the collateral is for your tax lien and/or if it is a property that you want to eventually own.

We are going to spend a chapter on how to buy tax liens at the tax lien sale. Depending on the area, different procedures are used. In actuality the tax lien sale is not a sale at all. Suffice it to say that you will have to compete with other bidders at a live real estate tax lien auction. We will explain to you the different bidding techniques in Chapter 7.

Buying after the Tax Lien Sale

There are three opportunities to buy tax liens after the tax lien sale. The first opportunity is called over-the-counter buying. The second opportunity is buying the tax liens through the mail. The third opportunity is approaching the winning bidder after the tax lien sale and making them an offer they cannot refuse.

Over-the-Counter Buying

The first opportunity to buy tax liens after the tax lien sale is when the tax liens offered for sale at the tax sale draw no interested buyers. In these cases, the tax liens revert to the county or appropriate taxing authority. The taxing authority then will be the holder of these tax liens.

The taxing authority will make the tax liens available to investors after the sale. No competitive bid will be required. When you buy tax liens from the taxing authority after the taxing authority has unsuccessfully attempted to auction them, this is called over-the-counter buying.

The procedures for over-the-counter buying vary by area. You will have to check with the taxing authority to find out when it accepts bids on these unsold tax liens. Sometimes the taxing authority will accept bids anytime after the auction is over. Other times bidding is restricted to certain time periods.

If your investment strategy is to acquire the property itself, it is even more important that you have seen the property. When a tax lien does not sell at the auction, it could be because there were not enough interested investors present. It could also be because the property is damaged or perhaps even worthless.

You must not make an over-the-counter purchase of a real estate tax lien that is worth more than the property. If you do, you have just thrown away your money.

Buying Tax Liens by Mail

The second opportunity to buy tax liens after the tax lien sale is when the taxing authorities will accept tax lien investor offers by mail. You can verify the procedure for this with a phone call. If the property is locatcd far from whcrc you live, purchasing by mail is a great way to keep your expenses down.

The obvious pitfall to purchasing a tax lien by mail is that you will not have looked at the property. Only by researching the area and everything about the property in particular can you safely make this kind of a tax lien purchase.

We suggest you contact a local real estate broker to help you with your research. The broker can provide you market data information about the area. The broker also can run comps on the property that is the security for the tax lien.

You may be able to get this information for free. The broker may agree to help you in order to create goodwill and generate future business. If you have to pay the real estate broker a small fee it will be well worth it. You may even get them to drive by the property and send you pictures.

Buying from the Winning Bidder

The third opportunity to buy tax liens after the tax lien sale is when you approach a winning bidder and make them an offer they cannot refuse. They may take an immediate cash return on their investment rather than wait for the tax lien to be paid off. You would be willing to do this because you are going to be paid very handsomely to wait.

Say the winning bidder bought a tax lien for $4,000. You offer them $4,500. They make an immediate $500 profit in a few hours. This $500 profit is a 12.5 percent return on their $4,000 investment. This is an astronomical 4,563 percent annual return!

Buying from the Winning Bidder

Winning Bidder Paid $4,000
Your Offer $4,500
Their Profit $500
$500 / $4,000 = 12.5%
Their Return in One Day 12.5%
12.5% X 365 Days = 4,563%
Annual Return = 4,563%

How do you make a profit? You have met with the property owner prior to the tax lien sale. The property is in good condition and is in a good neighborhood. You attempted to make a deal with them to buy the property. Unfortunately, that did not happen. So, you bought the tax lien from the winning bidder. The property owner has a two-year plan to be able to redeem the tax lien and keep their property. You actually helped them put the plan together!

Why not loan the property owner the money to pay off their tax lien? We do not recommend you loan the property owner the money to pay off the tax lien before the tax lien sale. You legally cannot charge the interest rate the taxing authority can. Most states have a maximum 10 percent annual interest rate on cash loans between private individuals. Good thing you bought the tax lien instead.

Suppose the interest rate the taxing authority lawfully sets to pay you as the buyer of the tax lien certificate is 18 percent. What would your profit be over two years? Amazingly, you would have a 16 percent annual return on your $4,500 investment!

Your Profit

Tax Lien Certificate $4,000
Interest Rate $\times$ 18%
First Year Profit $720
Second Year Profit $720
Gross Profit $1,440
$1,440 / $4,500 = 32%
32% / Two Years = 16%

In the next chapter we will teach you when to buy real estate tax liens. For some of you this will be the most fun part. Who says real estate investing cannot put a smile on your face? Read on!

CHAPTER 6

When to Buy Real Estate Tax Liens

I n this chapter we will look at when to buy real estate tax liens. We are going to complete the preparation process so you are clear about when to buy a tax lien and when to pass on buying a tax lien. We know you have completed the initial phase of the preparation process by doing a property evaluation.

Without completing this initial phase you are shooting from the hip as we say in Texas rather than taking careful aim at your investment target. You must also do the financial calculations before you pull the trigger on any real estate tax lien investment. Once you know the property and what your return on investment requirements are, then you are truly in a position to hit the bull's-eye!

Preparing to Buy

This is the part of buying real estate tax liens that we think is the most fun. You have already met with the property owner. You have determined the value of the property. You know the tax lien is a fraction of the property's value. Now you need to calculate how much money you are going to make.

First you will need to do several financial calculations to determine what you are going to bid. These calculations have to be based on the type of bidding used in your target area.

Say the bidding type is an interest rate bid. This means the winning bidder is the bidder who will accept the lowest interest rate on their investment. So you will need to calculate the minimum amount of interest you would need to make the investment worthwhile.

We recommend you consider the time and money you have spent finding the property, determining its value, and the time and money required to go to the tax lien sale. You must take this into account when you are doing your calculations.

Interest Calculations

The interest taxing authorities stipulate to be paid on real estate tax liens is normally stated as simple interest calculated on an annual basis. A 12 percent interest rate offered by the taxing authority on a tax lien means you earn 12 percent of the balance of the tax lien if it remains unpaid for one year.

Let us say the amount of the tax lien is $5,000 and the property owner redeems the tax lien after 12 months. You will receive your $5,000 back and 12 percent interest on that $5,000 or $600.

Tax Lien Amount	$5,000
Annual Interest Rate	×12%
Annual Interest	$600

Graduated Interest

In some states the interest is graduated over time. In Indiana the interest rate is 10 percent of the minimum bid if the property taxes are redeemed by the property owner within six months of the tax lien sale. The interest is 15 percent of the minimum bid if the property taxes are redeemed by the property owner between six months and one year of the tax lien sale.

The redeeming owner is also required to pay the difference between the amount you paid for the tax lien and the minimum bid, plus 10 percent annual interest on that amount. If you paid any additional property taxes after the tax lien sale, the redeeming property owner must pay you the additional property tax amount plus 10 percent annual interest on that amount.

Say that you bought a tax lien in Indiana that had a minimum opening bid of $5,000 for $5,500. The minimum opening bid is the face amount of the tax lien. After six months you pay an additional $2,500 in property taxes. Three months later the property owner redeems your tax lien. How much money would you make?

The first calculation you make is 15 percent of the $5,000 minimum bid. This is because the property owner is redeeming your tax lien between six months and one year of the tax lien sale.

First Calculation

Minimum Bid	$5,000
Interest Rate	×15%
Interest Made	$750

The second calculation you make is 10 percent annual interest for nine months on the $500 you paid for the tax lien above the minimum bid. You would be paid 7.5 percent interest on the $500 for the nine months. This represents 10 percent annual interest.

Second Calculation

Amount above Minimum Bid	$500
Interest Rate	×7.5%
Interest Made	$75.00

The third calculation you make is 10 percent annual interest for three months on the additional $2,500 in property taxes. You would be paid 2.5 percent interest on the $2,500 for the three months. This represents 10 percent annual interest.

Third Calculation

Additional Property Taxes Paid	$2,500
Interest Rate	×2.5%
Interest Made	$62.50

You get your $5,500 investment back. You would be reimbursed the $2,500 in additional taxes you paid. You would receive $750 in interest per the first calculation. You would receive $75.00 in interest per the second calculation. You would receive $62.50 in interest per the third calculation. The total interest you would receive is $887.50.

Total Interest Made

First Interest Made	$750.00
Second Interest Made	$75.00
Third Interest Made	$62.50
Total Interest Made	$887.50

Some taxing jurisdictions graduate their interest at other intervals. It could be adjusted at three months. It could be adjusted at six months. A rule of thumb would be to multiply the three-month interest rate by four to get an annual interest rate. A rule of thumb would be to multiply the six-month interest rate by two to get an annual interest rate.

If the three-month interest rate was 4 percent, what would the annual interest rate be?

$$4\% \times 4 = 16\%$$

If the six-month interest rate was 6 percent, what would the annual interest rate be?

$$6\% \times 2 = 12\%$$

Assumptions

We recommend you make two assumptions in your calculations. The first assumption we recommend is that you assume the tax lien will not be redeemed by the property owner until the very end of the redemption period. If the redemption period is three years, we want you to assume you will not be paid back for 36 months. If the redemption period is two years, we want you to assume you will not be paid back for 24 months. You get the picture.

The second assumption we recommend is that you assume you will have to pay any new property taxes that become due during the redemption period. By making this assumption you will not have any surprises.

In some areas the taxing authority will sell the subsequent tax lien to you automatically. In some areas the taxing authority will sell the subsequent tax lien to the highest bidder. In some areas the taxing authority will not make you pay the subsequent property taxes.

Expenses to Buy the Tax Lien

Say you are contemplating a real estate tax lien investment in Montana. The redemption period is three years. The interest rate is 10 percent annually. You are thinking about investing in a $4,000 tax lien.

Your investment strategy is to buy the tax lien for interest income. In the bidding procedure the highest bid wins. How to you make the interest calculation? You would assume that your rate of return should be equivalent to the interest rate paid in Montana.

Your assumption is correct. What about your expenses? You need to take into account any expenses beyond the actual tax lien purchase. Why? These expenses will lower your return.

If you have minimal expenses, you can assume your interest rate return is equivalent to the interest rate being paid. However, what if you have traveled to Montana from Texas and have significant travel expenses?

Say you have travel expenses of $500. You pay $4,000 for the tax lien. It is not redeemed for 12 months. What is your annual return? First let us do the calculation without the travel expenses.

Without Travel Expenses

Tax Lien	$4,000
Annual Interest	×10%
Annual Return	$400
Annual Yield	10%

As you can see, in this case, the annual interest and the annual yield are the same. To determine the annual yield we divide the $400 annual return by the amount of the tax lien investment of $4,000. This gives us our 10 percent annual yield.

Annual Yield

Annual Return	$400
Investment Amount	$4,000
Annual Yield	10%

Now let us do the calculation with the travel expenses included. To make the annual yield calculation we divide our $400 annual return by the amount of the tax lien investment of $4,000 plus the travel expenses of $500, or $4,500. The annual yield drops from 10 percent to 8.9 percent because of the $500 in travel expenses.

With Travel Expenses

Travel Expenses	$500
Tax Lien	$4,000
Investment Amount	$4,500

Annual Yield

Annual Return	$400
Investment Amount	$4,500
$400 / $4,500 = 8.9%	
Annual Yield	8.9%

Expenses to Buy the Tax Deed

What if your investment strategy is to buy the tax lien to eventually acquire the deed to the property? We recommend that you make a calculation of your expenses to acquire the deed and resell the property.

These expenses may include repairs, legal fees, loan costs, property taxes, insurance costs, brokerage fees, and closing costs. We recommend the value of the property be at least six times the total of these expenses plus what you have invested in the tax lien.

Let us say you pay $4,000 for the tax lien. You pay $500 in travel expenses. You have $1,000 in repairs. You have $700 in legal fees. You have an additional $4,000 in property taxes. You pay $200 in insurance costs. You pay $6,000 in brokerage fees. You pay $900 in closing costs. Total costs will be $17,300!

Tax Deed Expenses

Tax Lien	$4,000
Travel Expenses	$500
Repairs	$1,000
Legal Fees	$700
Property Taxes	$4,000
Insurance Costs	$200
Brokerage Fees	$6,000
Closing Costs	$900
Total Costs	$17,300

We say that you have to then multiply the total costs figure of $17,300 by the multiplier of six. We call this number the value floor. If this number is less than the current market value of the property, buy the tax lien. If this number is above the current market value of the property, find another tax lien.

Total Costs	$17,300
Multiplier	×6
Value Floor	$103,400

Bid Calculations

What is the maximum you should bid on a tax lien at the tax lien sale? The answer is it depends. Say you are bidding at a tax sale where the highest bid wins. Further, at this tax lien sale, every dollar you spend over the face amount of the tax lien does not earn interest. Therefore, your rate of return decreases as the amount of your bid increases.

Say your minimum acceptable return is 9 percent annually. You are interested in bidding on a $6,000 tax lien. The interest rate on the tax lien face amount is 12 percent annual interest. You have $600 in travel expenses.

Let us calculate the maximum amount you can bid, keeping your minimum acceptable return at 9 percent annually. Let us assume the tax lien is redeemed by the property owner after one year.

Multiply $6,000 by 12 percent and you get $720. Of $8,000, $720 is 9 percent. Subtract $600 in travel expenses from $8,000 and you get $7,400. Your maximum bid is $7,400.

Maximum Bid Highest Bid Sale

Tax Lien	$6,000
Interest Rate	×12%
Annual Return	$720
$720 / 9% =	$8,000
Travel Expenses	−$600
Maximum Bid	$7,400

Interest Rate Bid

If you are going to buy a tax lien in an interest rate bid state, you will again need to calculate what your minimum acceptable return is. Say you are looking at a tax lien in Illinois with a face value of $6,300.

Illinois uses a staggered interest rate schedule it can charge the property owner. You will bid a set interest rate that will remain in place until the property owner redeems your tax lien.

The bidder who bids the lowest interest rate is the winning bidder. The bidding starts at 18 percent per six-month period. Using our rule of thumb for a six-month interest rate, we multiply the 18 percent times two to determine the annual interest rate. That is 36 percent annually!

Rule of Thumb

$$18\% \times 2 = 36\%$$

You win the bid with a six-month interest bid of 11 percent. You have $500 in travel expenses. Your amount invested in the tax lien is $6,800.

Amount Invested

Tax Lien	$6,300
Travel Expenses	$500
Amount Invested	$6,800

The property owner redeems your tax lien after 24 months. How much interest will you make? Your interest will be calculated in six-month intervals on the amount you paid for the tax lien.

You paid $6,300 for the tax lien. You bid 11 percent interest for six months. The $6,300 will be multiplied by 11 percent. The resulting number is then multiplied by four. Four is the number of six-month periods in the 24 months it took the property owner to redeem your tax lien.

Amount Returned

Tax Lien	$6,300
Interest Rate	×11%
Six-Month Return	$693
Number of Six-Month Intervals	×4
Amount Returned	$2,772

To find your annual yield, divide the amount returned by the amount invested. Then divide this number by two because the amount returned is over two years. The amount returned is $2,772. The amount invested, including your travel expenses, is $6,800. Let us see: A 20.5 percent annual yield!

Annual Yield

$$\$2,772 / \$6,800 = 41\%$$
$$41\% / 2 = 20.5\%$$

Determining Your Minimum Interest Bid

To determine the minimum interest rate you can bid at an interest rate bid tax lien sale we recommend you use the same interest rate you set for the highest bidder tax lien sale. If you have minimal expenses, the amount of your return will be the interest rate you have bid.

If you have significant expenses, you will have to factor this into your calculations. This means you will increase your minimum interest bid to the point that interest earned on your total investment, including expenses, gives you the investment return you need.

We will use the same numbers from the highest bid tax lien sale. Let us say your minimum acceptable return is 9 percent annually. You are interested in bidding on a $6,000 tax lien. You have $600 in travel expenses.

Let us calculate the minimum interest rate you can bid that will keep your minimum acceptable return at 9 percent annually. Let us assume that the tax lien is redeemed by the property owner after one year. We are looking for $6,000 times what interest rate that will give us a 9 percent return on a $6,600 investment?

$6,600 times 9 percent is $594. This is your minimum amount of return for one year. We divide $594 by $6,000. Remember $6,000 is the tax lien amount that is earning interest. $594 is 9.9 percent of $6,000. We will round up to 10 percent. Your minimum interest rate bid is 10 percent.

Minimum Interest Bid

Tax Lien	$6,000
Travel Expenses	$600
Total Investment	$6,600
Minimum Interest	×9%
Minimum Return	$594
Minimum Interest Bid	$594 / $6,000 = 9.9%

Property Interest Bid

If you are going to buy a tax lien in a property interest bid state, you will again need to calculate what your minimum acceptable return is. Your annual return on a property interest bid will be the interest rate paid by that taxing authority. This interest rate must be converted to an annual interest rate if it is not already. Then you must take into account your expenses.

You are actually bidding for a percentage undivided ownership interest in the property. The taxing authority is trying to protect the property owner. Instead of the collateral for the tax lien being the entire property, the collateral for the tax lien is a partial interest in the property. The bidder who accepts the smallest percentage interest in the property wins the bid.

If your real estate tax lien investment strategy is to collect interest on the tax lien, then your ownership interest in the property is not too important. However, we caution you that something may prevent the property owner from redeeming the tax lien. Then the bigger your undivided ownership interest is, the more security you will have for your investment.

If your real estate tax lien investment strategy is to get the deed to the property, then the larger the undivided ownership interest you have in the property the better. Remember, if you do foreclose on your tax lien you will get a tax deed to the property. You will have a percentage interest in the property based on your original bid.

If your winning bid is for a 70 percent undivided interest in the property, then the property owner will retain a 30 percent ownership interest in the property. You and the property owner will be on the title as tenants in common. Our rule of thumb is that you want to have no less than a 50 percent undivided interest in the property to protect your investment. You will then never bid less than 50 percent for the tax lien.

In the next chapter we will show you where to buy real estate tax liens. This is where some of you will be able to combine business with pleasure. Are there any skiers out there? How about sun worshippers?

CHAPTER 7

Where to Buy Real Estate Tax Liens

Where to begin? Where to start? Almost every county or municipality in the tax lien states or provinces has tax sales every year. There are tens of thousands of real estate tax lien buying opportunities waiting for you. Our point is that you must get started to make any money.

We recommend you begin by calling your local taxing authority. It does not matter if you live in a tax lien or a tax deed area. Ask them for information regarding local real estate tax lien sales. You may be surprised by the wealth of information they provide to you.

If you live in an area that does not conduct real estate tax lien sales, no problem. Choose an area or state that is close to where you live. Some real estate tax lien investors research the population and even ages of their target county and neighboring counties before they invest. We think this is overkill.

Their point is to find areas with limited population or large population. Limited population may mean less competition. Large population may mean a plethora of tax lien investment opportunities.

An aging population may mean older neighborhoods that are declining. Therefore, the underlying property may not be good security for the tax lien being redeemed. A younger population may mean newer neighborhoods that are on the upswing. This may provide better security for the tax lien being redeemed.

Types of Property

Some tax lien investors find some types of property more profitable than other types of property. We recommend you start out with what are generally regarded as the more profitable types of property. We also recommend that you avoid starting out with the less profitable property types.

Profitable Properties

Single-family, one to four units, owner-occupied, mortgaged properties are the most profitable real estate tax lien investment properties. We know we just said a mouthful and an earful. Let us break it down to bite-size pieces.

Remember, we are making these distinctions in the context of real estate tax lien investing. We provide these distinctions to you to help you save time and money. These distinctions may not translate to a different real estate investment context, like buying apartments.

Single-Family Properties

Single-family properties are properties where a single family occupies and uses the property. Single-family properties make up the vast majority of all the real estate parcels subject to tax liens.

Single-family properties are the opposite of multifamily properties. Single-family properties are homes. Multifamily properties are apartments. The owners of single-family properties are people. The owners of multifamily properties are businesses.

One to Four Units

One to four units are the maximum-size property on which we recommend you buy the tax liens. This recommendation, as with all the recommendations in this section, is based on us wanting two things to happen for you.

First, we want to increase your potential real estate tax lien investment returns. Second, we want to increase the amount of security you have in making the real estate tax lien investment. As we said in Chapter 3, super-high returns with super-low risks. One to four units are your best bet to have this combination. The property tax burdens on one-to-four-unit properties are generally much more manageable than the tax burdens on larger properties.

Owner-Occupied

Owner-occupied property is the crème de la crème of real estate tax lien profitable properties. An owner-occupied property is a property wherein the property owner has more than just an ownership stake in the property.

The owner of the owner-occupied property is living in the property. The property is their home. They may be raising a family in the property. They are completely emotionally attached to the property.

If they lose the property, they are losing more than a piece of real estate. They are losing more than just their equity in the property. The owner of the owner-occupied property is losing their lifestyle if they lose the property.

They will fight to keep the property. That means you have better odds in your favor that the tax lien will be redeemed by the owner of the owner-occupied property. The non-occupying property owner may have no attachment to the property whatsoever.

Mortgaged Properties

A mortgaged property will be redeemed. Your ace in the hole is the mortgage lender. Once in a while even a property owner who is an owner-occupant will sometimes be forced to give up their home because of circumstances beyond their control.

A mortgage lender will never walk away from a property that is the security for their loan. They will redeem the real estate lien on the property. Then they will foreclose on their loan. The borrower will have to pay the mortgage arrcarages and the delinquent property taxes to the mortgage company in order to reinstate their loan.

There is one caveat to this. A mortgage lender may walk away from a property if they are upside down in the property. Upside down means the loan amount is higher than the property value. And the loan amount would have to be much higher than the property value. This could happen when a property has been contaminated in an environmental disaster.

Unprofitable Properties

Then there are just plain unprofitable properties in the real estate tax lien investment world. These properties in and of themselves are not unprofitable properties. However, in the context of real estate tax lien investing we are labeling them as unprofitable so you will avoid them as you get started.

Obviously, a property you evaluate and then decide that you are not going to pursue the tax lien could be considered an unprofitable property. That is not what we are talking about here.

In fact, for us, this is a profitable property in the sense that because you spent the time to do your investment due diligence and passed on investing, you saved yourself a likely investment loss. One or two investment losses can put a serious dent in your investment gains!

Raw Land

Some pieces of vacant property are worth less than the taxes due on them. The owners may have raw land that is land-locked. They have no way to get into or out of their property without going on someone else's property.

Many times raw land has no utilities that serve it. It is so far out of the path of progress that it will never have any value. Can we offer you some property in the west Texas desert? These types of properties have no value, so the property owner stops paying the property taxes. Then the taxing authority taxes over ownership.

Undeveloped lots can be profitable. There are just too many factors outside your control. The risk is super-high and the rewards are super-low. That is bass ackwards for your real estate tax lien investment strategy. Pass on tax liens on raw land.

Commercial Property

Commercial properties are less risky than raw land. Strip shopping centers, medical office buildings, and retail space are examples of commercial property. Unless you already have an extensive background in commercial real estate, you should avoid these properties.

There are large investment groups that invest in commercial real estate. We recommend you leave these properties to the big boys and girls. Typically, they have lots more money to throw at the properties that are worth something. You just cannot compete.

Buying at the Tax Lien Sale

If your investment strategy is to buy real estate tax liens for high-interest yields, you will have to attend the tax lien sale. Most taxing authorities conduct their tax lien sales in the form of an auction. We will present the information you need to prepare for these tax lien auctions. We will also teach you what to do at the auction itself.

Preparing for the Tax Lien Auction

There are two things you need to do to prepare for the tax lien auction. The first thing you need to do is actually register for the auction as a bidder. The second thing you need to do is get the bidder information packet from the taxing authority conducting the tax lien auction.

Register as a Bidder

Registration can be done before the tax lien sale or on the day of the auction. If registration information is not published with the tax sale property information, contact the taxing authority as soon as you know the date of the sale and ask when you can register.

Some taxing authorities may ask you to post a deposit when you register. The amount of the deposit depends on the area. Some areas will ask for a deposit in the form of a cashier's check of up to 25 percent of your proposed bid. Call ahead to clarify this information. This will save you extra trips.

Procure the Bidder Information Packet
Each tax jurisdiction has a different procedure for registering to bid. They also have their set way of conducting the bidding process itself. After you register you will be given an information packet detailing these procedures. Ask for the information packet if one is not automatically given to you.

Do not assume that because you have bid at a previous tax lien sale in a tax jurisdiction everything is still the same. There may be new procedural information that will be necessary for you to know in order to make a successful bid.

Seven Pieces of Information
The bidder information packet will contain seven pieces of critical information. These include the number of tax liens you can buy, the acceptable methods of payment for the tax liens, the way the interest is paid on the tax liens, when the interest is paid on the tax liens, the kind of paperwork you will receive after you buy tax liens, what you need to record to protect your tax lien investments, and whether you have to be present at the tax lien sale in order to be the winning bidder.

1. How Many Tax Liens Can You Buy?
Some taxing authorities put a limit on the number of tax liens an individual investor can buy. Most taxing authorities place no limit on the number of tax liens you can buy. They want the money! The limitation will be more a function of how much money you have to make investments.

2. How Do You Pay for the Tax Liens?
Each taxing authority mandates when the payments for the tax liens need to be made. They also mandate what form of payment they will accept. Whatever the form of the payment, you pay the purchase price to the taxing authority.

You have no direct contact with the property owner at the tax lien sale. As a rule of thumb, most taxing authorities require that you pay immediately for the tax liens you buy. They want you to pay for the tax liens with cash, cashier's check, or money order. See Chapter 14, "Tax Lien States" for the information about your area.

3. How Are You Paid Interest?

You will be paid the amount you invested in the tax lien plus the interest by the taxing authority. This assumes the property owner redeems the tax lien. Some taxing authorities have notice requirements.

This means they have to tell you within a certain time frame if the property owner has redeemed the tax lien. Once the property owner redeems the tax lien, the taxing authority processes the property owner's payment. They then send the money to you.

4. When Will You Be Paid?

You are paid only if the property owner redeems the tax lien. The taxing authority does not make interest payments to you. You will receive a one-time payment of principal and interest.

5. What Paperwork Will You Receive?

You will receive some type of paperwork from the taxing authority. The states and territories refer to this paperwork by different names. These names include tax lien, tax certificate, tax lien certificate, certificate of purchase, certificate of sale, tax claims, certificate of delinquency, receipt showing the amount paid, receipt for the purchase money, tax sale receipt, and tax sale certificate.

Keep this paperwork in a safe place. This paperwork is the evidence that you bought and paid for the tax lien. You will need to present this paperwork to the taxing authority in order to receive your money. Finally, this paperwork can be assigned to another investor for a fee (see Chapter 8).

6. What Do You Need to Record?

Each state specifies what you need to do to protect your tax lien investment. In some areas you will have to record specific documents with the recorder's office that become part of the public record. You also may need to notify the property owner within a certain period of time after you have purchased the tax lien on their property.

7. Do You Have to Be Present to Bid?

In the vast majority of areas, the taxing authority requires you to be present at the auction to bid. Some states even require you to be a resident of the state to bid in the auction. There are a few areas that will accept bids by mail.

We recommend you attend an auction before you actually make a bid. This may prove inconvenient because most tax lien sales are held only once a year. As an alternative, we suggest you attend a foreclosure sale in your area. These are typically held on a monthly basis.

At the Tax Lien Auction

Tax lien auctions are held in a public place. Many times tax lien auctions such as foreclosure sales are held on the steps of the county courthouse. The first thing you need to do is check in with the official conducting the tax lien auction. You will register with them and you may receive a bidder card. You will use the bidder card to signal your bid.

Overview

Here is an overview of what will happen at the tax lien auction.

1. You will register and receive your bidder card.
2. The auctioneer will begin the auction following a preset order of properties.
3. You and the other bidders will use your bidder cards to make bids.
4. The auctioneer will accept the best bid based on the type of bidding used.
5. After your bid is accepted you will show your bidder card to the auctioneer.
6. You will sign a receipt for the transaction.
7. You will pay your bid amount to the treasurer.
8. You will receive paperwork evidencing your tax lien purchase.

Competition

Remember that the real estate tax lien auction is a competition. There are other investors who are interested in the same properties in which you are interested. The larger the taxing jurisdiction, the more investors will attend the auction. If you are attending an auction in a very large jurisdiction, expect it to be crowded.

You may find that you are more comfortable with smaller tax lien auctions. Smaller areas may not have institutional investors present with deep pockets. Because most interest rates on tax liens are set by the state and not the county or municipality, you will receive the same yields by competing with two other bidders at the smaller auction as you would competing with 15 other bidders at the larger auction.

By preparing for the competitive situation at the tax lien auction, you will be in more control of yourself once the bidding starts. You want to guard against letting yourself get carried away.

You have done the hard work and you know what the tax lien is worth to you. You have determined how much you can invest. You know what your yield requirements are. Your investment strategy is to make a profit. If another bidder outbids your predetermined maximum bid, then stop bidding. We promise you there will be tons of other tax liens for you to bid on.

Georgetown, Texas

We share with you one of our experiences at a real estate auction in Georgetown, Texas. While this was not a tax lien auction, we present it here to give you an example of how to bid and when to bid.

We were in Georgetown doing a marketing promotion and were doing some sightseeing. We drove past an old Victorian home with signs in the front yard announcing an estate sale for the weekend. We stopped to look and discovered two things going on.

An estate auctioneer had rented the vacant property and brought their inventory of estate sale items to this property. The auctioneer wanted the ambiance of the property to create an atmosphere for the estate sale. We actually thought this was a very smart marketing ploy.

We also discovered that on Sunday afternoon at the conclusion of the estate sale auction, the auctioneer was going to hold an auction for the property. This was now becoming very exciting!

We toured the house and grounds and decided to participate at the property auction. We had determined that the property needed work. The property needed about $150,000 in renovations. Once the work was completed we felt the property would sell in the $450,000 to $600,000 range.

The auction was conducted in the backyard under a canopy. We registered for the auction and got our bidding card. There were 30 to 40 people sitting in chairs at the back of the auction area. We walked in and sat down toward the front so we would have an unobstructed view of the auctioneer.

The auctioneer made an announcement that there would be a bidder making their bids over the phone to one of the members of the auctioneer's staff. The auctioneer then began the auction by asking for an opening bid of $400,000.

When no one would bite, the auctioneer asked the bidders to make an opening bid.

The first bid was for $50,000. The second bid was for $100,000. The third bid was for $150,000. We were watching and listening and waiting. Finally there were only two bidders bidding: the bidder on the phone and one of the bidders on-site. They were bidding back and forth in $5,000 increments.

The bidder on the phone bid $195,000. The auctioneer asked for a $200,000 bid. The bidder on-site said nothing. The auctioneer announced, "$195,000 going once. $195,000 going twice." That is when Bill raised his bid card from his lap and held it in front of him.

The auctioneer pointed at Bill and said, "$200,000." Our bid was relayed to the phone bidder. You could tell they were stunned by our bid from the reaction of the auctioneer's staff member. Finally, they came back with a bid of $205,000. We immediately bid $210,000.

This was going to be our final bid no matter what. We had determined that we would bid no more than $210,000 before the auction started. The auctioneer asked for a $215,000 bid. None was forthcoming. The auctioneer announced "$210,000 going once. $210,000 going twice. $210,000 going three times."

"Sold for $210,000."

We had won the bid. We were very happy. People came up and congratulated us. What we want you to learn is our technique for bidding. We made sure we were well situated to be seen by the auctioneer. We did not bid until the end of the bidding process. We knew what our top bid was going to be. We did not go over our predetermined top bid.

Fairness of the Bidding Process

Many taxing authorities enforce regulations designed to ensure that the bidding process is a fair process for everyone involved, including the property owner. These regulations can assess penalties on a bidder for bidding on a tax lien with no intention of buying it.

You can be assessed a penalty if your bid is accepted and you do not pay for the tax lien within the appropriate time frame. This penalty is a percentage of the winning bid and can be up to 25 percent of that bid.

Some areas have strict rules on collusion between bidders. This is particularly important to the property owner in property interest bid states. These rules make it illegal for a group of bidders to decide ahead of time not to bid against each other on the tax liens. They divvy up who will bid on what tax lien so that each investor receives an undivided 100 percent interest in the property.

Types of Bidding

The types of bidding used at tax lien auctions are specified by the taxing jurisdiction. There are four types of bidding used. These are highest bid, buyer's bid, interest rate bid, and property interest bid. No matter what the type of bid, the taxing jurisdiction will set a minimum bid that will cover the delinquent property taxes, penalties, costs, and fees.

Highest Bid

The bidder who makes the highest bid over the amount due for the tax lien is the winning bidder. Any amount you pay for the tax lien beyond the amount due is put into an account that earns interest over time.

This excess amount is called the bid premium. If the property owner redeems the tax lien, this money and the interest it has received are transferred to you. This is in addition to the tax lien face amount and the interest that is paid back by the property owner.

There is one caveat on the bid premium being transferred to you. If the tax lien is not redeemed by the property owner, and you are issued a tax deed, the property owner may have the right to these funds.

Highest Bid Example

Bidder 1, bidder 2, and bidder 3 are bidding on a tax lien that has a face amount of $3,700. Bidder 1 bids $4,100. Bidder 2 bids $4,150. Bidder 3 bids $4,200. No further bids are forthcoming.

Bidder 3 wins the bid at $4,200 and receives the tax lien. If the property owner redeems the tax lien, bidder 3 will receive $3,700 plus interest on that amount. Bidder 3 also will receive another $500 back, the bid premium, plus interest returned on the $500.

Highest Bid

Winning Bid	$4,200
Tax Lien Amount	$3,700
Bid Premium	$500

Buyer's Bid

The buyer's bid is similar to the highest bid. You will bid a dollar amount for the tax lien. However, the amount of your bid that is in excess of the amount due on the tax lien will not be returned to you if the property owner redeems the tax lien. The more you pay for the tax lien, the lower your investment yield will be.

Buyer's Bid Example

Bidder 1, bidder 2, and bidder 3 are bidding on a tax lien that has a face amount of $3,700. Bidder 1 bids $4,100. Bidder 2 bids $4,150. Bidder 3 bids $4,200. No further bids are forthcoming.

Bidder 3 wins the bid at $4,200 and receives the tax lien. If the property owner redeems the tax lien, bidder 3 will receive $3,700 back plus interest on that amount. Bidder 3 will not receive any other money. Their $500 becomes part of the cost of doing business.

Buyer's Bid

Winning Bid	$4,200
Tax Lien Amount	$3,700
Amount Returned	$3,700
Cost of Doing Business	$500

Interest Rate Bid

Bidders bid on the minimum interest rate that is acceptable for them to receive. Bidders do not bid a tax lien amount. If you are the winning bidder you will have to pay the delinquent taxes and penalties in full.

You will receive a tax lien for that amount. The interest you receive is what you bid. You cannot bid an interest rate that is higher than what the taxing authority can legally charge the property owner.

Interest Rate Bid Example

Bidder 1 and bidder 2 are bidding on a tax lien that has a face amount of $3,000. Bids begin at 18 percent per six-month interval. Bidder 1 will bid down to 7 percent for the six-month interval, or 14 percent annually. Bidder 2 will bid down to 6.5 percent for the six-month interval, or 13 percent annually.

Bidder 2 wins the bid. Bidder 2 pays $3,000 and receives the tax lien. If the property owner redeems the tax lien after 18 months, Bidder 2 will receive $3,000 plus $195 in interest for three six-month intervals.

Interest Rate Bid

Tax Lien	$3,000
Interest Rate	6.5%
Six-Month Intervals	3
Interest	$585
Yield	13%

Property Interest Bid

Bidders bid for an interest in the property. The bidder who is willing to take the smallest portion of undivided interest in the property will win the tax lien. The idea is to protect the property owner. If the property owner does not redeem the tax lien, you can foreclose on your interest in the property.

If you have a 90 percent interest in the property you obviously have more security for your tax lien than if you had a 60 percent interest in the property. Remember, our rule of thumb says to have at least a 50 percent interest in the property.

Property Interest Bid Example

Bidder 1 and bidder 2 are bidding on a tax lien that has a face amount of $5,000. Either bidder will have to pay the $5,000 tax lien amount. Let us say the tax lien pays 14 percent annual interest.

Bidder 1 will not take less than an 85 percent interest in the property. Bidder 2 will take an 80 percent interest in the property. Bidder 2 will be the winning bidder. When the property owner redeems the tax lien, bidder 2 will receive the $5,000 and 14 percent annual interest.

However, if the property owner does not redeem the tax lien, bidder 2 will have to foreclose on the property. Bidder 2 will then have an 80 percent undivided interest in the property. The property owner will retain a 20 percent undivided interest in the property.

We will do two calculations. The first calculation will be if the property owner redeems the tax lien. The second calculation will be if the property owner does not redeem the tax lien. Either way if you are bidder 2 you come out ahead.

Property Interest Bid / Tax Lien Redeemed

Tax Lien	$5,000
Interest Rate	$\times 14\%$
Interest (one year)	$700

Property Interest Bid / Tax Lien Not Redeemed

Investor Ownership Interest	80%
Property Owner Interest	20%
Property Value	$100,000
Investor Value	$80,000

In the next chapter we will show you how to turn your real estate tax liens into a gold mine. Hint: We want you to look for a sign.

CHAPTER 8

How to Turn Your Real Estate Tax Liens into a Gold Mine

This is the chapter that delivers on this book's title. We are going to teach you how to assign your real estate tax liens to other investors for a profit. You are certainly welcome to do real estate tax lien investing in the traditional way. In fact, for most of you the traditional way will be your preferred way to invest in real estate tax liens.

However, for some of you, what we are about to present will have lightbulbs going off in your heads like flashbulbs at a Hollywood premier. Our overall real estate investment strategy is Quick Cash. No matter what real estate vehicle we are investing in, we want to make money quickly. Investing in real estate tax liens is no different.

The quickest way to make money in any real estate investment is through assigning the deal to another investor. You find a good real estate deal. You put the deal under contract. Then you assign your good deal for a fee. We are going to show you how to turn your real estate tax lien investing into a gold mine.

Assigning will work when you are negotiating with the property owner before the tax lien sale. Assigning will work after you have bought a tax lien at a tax lien sale. Assigning will work when you have acquired the deed to the property after foreclosing at the expiration of the redemption period.

Flipping

Many real estate investors are familiar with the term *flipping*. Flipping is getting in and out of a real estate investment quickly. You can buy a property, fix it up, and immediately put it back on the market. You can buy a property, skip the fix-up, and immediately put it back on the market.

The number one way we flip real estate is through assigning real estate contracts. This is a way to flip real estate without buying or owning the property. You may not even have to close escrow. We really are not flipping real estate at all. To flip real estate, technically, you need to own the real estate.

We are flipping real estate contracts. Real estate contracts are personal property. We own the contracts. Once you know how to assign contracts, your real estate investing career is going to take off.

We will give you the information you need to understand assigning contracts. We will talk about the types of contracts you can assign. We will then apply assigning to the real estate tax lien arena and show you how to make quick cash assigning your real estate tax lien contracts.

What Is Assigning?

Assigning a real estate contract transfers your position in the contract to another person for a fee. Technically, assigning a real estate contract allows you, the assignor, to assign the contract to a new person, the assignee. An assignment transfers your rights to purchase a property under the terms of a real estate purchase contract to a new buyer.

The new buyer literally steps into your shoes and can buy the property under the same terms and conditions you negotiated with the seller. The assignor gives paperwork, the assignment, to the assignee, who receives the paperwork in return for money or other valuable consideration.

Assignment Fees

The money you receive for assigning a contract is called an assignment fee. The fee is negotiable between you, the assignor, and the person you assign the contract to, the assignee. The other party to the contract you have had accepted—seller, lessor, optionor, lender, taxing authority, or whoever—has no say so in your negotiations with your assignee.

What kind of dollar amount should the fee be that you receive for assigning a contract? We have assigned a contract for as little as $1,000. We also have assigned a contract for as much as $100,000. Typically, the fees we have received for assigning contracts range between $5,000 and $15,000.

Types of Real Estate Contracts that You Can Assign

Virtually every type of real estate contract can be assigned. You can assign purchase contracts, options, leases, lease options, mortgage contracts, trust deeds, tax liens, the list goes on. You can even assign an assignment contract! If it is a contract involving real estate, you can figure out a way to assign it. Assigning a contract is the easiest and quickest way to flip real estate.

Purchase Contracts

The complete name for this contract is actually purchase contract for real estate and deposit receipt. This is the contract that contains the terms and conditions to which you and the seller agree when the seller accepts your offer to purchase their property.

You can copy the blank purchase contract in Appendix C. You can access the Texas Real Estate Commission's contract at www.trec.state.tx.us. Office supply stores in your area may carry a generic real estate purchase contract. Or, you can use a purchase contract from a local real estate company.

The truth of the matter is that you can use a napkin at a restaurant to write a real estate offer. We do not recommend using napkins to write your offers, however; the ink runs on the napkin when it gets wet. (We have had it happen.) As long as the purchase contract is in writing, it is valid. Every state has a statute of frauds that says for a real estate contract to be valid, it must be in writing.

If you are working with a real estate agent and they want to use their contract, then use their contract. It is not worth the aggravation spending the time to educate a real estate agent on why you should use your contract. Just make sure everything you want in the contract is communicated by whatever purchase contract you use.

You will want to include everything you can possibly think of in your purchase contract. Every blank space is either filled in, or the letters *NA* (not applicable) are written in. You are negotiating not just for yourself but also for the buyer you are going to assign the contract to.

Believe us when we tell you that the new buyer wants a really good deal! How the new buyer gets a really good deal is when you write a really good contract that has been accepted by the property owner.

There is one caveat we will give you when you are negotiating with a property owner before the tax lien sale. If they are delinquent on their property taxes, they may also be behind on their mortgage payments. This is not necessarily a deal killer.

However, if the property owner has received an official notice of default from their mortgage holder your state may require special wording in the real estate contract if you are purchasing a homeowner's equity in preforeclosure. If you do not, the courts can void your deal plus impose fines and penalties against you. Remember, the preforeclosure phase lasts until the foreclosure sale occurs no matter what state the property is in.

We have included the requirements for your purchase contract if you are negotiating with a California homeowner who not only has a delinquent property tax problem but also has received a notice of default from their mortgage holder.

Deposit Receipt

There is a deposit receipt section in every real estate purchase contract. Sometimes this is referred to as the earnest money

Notice Required by California Law

Until your right to cancel this contract has ended _____
(buyer) or anyone working for _____ (buyer) CAN-
NOT ask you to sign or have you sign any deed or any other document.
You may cancel this contract for the sale of your house without any penalty
or obligation at any time before _____ (AM/PM) on _____, 20_____. See
the attached notice of cancellation form for an explanation of this right.

NOTICE OF CANCELLATION

_____

(Enter date contract signed)

You may cancel this contract for the sale of your house, without penalty
or obligation, at any time before _____
To cancel this transaction, personally deliver a signed and dated copy of
this cancellation notice, or send a telegram to _____ (buyer) at
_____ (address)
NOT LATER THAN _____
I hereby cancel this transaction _____ (date)

_____

_____

(Sellers signatures)

deposit. This is where the buyer includes some type of valuable consideration with the contract to show good faith to the
seller. In other words, the deposit the buyer attaches to the
offer shows that they are earnest about buying the property.

We recommend you use a promissory note as your deposit instrument for all you contracts. We recommend you use
a promissory note for two reasons. First, by using a promissory
note you protect your cash. Second, you do not want 10, 15, or
20 personal checks out there accompanying all those offers
you are writing and presenting.

You only have to turn the promissory note into cash if
your offer is accepted and you are going to open an escrow. If
you assign your purchase contract before you open escrow,
then the promissory note never gets cashed.

The promissory note we recommend you use can be found in Appendix C. It is in the format of a check. You may be able to find a similar promissory note in the legal forms section of an Office Depot or Office Max.

This is a much simpler version than the promissory note used by lenders as evidence of the debt for a real estate loan. The main idea here is to have something attached to the purchase contract that represents consideration. This gives validity to your contract.

Option Contracts

A real estate option contract says you will buy a property within a certain time frame. You will commit funds in the form of an option fee or option money to keep the option open for the period of time agreed.

Option contracts have a unique feature among all the different real estate contracts. All contracts are bilateral to begin with. Consent in the form of mutual agreement on both the seller's part and the buyer's part is necessary for validity. Once the option has been agreed to, only the buyer can exercise it.

The seller cannot back out of the deal if the buyer exercises the option. The optionee (buyer) can back out of the deal and not be sued for specific performance. The optionor (seller) gets to keep the option fee the optionee put up, but that is all.

We use an option contract that is designed to be assigned by the wording of the contract itself. See Appendix C for a copy of this option contract. In the event you are using an option contract that is not set up to be assigned, all you have to do is add the words *and/or assigns* to the buyer's name portion of the contract.

Leases, Lease Options, Mortgages, Trust Deeds, Tax Liens

Every type of real estate contract can be assigned. Leases, lease options, mortgages, trust deeds, and tax liens can be assigned.

In fact, the tax lien you buy from the taxing authority is assigned by them to you!

Car dealers use assignments in their rebate programs. Assigning contracts is everywhere in the business world. The point is we want you to feel comfortable assigning real estate contracts.

How to Assign a Contract

Assigning a contract begins when you write the initial offer. In the initial offer you make to the owner, whether it is a purchase contract, an option contract, a mortgage contract, a trust deed, or a tax lien, you use the terminology *and/or assigns* in the contract.

You have a new name from this day forth. Think of it as if you are being given a royal title. This title is much better than *sir* or *madam.* It is even better than *your royal highness.* It is more powerful than *your majesty.* From now on, as a real estate investor writing contracts, you will be known as *Your Name and/or assigns.*

Assignment Contract

We have shown you how to assign a real estate contract using the *and/or assigns* name addition. What about an actual assignment contract? We find that having an assignment contract available makes assigning any contract a more viable option.

You still want *and/or assigns* in the buyer's name section in whatever contract you are writing. By using the assignment contract in conjunction with *and/or assigns,* you build an added layer of written protection for yourself, the owner of the property, and the new buyer.

Assigning a contract is completely above board and legal. When an owner asks you what *and/or assigns* means, this is what you should say:

And/Or Assigns Script

"_____ (Owner's Name), the and/or assigns clause gives both you and us the added flexibility of bringing in additional buyers or money partners to succesfully close our transaction. Would that be all right with you?"

In our experience, the owner's answer has always been yes. Sometimes we have had to work with the owners a while and educate them on the benefits that this phrase has for them. All you are trying to do with *and/or assigns* is create flexibility.

What do you do if the owner's answer is no? You want to make sure the owner understands what you are trying to do by having the ability to assign your contract. Flexibility is the name of the game in making a real estate deal work.

Flexibility on your part and on the owner's part is especially important in a tax lien preauction real estate deal. If the owner will not agree to give you the flexibility you need by having *and/or assigns* in your contract, let the owner know that you will not proceed to present the rest of the contract.

You must stick to your guns on this point. *And/or assigns* is that important to your real estate investing success. It is much harder to come back to the negotiating table after you have already reached an agreement with the owner. Have *and/or assigns* part of your agreement from the beginning. See Appendix C for a copy of our assignment contract.

Why Use an Assignment?

There are four main reasons for using an assignment. Assigning a purchase contract makes you money without buying the property. Assigning is the fastest way to flip a property. Assigning is the quickest way to make money in real estate investing. Assigning avoids all the pitfalls of real estate ownership.

Assigning Makes You Money without Buying Property

Assigning a real estate contract makes you money without buying property. In a traditional real estate investment, you (the investor) make money by finding a property, writing and having your offer accepted by the seller, opening and successfully closing an escrow, fixing up the property (if necessary), and then selling the property to a buyer. This is what a timeline would look like for buying real estate to make money:

Buying Timeline for Buying Real Estate to Make Money

Find Property	Write Offer	Offer Accepted	Open Escrow	Close Escrow	Fix Up	Sell Property
				Spend Money	Spend Money	Make Money

We are being rather generous with the timeline. It is actually harder than that. The reality of making money when you buy real estate the traditional way begins with that timeline. You really do not make any money until you do the following: Advertise and show the property, receive and accept an offer, and open and close an escrow. Then, and only then, do you make money.

Selling Timeline for Buying Real Estate to Make Money

Advertise Property	Show Property	Receive Offer	Accept Offer	Open Escrow	Close Escrow
Spend Money					Make Money

Assigning Is the Fastest Way to Flip Property

Assigning a real estate contract is the fastest way to flip property. Face it. Paperwork is the name of the game in real estate investing. The less paperwork involved in a real estate transaction, the better.

The less paperwork involved in a real estate transaction means the less time it takes to complete the transaction. The less time involved on your part and on the part of the real estate investor or retail buyer you are assigning the contract to means a faster turn around time for you.

Paperwork for Flip without Escrow

This is the paperwork involved in the simplest flip we do. This is a no-money-down deal. There is no escrow involved. We write a purchase contract and promissory note, which we present to the property owner. The owner accepts our offer. They give us back our promissory note and a quitclaim deed to transfer title to the property. This makes three distinct pieces of paperwork for the buying side.

Flip Paperwork for Buying Property

1. Real estate purchase contract.
2. Promissory note.
3. Quitclaim deed.

We receive a purchase contract and a personal check as an earnest money deposit from an investor to whom we flip the property. We give the real estate investor a quitclaim deed.

The investor gives us a cashier's check. We give the investor back their personal check. Again, we do not have an escrow between the investor and us. We have an additional four distinct pieces of paperwork on the selling side.

Flip Paperwork for Selling Side

1. Real estate purchase contract.
2. Personal check.
3. Quitclaim deed.
4. Cashier's check.

Now we have a total of seven distinct pieces of paperwork involved in this transaction. There are three pieces of paperwork on the buying side. There are four pieces of paper on the selling side.

Paperwork for Assignment

What if we were able to have assigned our purchase contract instead of doing a traditional flip where we actually owned something? Would we speed up the flip by doing an assignment? How much paperwork is involved if we assign our purchase contract?

We write a purchase contract and a promissory note, which we present to the owner. The owner gives us back our promissory note. So far everything is the same as doing a flip.

Here is where the assignment transaction changes the paperwork. The owner does not give us a quitclaim deed. The owner gives a quitclaim deed to transfer title to the investor to whom we assign the purchase contract. We now have one less quitclaim deed using the assignment.

The next paperwork that changes with the assignment is there is no second purchase contract. We do not receive a purchase contract from the investor. The investor takes over our position in the first purchase contract.

The investor does not write a personal check to accompany their offer to us. We receive a cashier's check from the investor. The investor receives the quitclaim deed from the owner.

Assignment Paperwork

1. Real estate purchase contract.
2. Promissory note.
3. Quitclaim deed.
4. Cashier's check.

The difference in the amount of paperwork for a flip and an assignment is substantial. The flip paperwork runs to seven items. The assignment paperwork runs to four items.

Our point is that assigning a contract is the fastest way to flip property. Assigning a contract is flipping property! Flipping is good. When you use assigning as a flipping tactic, you will streamline the paperwork and reduce the time involved in the transaction. You will also make the same amount of money on the deal.

Assigning Is the Quickest Way to Make Money

Assigning a real estate contract is the fastest way to make money in real estate investing. When you have a Quick Cash strategy, time is definitely of the essence.

The timeline for assigning contracts is substantially shorter than the timeline for a traditional real estate investment. Even with flipping a property, you cannot make money as quickly as when you assign contracts. As you can see, you can make money more quickly and at more junctures along the way than with a traditional real estate investment strategy of buying the property, owning the property, and selling the property.

Assigning Timeline
Assigning Contracts to Make Money

Find Property	Write Offer	Offer Accepted	Open Escrow	Close Escrow	Fix Up	Sell Property
		Make Money	Make Money	Make Money	Make Money	

Assigning Avoids the Pitfalls of Real Estate Ownership

Assigning a contract avoids all the pitfalls of real estate ownership. We feel that assigning is the best strategy for the tax lien investing arena. Assigning tax lien contracts has multiple advantages to the traditional tax lien investment strategy.

These advantages include no landlording, no monthly mortgage payments, no property taxes, no hazard insurance, no maintenance costs, no homeowner's association dues, no lawsuits, no extensive record keeping, and no income tax problems.

When to Assign a Contract

You can assign a real estate contact before, during, and after the closing. Assigning a contract before the closing is the way we like to do our own transactions. You tie up a property with an accepted contract and immediately search for a buyer to whom to assign the contract.

Assigning a contract during the closing is our second favorite way we like to do our transactions. You tie up the property and assign the contract before the closing takes place. The assignee takes your place in the closing and then winds up closing the escrow.

Assigning after the closing is the final way we like to do our transactions. Again, you tie up a property with an assignment clause in the contract. If you do not find a buyer before closing and wind up closing the property yourself, you can quickly transfer your interest in the property to another buyer after closing. Essentially, you are going to flip the property using what we call an assignment deed.

Look at the timeline for assigning contracts. This will give you a way to visualize the different times you can use an assignment. Anytime you can assign a contract and make money is a good time to do an assignment.

The timeline is the same for assigning in the real estate tax lien arena. You can assign your contract after you write the offer to buy the owner's equity and before an escrow is opened. You can assign your contract to buy the owner's equity during the escrow. And, you can assign your contract to buy the owner's equity after closing escrow.

Timeline for Assigning Contracts

Write Offer	Open Escrow	Close Escrow
Assign Before Closing	Assign During Closing	Assign After Closing

Assignment Before Closing

We do not ever want to close an escrow. At least not in the traditional way most real estate investors do. We want to close our deals in a different way. In the normal course of events, a real estate transaction goes like this: A real estate investor finds a potential property. The investor writes an offer on the property and presents it to the owner. There is a negotiation back and forth between the owner and the investor. There is an agreement as to price and terms. Then the owner and the investor open an escrow or go to a closing.

Once the escrow is complete, the escrow closes. The owner receives money or other valuable consideration from the investor. The investor receives the title to and possession of the property.

Close by Assigning

We close our deals by assigning our owner-accepted real estate contracts. By using an assignment of contract, we use a one-page escrow instruction between us and the buyer to whom we are assigning the contract. In the case of a tax lien we have the owner give a quitclaim deed to the new buyer.

Assignment during Closing

An assignment during closing is a very common occurrence in our real estate investing. We have said our favorite time period to do an assignment is before closing, but doing an assignment during closing runs a close second.

The difference between assigning before closing or during closing is whether you have formally opened escrow or not. An assignment before closing means you have written an offer and had it accepted but have not opened escrow before you assign the contract. An assignment during closing means you have done all of the above and opened an escrow.

The new buyer steps into your position as the buyer in the escrow. The assignment fee can come to you through the escrow or outside the escrow. Either way is fine.

An escrow will be opened for two reasons. If the owner requests an escrow, an escrow will be opened. If the new buyer requests an escrow with the owner an escrow will be opened.

Assignment after Closing

At first blush it might seem out of place for us to talk about assigning after the closing. However, as we have taught you to do with every contract you write, you used the clause *and/or assigns* when you wrote the purchase contract.

What do you do if you decide to close the transaction yourself because it is such a good deal or you have not found a new buyer before the closing date comes? The fastest way to assign your interest in a property after you have closed escrow is to quitclaim the property to a new buyer. Whatever interest or title you have in the property is transferred to the buyer.

No one but us will tell you that you can assign a piece of real estate after you have closed escrow. We call a quitclaim deed an assignment deed. We use this deed when we want to get out of a property quickly that we wind up owning.

Once you assimilate the assigning tactic into your tax lien investing strategy, you will begin to find all kinds of contracts to assign. Real estate contracts to assign will begin to find you. We look to assign every tax lien contract we write.

Assigning Real Estate Tax Liens

We have already talked about assigning contracts in the real estate tax lien arena in two of the three tax lien investment areas. You may put together a deal with a property owner in the tax lien preauction phase. You then assign your deal to another investor and receive an assignment fee.

You may wind up foreclosing on your tax lien after the property owner's redemption period expires. Rather than keeping the property for rental income or future appreciation, you give an assignment deed, a quitclaim deed, to another investor and receive an assignment fee.

What about assigning your tax lien after you make the winning bid at the tax lien auction? The taxing authority actually assigns their lien against the property to you after you pay the delinquent property taxes, interest, penalties, and fees. Why not assign your assignment?

Say you make the winning bid on a $5,000 tax lien. The interest being paid on this tax lien is 11 percent every six months. That is 22 percent annual interest. The property owner has a three-year redemption period.

What if you assign your tax lien certificate to another investor a week after the tax lien auction for $500? You get your $5,000 back plus a $500 profit. That is a 10 percent return on your investment in one week! What would the annual yield be?

Assign Your Tax Lien

Tax Lien	$5,000
Assignment Fee	$500
Your Return	10 percent
Annual Yield	520%!

How would the investor to whom you assigned your tax lien make out? Say the property owner redeems the tax lien after two years. The investor would have $5,500 invested in the tax lien: $5,000 for the lien itself and $500 to you for the assignment fee. The investor would receive 11 percent interest on $5,000 for four six-month intervals: $2,200 over the 24 months. This would be a 20 percent annual return.

Investor Return

Investment amount	$5,500
Tax Lien	$5,000
Interest Rate	×11%
Six-Month Return	$550
Six-Month Intervals	×4
Investor Return	$2,200
Annual Yield	20%

In the next chapter we will show you how to foreclose on your tax liens if the property owner does not redeem. As we have already said, after you foreclose you can quitclaim your interest in the property to another investor for quick cash. Are you excited or what?

CHAPTER 9

Foreclosing on Your Real Estate Tax Liens

We are going to spend the first part of this chapter training you in the foreclosure process. Every state has a slightly different method on how they go through their foreclosure procedures. However, the basic process is the same in every state.

What varies from state to state is the time periods allowed for foreclosure. Do not get too caught up in what may seem to be very technical information. We present this information so you can get the flavor of what is involved in a foreclosure.

We will then get into how to foreclose on real estate tax liens. In some tax jurisdictions you get a tax deed from the treasurer automatically at the end of the property owner's redemption period. In other taxing jurisdictions you may have to get an attorney and go to court to be able to foreclose on your tax liens.

Foreclosure

There is no more dreaded word in the real estate world than foreclosure. It does not matter if you are the real estate borrower or the real estate lender. No one likes to be in the foreclosure situation.

Foreclosure is a real estate lender, whether an institutional real estate lender or a private real estate lender, taking the title to a property away from the borrower in lieu of receiving mortgage payments. Said more formally, when all else has failed, a real estate lender will pursue allowed legal prerogatives to recover the collateral for the real estate loan in order to sell it and recoup their loan proceeds.

The definition of foreclosure is to shut out, exclude, bar, or deprive a person of the right to redeem a mortgage. Foreclosure is not only a process to recover a lender's collateral but also a procedure whereby a borrower's rights of redemption are eliminated and all interests in the subject property are removed.

Power of Sale Foreclosure

A foreclosure is based on the terms of the deed of trust or the mortgage contract, giving the lender, or the trustee, the right to sell the collateral property without being required to spend the time and money involved in a court foreclosure suit.

Texas

In Texas, for example, these nonjudicial foreclosures are more common than judicial foreclosures (lawsuits in court). The right to exercise the power of sale must be created in writing and is usually part of the deed of trust, which must clearly state that there is a right of nonjudicial foreclosure. The power of sale foreclosure is popular in Texas because it allows the trustee to sell the property more quickly and thus recover the lender's collateral in a timely manner.

In Texas the trustee named in the deed of trust has the power to sell the defaulted mortgaged property upon the request of the real estate lender or beneficiary of the trust deed. The trustee must then carefully follow the terms and conditions stated in the deed of trust for the foreclosure. The foreclosure sale must also follow the legal procedures of the state of Texas.

Texas Property Code

The Texas Property Code contains the following procedures for nonjudicial foreclosure. You can check what your state procedures are by contacting a real estate attorney or your local title insurance company.

1. The trustee must notify the debtor of the foreclosure sale at least 21 days before the date of the sale. This notice is to be sent by certified mail to the debtor's last known address.
2. Notice must be posted at the courthouse door of the county in which the property is located and filed in the county clerk's office where the sale is to be held.
3. The sale must be a public auction held between 10:00 A.M. and 4:00 P.M. on the first Tuesday of the month.
4. The sale must take place in the county where the property is located.
5. The holder of the debt on residential property must give the debtor at least 20 days to cure the default before the entire debt can be accelerated and declared due and the notice of sale given.

At the Foreclosure Sale

At the foreclosure sale, the trustee has an obligation to act impartially and can take no action that would discourage bidders. This is to be a public auction open to all persons, including the lender and the trustee.

There is no requirement in Texas that the auction generate fair market value; therefore, the property will go to the highest cash bidder. The purchaser of the foreclosed property takes the title without any covenants through an instrument called a trustee's deed.

The proceeds from the sale will be used to pay the trustee and any expenses of the trustee's sale. Then the lender who is foreclosing will be paid. If there is money still left, those creditors who had filed liens against the property will be paid. And finally, any surplus monies must be returned to the borrower/debtor.

In Texas, as in every other state, if a senior tax lien holder forecloses, all junior lien holders' interests terminate. If a junior lien forecloses, they get the title to the property subject to the senior lien holder's interest in the property.

Judicial Foreclosure and Sale

This legal procedure involves the use of the courts and the consequent sale of the collateral. Foreclosure by court order is an alternative method that may be used in Texas and other states, although it is not favored by commercial lenders. It is the only remedy if a deed of trust does not contain a power of sale provision.

How It Works

The delinquent mortgagors are notified of the default and the reasons for it. They are informed that an immediate solution is required and that all their efforts must be expended to solve the problem as quickly as possible.

However, if all attempts fail, a complaint is filed by the lender in the court for the county in which the property is located and a summons is issued to the borrowers. This initiates the foreclosure process. Simultaneously with this activity, a title search is made to determine the identities of all the parties having an interest in the collateral property and a lis pendens (literally, a legal action pending) is filed with the court, giving notice to the world of the pending foreclosure action.

Notice is sent to all parties having an interest in the property, requesting that they appear in court in order to defend their interests, or else they will be foreclosed (the literal definition we mentioned earlier) from any future rights by judgment of the court. It is vitally important for the complainant lender to notify all junior lien holders of the foreclosure action so they will not be enjoined from participation in the property auction. If junior lien holders are not given proper notice, they acquire the right to file suit on their own at some future time.

Jurisdiction

Depending upon the number of days required by the presiding jurisdiction for public notice to be given to inform any and all persons having an unrecorded interest in the subject property that a foreclosure suit is imminent, and depending upon the availability of a court date, the complaint is eventually aired before a presiding judge. In most instances, the defendant borrower does not appear in court unless special circumstances are presented in defense of the default.

Those creditors who do appear to present their claims are recognized and noted, and a sale of the property at a public auction by a court appointed referee or the sheriff is ordered by means of a judgment decree. The proceeds from the sale will be used to satisfy the parties named in the judgment. In Texas, the borrower's right to redeem the property continues for a reasonable time after the sale.

In a judicial foreclosure a junior lien holder's interest in the property is not automatically eliminated. If the junior lien holder did not join in the foreclosure suit, the property is sold, subject to the junior lien. If, however, the junior lien holder was a party to the foreclosure suit, this interest ends at the sale in the same way as the senior lien holder's interest does.

Insured Conventional Mortgage Foreclosure

Under the terms of the insurance policies of most private mortgage guarantee companies (private mortgage insurance, or PMI), a default is interpreted to be nonpayment for four months. Within 10 days of default, the lender is required to notify the private mortgage insurer, who will then decide whether or not to instruct the lender to foreclose.

When an insured conventional mortgage is foreclosed, the lender who is insured is the original bidder at the public auction of the collateral property. Under these circumstances, the successful bidder lender files notice with the insurance company within 60 days after the legal proceedings have transpired.

Loss Recovery

If the insurance company is confident of recovering any losses by purchasing the collateral property from the lender and then reselling it, it will reimburse the lender for the total amount of the lender's bid and receive title to the property. If, however, the private mortgage insurance company does not foresee any possibility for recovery, it may elect to pay the lender the agreed-upon amount of insurance, and the lender retains ownership of the property. The lender then sells the property to recover any balance still unpaid.

Remember that in any and all cases of judicial foreclosure and sale, any ownership rights acquired by the successful bidder at the foreclosure auction will still be subject to the statutory redemption rights of the defaulted mortgagor. A full fee simple absolute title cannot vest in the bidder until these redemption rights have expired.

Federal Housing Administration Insured Mortgage Foreclosure

Foreclosures on Federal Housing Administration (FHA) insured mortgages originate with the filing of form 2068 Notice of Default by the lender. This form must be given to the local FHA administrative office within 60 days of default. The notice describes the reasons for the mortgagor's delinquency, such as death, illness, marital difficulties, income loss, excessive financial obligations, employment transfers, or military service.

In many cases involving delinquent FHA insured mortgages, loan counselors from the local FHA office will attempt to design an agreement between the lender and the borrower for adjustments to the loan conditions in order to prevent foreclosure. The most common technique used in circumstances where default is beyond the borrower's control, but deemed curable, is forbearance of foreclosure.

Default Not Cured

If the problems causing the default are solved within a one-year period, the lender informs the local FHA office of that fact. If not, a default status report is filed and the lender must initiate foreclosure proceedings. If the bids at the foreclosure auction are less than the unpaid mortgage balance, the lender is expected to bid the debt, take title to the property, and present it to the FHA along with a claim for insurance, which may be paid in cash or in government securities. In some cases, with prior FHA approval, the lender may assign the defaulted mortgage directly to the FHA before the final foreclosure action in exchange for insurance benefits.

In any case, if the property can be sold easily at a price that would repay the loan in full, the lender simply would sell the property after bidding at the auction and would not apply for FHA compensation. If the FHA ends up as the owner of the property, the collateral may be sold as is. FHA may repair or refurbish (fix up the property) if they feel it can be resold at a higher price and minimize the losses to FHA.

Veterans Administration Guaranteed Mortgage Foreclosure

Unlike the FHA insured mortgage, whereby a lender's entire risk is recovered from the insurance benefits, a Veterans Administration (VA) loan is similar to a privately insured loan in that a lender receives only the top portion of the outstanding loan balance, up to a statutory limit. In the event a delinquency of more than three months on a VA loan, the lender must file proper notification with the local VA office, which may then elect to bring the loan current if it wishes.

If this occurs, the VA can come against the defaulting veteran for repayment of the funds advanced. Subrogation rights are given the lender against the mortgagor for the amount advanced. This means that the VA claim against the defaulting veteran takes priority over the rights of the lender to these funds.

Like FHA

Much like the FHA, VA lenders are required to make every effort to help the borrower through forbearance, payment adjustments, a deed in lieu of foreclosure (more about this shortly), or other acceptable solutions. Actual foreclosure is considered only as a last resort.

In the event of a foreclosure, the lender usually will be the original bidder at the auction and will submit a claim for losses to the local VA office. The VA then has the option to pay the unpaid balance, interest, and court costs, if any, and take title to the property. Or the VA can require that the lender keep the property and will pay the lender the difference between the determined value of the property on the date of the foreclosure and the mortgage balance. The latter alternative is usually chosen when the property is badly deteriorated, reinforcing the importance for a lender to supervise the condition of the collateral property.

Second Mortgage Foreclosure

Defaults of second mortgages and other junior mortgages are handled exactly in the same manner as are conventional first mortgages. Here, however, the relationship is usually between two individuals rather than between an institutional lender and an individual borrower.

A second mortgagee will usually seek the counsel of an attorney to manage the foreclosure process against a second mortgagor. The delinquent borrower will be requested to cure the problem within a certain time period. If a cure cannot be accomplished, notice is given to all persons having an interest in the property, and the attorney then files for judicial foreclosure.

The second mortgagee generally is the original bidder at the public sale and secures ownership of the collateral property subject to the lien of the existing first mortgage. They can then continue to maintain the integrity of this first mortgage by making any payments required, while seeking to sell the collateral to eliminate, or at least offset, any losses.

Deficiency Judgments

If the proceeds from a foreclosure sale are not sufficient to recover the outstanding loan balance plus the costs incurred as a consequence of default and interest to date, a lender may, in most states, sue on the mortgage for the deficiency. If the foreclosure is by court order, the judge normally awards the lender a judgment against the debtor in the amount of the deficiency. If a power of sale foreclosure takes place, the lender must then file suit against the debtor to collect any deficiency.

Texas

In Texas a lender would consider several things before pursuing legal action for a deficiency balance because the amount of the deficiency and the ability of the debtor to pay after the suit would be important factors. The homestead laws in Texas, and other states, would protect most of the debtor's basic possessions from this type of judgment. In most cases, a defaulted borrower does not have any nonexempt assets to make up this deficiency. Otherwise, they would have been put to use in order to prevent the default in the first place.

Current Trend

The current trend is to rely less on collecting deficiencies and more on limiting a borrower's personal liability on a real estate loan to the equity in the collateral property. Especially on purchase money loans, lenders may be limited to recovering only the collateral property and nothing more.

One reason for this trend is the tendency of a deficiency judgment to penalize those borrowers who make good on their debts. Because such judgments can become liens against any property a borrower holds or may acquire in the future, dishonest debtors may avoid payment by simply making certain they do not own any property in their own names.

Lender Adjustments

A lender will usually attempt to adjust the conditions of a loan in order to help a troubled borrower over short-term difficulties. Delinquent mortgage payments are the most common cause for a default. The nonpayment of property taxes or hazard insurance premiums, lack of adequate maintenance, and allowing priority liens to vest are also cause for default.

To offset the possibility of a foreclosure on delinquent mortgages, many lenders will exercise forbearance and waive the principal portion of a loan payment for a while or even extend a moratorium on the full monthly payment until a borrower can better arrange their finances. Other adjustments in terms of a delinquent mortgage that might aid the defaulted borrower include an extension of time or a recasting of the loan to reflect the borrower's current ability to pay under circumstances of financial distress.

Deed in Lieu of Foreclosure

Sometimes all efforts at adjusting the terms of a mortgage to solve a borrower's problems fail. A lender may then attempt to sell the loan. This creates further opportunities for you as a real estate investor. (See our book *Quick Cash in Foreclosures* for a great Brain Trust idea.)

If the lender cannot find a buyer willing and able to buy the loan, a lender may seek to secure a voluntary transfer of title to the property from the borrower. This action prevents the possibly costly and time-consuming process of foreclosure.

By executing either a quitclaim deed or a grant deed, a borrower can eliminate the stigma of a foreclosure suit, maintain a respectable credit rating, and avoid the possibility of a deficiency judgment. Real estate lenders are fully aware of the difficulties with evictions and the costs and time involved in a full foreclosure process. Most often, the lender encourages a hopelessly defaulted borrower to transfer a deed voluntarily.

However, the lender must take care to be protected against any future claims of fraud or duress by the borrower. In addition, the lender must be aware of the possibility of the existence of any other liens against the property. A quitclaim deed does not remove junior liens as does a completed foreclosure.

Tax Lien Foreclosures

When you foreclose on your real estate tax lien, you are foreclosing or shutting out the property owner's right of redemption. Just because you foreclose on your tax lien does not mean you automatically wind up with the property.

In some tax jurisdictions, when the property is auctioned at the foreclosure sale, you are paid the amount you are owed for the tax lien plus penalties, interest, costs, and fees. Any remaining equity is returned to the owner.

As we have said, some tax jurisdictions require you to obtain a court order before you can foreclose on your tax lien. Other tax jurisdictions allow nonjudicial foreclosure on your tax liens.

Whether you are foreclosing judicially or nonjudicially, you will have to follow public notice and filing requirements. If you fail to perform these requirements you may forfeit any right you had to the property. We recommend you work with an attorney to protect your rights.

If you file a foreclosure action with the court, a lis pendens is recorded against the title to the property. A lis pendens literally means a legal action is pending. This effectively clouds the title to the property.

A court date will be set and your motion to foreclose on your tax lien will be heard. The court then will make a judgment, hopefully in your favor, and schedule a foreclosure sale. The court will notify the property owner of the foreclosure sale.

If you are not required to file a foreclosure action with the court, you may have to file a notice of default with the local recorder. This gives all interested parties public notice of the foreclosure sale.

Bidders

In some states you are the only person allowed to bid at the foreclosure sale! Except in Florida, there is no public oral bid auction sale of the real estate. There is no opportunity for anyone else to bid up the price of the property. Your credit bid, which is the amount you are owed for the tax lien plus subsequent taxes and fees paid plus interest and foreclosure costs, is the winning bid. All private party-deeds of trust and mortgages are wiped out. That means they are removed as liens against the property title. You could wind up with a property with no mortgages.

The statistics say that only a very small percentage of property owners will let their properties go to a tax lien foreclosure sale. We have already mentioned that between 95 percent and 98 percent of tax liens will be redeemed by the property owner.

Costs

We recommend you calculate how much it will cost you to obtain the title to the property in the event you do have to foreclose. Find out if you even have to begin a foreclosure proceeding. If you do have to start a foreclosure, how much will an attorney cost you?

What are the filing fees, court costs, and taxing-authority-mandated expenses to obtain the property title? Also, some states do not guarantee the quality of the title you receive. Will you have further costs getting marketable title after the foreclosure sale?

One of the most important factors to consider is the length of time from the beginning to the end of the process. Obtaining a marketable title can be a lengthy procedure. While we think there is a super-low risk in tax lien investing, you must allow yourself enough time to recoup your investment and profit from it.

New Property Taxes

In some tax jurisdictions you are responsible for paying the property taxes over the next two years if the property owner does not. In other jurisdictions, you will have the option of paying the subsequent taxes.

If you do not pay the subsequent taxes, the county may sell a subsequent tax lien to another investor. Having an additional tax lien holder on the same property may complicate your attempts to obtain the deed. However, your tax lien would be considered the senior lien. If you do pay the subsequent taxes, that amount will be added to your lien.

We recommend that you find out what responsibilities you take on by buying the tax lien with regard to the subsequent property taxes. If you do not want to pay additional property taxes, buy tax liens in areas that do not require you to pay the subsequent taxes.

Tax Lien Security

How much security do you have for your investment when you buy a real estate tax lien? So far we have talked about the security of the property being 10 times the value of your tax lien investment. That is why we said tax lien investing has a super-low risk.

Let us look at the quality of the tax lien itself apart from the underlying property. The security for any particular tax lien depends on several factors. These include the priority of the tax lien under state law, if there are liens that can be senior to the tax lien, and whether any such lien exists against the property at the time of the foreclosure sale.

Arizona law states:

> The (tax) lien shall be prior and superior to all other liens and encumbrances upon the property, except liens or encumbrances held by the state.

It is possible that a property that is the security for your tax lien could at the time of your foreclosure be encumbered by a superior state of Arizona lien. If this lien is in an amount greater than the current fair market value of the property, then the underlying security for the tax lien is worthless. Just like with a mortgage greater than the value of the property, we would say that the property is overencumbered.

Let us say you hold a $5,000 real estate tax lien on a property. The property is worth $15,000. The state of Arizona has a $13,000 lien encumbering the property. How much security do you have in the property for your tax lien?

Tax Lien Security

Property Value	$15,000
Arizona Lien	$13,000
Your Security	$2,000
Your Tax Lien	$5,000
Overencumbered	$3,000

In many states the tax lien is a higher-priority lien. A superior lien to the tax lien is practically an impossibility.

Iowa law states that a treasurer's deed:

> ... shall vest in the purchaser all the right, title, interest, and estate of the former owner in and to the parcel conveyed, subject (only) to all restrictive covenants, resulting from prior conveyances in the chain of title to the former owner, and all the right, title, interest, and claim of the state and county to the parcel.

Restrictive covenants are covenants like utility easements, zoning, and restrictions on discrimination.

Under the laws of Iowa, Louisiana, Massachusetts, New Hampshire, and Rhode Island, if two or more investors want to buy a particular tax lien, the investor willing to accept the smallest undivided interest in the real estate wins the bid. In Massachusetts, the successful bidder at a tax lien sale is the investor who offers to pay:

> ... the amount of taxes and interest, if any, and necessary intervening charges ... for the smallest undivided part of the land.

Investors are often reticent to bid on tax liens in states using this system. When they have to foreclose they have only a partial ownership interest in the property. Because of this, treasurer's offices in some states use a random selection process to determine who will get a particular tax lien.

In Alabama, Connecticut, Colorado, Delaware, the District of Columbia, Georgia, Guam, Hawaii, Indiana, Maryland, Michigan, Mississippi, Missouri, New Brunswick, South Carolina, Tennessee, Texas, Vermont, and West Virginia, a bid in excess of the amount due for the delinquent taxes and any penalties, interest, fees, and costs is used to determine the successful bidder. We have previously called this a high bid real estate tax lien auction.

Time to Foreclosure

Before a real estate tax lien holder can foreclose on a property owner's right of redemption, the tax lien holder will have to bring current all delinquent real property taxes plus any penalties, interest, fees, and charges due. The longer it takes to foreclose out the right of redemption, the greater the accumulated amount of those taxes, penalties, interest, fees, and charges. The greater that amount, the less security cushion in the property.

In Wyoming it takes four years before you can foreclose. In Arizona you can start the judicial foreclosure process after three years. In Colorado it also takes three years. In Iowa it takes 21 months. In Maryland and Massachusetts it takes six months.

Title Insurance

When you buy real estate at a mortgage-lender-held foreclosure sale, you get a title to the real estate that a title insurance company will insure. You will receive a sheriff's deed from a mortgage foreclosure. You will receive a trustee's deed from a trust deed foreclosure. However, that is not the case when you obtain the property title through the tax sale foreclosure process.

In every state it is more difficult to get title insurance on a property foreclosed in the tax lien foreclosure sale than it is to get title insurance at a foreclosing lender sale. This is especially true if the foreclosure process used to acquire the property title is nonjudicial.

It is usually the case that title insurance companies will be unwilling to insure the property title. You will have to have your attorney file a quiet title lawsuit in court in order to get title insurance for the property.

Lien Priority

A real estate tax lien is usually considered the first or senior lien against the title to a property. If a first or senior lien is foreclosed, any junior liens are wiped out. If the tax lien you are foreclosing on is the first or senior lien, you will take title to the real estate free and clear of all other liens.

Connecticut law states:

Within sixty days after such sale, the collector shall cause to be published in a newspaper having a daily general circulation in the town in which the real property is located, and shall send by certified mail, return receipt requested, to the delinquent taxpayer and each mortgagee, lien holder and other record encumbrancer whose interest in such property is affected by such sale, a notice stating the date of the sale, the name and address of the purchaser, the amount the purchaser paid for the property and the date the redemption period will expire. The notice shall include a statement that if redemption does not take place by the date stated and in the manner provided by law, the delinquent taxpayer, and all mortgagees, lien holders and other record encumbrancers who have received actual or constructive notice of such sale as provided by law, that their respective titles, mortgages, liens and other encumbrances in such property shall be extinguished.

Florida law states:

All taxes imposed pursuant to the State Constitution and laws of this state shall be a first lien, superior to all other liens, on any property against which the taxes have been assessed and shall continue in full force from January 1of the year the taxes were levied until discharged by payment or until barred under Chapter 95.

Hawaii law states:

Every tax due upon real property . . . shall be a paramount lien upon the property assessed, which lien shall attach as of July 1 in each tax year and shall continue for six years.

Maryland law states:

From the date property tax on real property is due, liability for the tax and a 1st lien attaches to the real property in the amount of the property tax due on the real property.

We could go on with more examples from other states. We think you get the picture. Your safest tax lien investment is in those states where, by law, the tax lien has priority over any other liens against the title to the property.

Laws controlling the priority of the real property tax lien for any given jurisdiction can be confusing. Your attorney may have to know not only the statutory law but also the court decisions interpreting tax lien priority.

What if your real property tax lien is not the senior lien? In that jurisdiction you would take title to the real estate subject to any balance due on any such senior liens. These senior liens could be junior liens that are given priority by law.

Wyoming law states:

The lien is superior to all other liens except those created by junior tax sales or payment of subsequent taxes by another person.

In the next chapter we will show you how to redeem your tax liens. We have talked about the property owner redeeming the tax lien. How do you redeem your real estate tax liens? Read on!

CHAPTER 10

How to Cash in on Your Real Estate Tax Liens

After you make an investment, one of the best things that can happen is getting your investment back. One of the great things that can happen is that your investment makes a profit. The greatest thing that can happen is your initial investment is returned to you and you make a super profit!

In the real estate tax lien investment arena 95 percent to 98 percent of the time you will get your investment back. This is because that percentage of the time the property owner will redeem your tax lien against the title to their property.

At the same time you get your tax lien investment back, you also receive the profit on the investment. Unlike most other investment vehicles, with real estate tax liens the investment and the profit are linked. When you get your real estate tax lien investment back, the profit is attached to it.

The property owner does not get clear title to the property until they pay everything associated with the real estate tax lien. They must pay the face amount of the tax lien, penalties, interest, fees, and costs. The property owner cannot pay just the tax lien and your investment but not pay the interest and everything else—your profit. This is a package deal.

Where the Money Comes From

You receive your investment return and profit from the taxing authority that sold you the real estate tax lien. The property owner pays the taxing authority. The property owner does not pay you. The taxing authority pays you.

Because the vast majority of real estate tax liens are redeemed by the property owner, you seemingly do not need to do anything other than wait for your check from the taxing authority. You know, the check that is in the mail.

Communication Is the Key

We recommend you be proactive in your real estate tax lien investing. Know the procedure for foreclosing on your tax lien. Know how to obtain a tax deed if the property owner does not redeem your tax lien.

After you buy a tax lien find out about giving notices. Set up a checklist of key dates. Make sure you follow up with all notice and filing requirements. Do this even if your investment strategy is only to make an investment return and not to own the property.

There is no way to know for sure if the property owner will redeem your tax lien. You have to protect your investment. You may need to hire an attorney. Being prepared and in communication is your best course of action.

Communicating with the Property Owner

As we have already said, we recommend you meet with the property owner and view the property that is going to be the security for your tax lien investment before you buy the tax lien. If you follow this recommendation you will already be in communication with the property owner.

Some of you will make a deal with the property owner early on. You will buy the property owner's equity. We talked about how to do this in Chapter 5. The property owner will give you a quitclaim deed to the property. You then will own the property.

Buy the Owner's Equity

Let us say the property is worth $210,000. The loan balance is $150,000. The owner is behind $8,000 in property taxes. Their equity position is $52,000.

Owner's Equity

Property Value	$210,000
Loan Balance	$150,000
Behind in Taxes	$8,000
Owner's Remaining Equity	$52,000

You offer the owner $11,000 for their remaining equity. You will have to come up with an additional $8,000 to pay the back taxes. You would be paying $169,000 for the property.

Purchase Price

Loan Balance	$150,000
Behind in Taxes	$8,000
Equity Offer	$11,000
Purchase Price	$169,000

If the property has a value of $210,000, this looks like you have $41,000 in equity.

Your Equity

Property Value	$210,000
Purchase Price	$169,000
Your Equity	$41,000

You could flip the property or your contract with the property owner before the tax lien sale. You would not have to pay the delinquent taxes. Let us say you make a deal to flip the property to an investor. The investor agrees to buy the property from you for $175,000. What would this look like?

You have actually bought the property for $161,000. Remember, you have not paid the $8,000 in delinquent property taxes. So your profit will be $14,000.

Flip Property

Sales Price	$175,000
Your Price	$161,000
Your Profit	$14,000

You would get your $11,000 investment back. The $14,000 profit would be on top of that. A $14,000 profit on an $11,000 investment is a 127 percent profit. If you made this return in 30 days, that would be more than a 1,500 percent annual return!

Your Profit Percentage

$14,000 / $11,000 = 127%$ in 30 Days
Annual Percentage
$127\% \times 12$ Months $= 1,527\%$ in One Year

What if you assigned your contract to an investor? You have a contract with the property owner to buy their equity. You have not actually executed the contract. You would not have $11,000 out of your pocket. The investor would have to come up with that. You would not have $8,000 in delinquent property taxes out of your pocket. Again, the investor would have to come up with that.

Let us say you assigned your contract to the investor for $7,000. The investor would step into your shoes and buy the property owner's equity for $11,000. They would pay you an assignment fee of $7,000. The investor's purchase price would be $168,000.

Assign Contract

Your Contract Price	$161,000
Assignment Fee	$7,000
Investor Purchase Price	$168,000

Your profit percentage would be infinity. You made $7,000 with no money out of your pocket.

Your Profit Percentage

$7,000 / 0 = Infinity in 30 Days
Annual Percentage
Infinity $\times$ 12 months = Ridiculous in One Year

Buying the Tax Lien and Collecting on It

Let us say you do not make a deal with the property owner before the tax lien sale. You go to the sale and purchase the tax lien. It looks like you will have no further communication with the property owner. We have said that how the property owner redeems the tax lien is by paying the money to the taxing authority. The taxing authority will then pay you.

However, we recommend you keep in communication with the property owner on a regular basis during the redemption time period. This serves two purposes. The first purpose served is you will know when and, perhaps more importantly, if the property owner is going to be able to redeem your tax lien.

The second purpose served is you will have additional opportunities to make a deal to buy the property owner's equity. If your investment strategy is to acquire the property, then you may be able to acquire the property sooner.

In addition, instead of waiting till the end of the property owner's redemption period, you can begin renting out the property sooner. It may also save you the additional expenses of retaining an attorney and going through a foreclosure proceeding to get the property deed.

We recommend you be in communication with the property owner every 90 days. For those of you who are very business minded, think of it as being in communication with the property owner on a quarterly basis.

Legal, Moral, Ethical

We know we have to handle something right now for some of you. We can hear some of you thinking: Is it legal to talk to the property owner during the redemption period? Is it moral to talk to the property owner before the tax lien foreclosure sale? Is it ethical to talk to the property owner if they are experiencing tough times financially?

The answer is yes, yes, and yes! You are protecting your tax lien investment. After all, who is going to pay you? The property owner is going to pay you. Yes, the taxing authority may be the conduit for the payment, but the taxing authority is not going to give you your money back. They already took your money!

Let us say six months have gone by since you bought the tax lien. You talked to the property owner by phone after three months. They felt they would be in better financial shape soon. You call again to see how they are doing.

Things have gotten worse for them instead of better. In fact now they are three months behind in their mortgage payments and have received a notice of default from their mortgage lender. The mortgage lender is going to foreclose on their loan. This may help you cash in on your tax lien sooner.

By being in communication with the property owner, those of you wanting the deed to the property may be able to make a better deal for yourself. You can truncate (cut off) the property owner's redemption period.

Mortgage Foreclosure Alternatives

There are eight actions the property owner can take in response to a notice of default. We use a foreclosure alternatives presentation once we are in front of the property owner. We want them to sell us the property.

We recommend that you put each of these eight alternatives on a separate sheet of paper. We will refer to the Texas and California foreclosure timeline for the time periods to implement these alternatives.

1. Reinstatement

The reinstatement alternative gives the property owner the opportunity to make up back payments plus any incidental charges such a filing or posting notices and trustee service charges. The payment of the reinstatement amount will cancel the mortgage foreclosure and enable the borrower to continue as if no default occurred.

In Texas the borrower may reinstate their loan within the 20 days from receiving the first official letter from the lender and before receiving the second official letter. Once they receive the second letter from the lender, reinstatement is only possible if the lender agrees to the reinstatement. We are going to match the eight foreclosure alternatives with where in the foreclosure timeline they can be done.

Texas Foreclosure Timeline

2–3 Months	20 Days		Can Be 1 Day	21 Days Minimum
No Payments	First Official Letter	Second Official Letter	Posting at Courthouse	Sale First Tuesday

1. Reinstatement _____
2. Redemption _____
3. Deed in Lieu of Foreclosure _____
4. Legal Delay _____
5. File Bankruptcy _____
6. Renegotiate _____
7. Sell the Property _____
8. Do Nothing_____

2. Redemption

In order to redeem the loan, the borrower must pay off the loan in full. This may be accomplished through refinancing (with a cosigner perhaps) or by a relative or friend bailing out the owner in return for an equity position.

Most states permit redemption up to the foreclosure sale. In California the owner must redeem after they receive the posting at the courthouse and have up to the date of the foreclosure sale, unless the lender agrees to reinstatement.

California Foreclosure Timeline

2–3 Months	3–4 Weeks		3 Months	20 Days	Next Day
No Payments	First Official Letter	Second Official Letter	Posting at Courthouse	Redeem Only	Sale

2. Redemption _____

3. Deed in Lieu of Foreclosure

For the owner who knows they will have no opportunity to reinstate, redeem, or even sell their property and just wants out of the property, a deed in lieu of foreclosure may be a viable foreclosure alternative. Sometimes the owner can turn the ownership of the property over to the bank and avoid the trauma of mortgage foreclosure. This action will reduce the negative impact on the owner's credit. In most states, as in Texas, an owner can execute a deed in lieu of foreclosure up until the foreclosure sale.

When a lender takes a deed in lieu of foreclosure from a borrower, the lender receives the property subject to all junior and senior liens. This can be potentially hazardous to the lender. The property could be overencumbered with tax liens and judgments. Remember, your tax lien is a senior lien. It is most important for the lender to get an up-to-date title report the day the deed is to be accepted.

If the title report shows trouble that the lender does not want to deal with, the lender would proceed with the foreclosure sale rather than accept the deed. On the other hand, if there are no other liens shown on the title report but the lender's, the lender may choose to accept the deed.

Brain Trust

Mortgage lenders will typically not accept a deed in lieu of foreclosure. The debtor could later claim that the lender took unfair advantage of them by offering no or low compensation for the equity they had in the property. The courts have been known to rule in favor of the former property owner and allow them to reclaim the property or to cloud the lender's title with a lawsuit.

Lenders, to protect themselves, will request a written acknowledgement from the borrower stating that the borrower has received fair consideration for the property. You can do the same thing after you make a deal with the property owner. You are actually in a better position than the mortgage lender because your tax lien is the senior lien and must always be paid.

4. Legal Delay

If the owner can prove that the amount in default is inaccurate, often they can delay the foreclosure proceeding and gain additional time to find a more acceptable solution. The maximum time extension is effectively the time it would take to start the foreclosure process over again. The owner may also cause a legal delay up to the foreclosure sale itself. This action is possible in California and every other state as well.

5. File Bankruptcy

Bankruptcy is a serious event that could affect the timing and ultimate outcome of any foreclosure. Bankruptcy is a legal procedure established by federal law to assist debtors who can not meet their financial obligations.

Although this is not a permanent cure for the property owner, filing bankruptcy can temporarily halt the mortgage foreclosure process. Before considering this option, the owner should seek the advice of an attorney. The owner may file bankruptcy up to the day of the foreclosure sale. Bankruptcy also can halt your tax lien foreclosure sale. In the next chapter we will cover the specifics of bankruptcy as it relates to tax lien foreclosures.

6. Renegotiate with the Lender

The most overlooked of all the foreclosure alternatives an owner has is the opportunity to renegotiate with the lender. The lender does not want the property, and any effort by the owner to negotiate a plan that will enable the loan to be back in service for the lender's loan portfolio will be looked upon with great favor by the lender.

Generally, the current month's payment, plus a portion of the past-due amount will be considered. The borrower can renegotiate with the lender right up to the mortgage foreclosure sale in Texas and all the other states.

7. Sell the Property

For the owner who does not care to save their property or who has no other choice but to let the property go, selling the property may be the smartest choice. This is true even if they have to sell the property at a bargain price.

This is better for the owner than losing their entire equity and damaging their credit at the same time. Your purpose with the mortgage foreclosure alternatives presentation is to have the owner come to the conclusion that selling you their property is their best and most profitable foreclosure alternative. The owner can try to sell their property right up to the foreclosure sale in Texas and elsewhere throughout the country.

8. Do Nothing

The owner always has the choice of just letting things happen. They surely will lose their hard-earned equity and damage their credit. They can just about forget about getting a new home anytime in the foreseeable future.

Unfortunately, we have encountered more than a few people who just put their heads in the sand. They think they are going to win the lottery. They procrastinate until there are no viable options left to prevent the foreclosure sale.

If you can not persuade the property owner to sell you the property before the mortgage lender forecloses, you are still in the driver's seat with your real estate tax lien. The lender will now have to pay everything due to you on the tax lien.

Communicating with the Taxing Authority

Being in communication with the taxing authority is as important as being in communication with the property owner. From the initial publication of the tax lien sale to bidding at the tax lien auction to receiving your investment return and your profits to foreclosing on your tax lien, you will be involved with the taxing authority.

The taxing authority sets the rules of the game for real estate tax lien investing. How much profit you will make is directly related to your understanding of these rules. We have already mentioned that you need to calculate your potential profit before you get involved in the tax lien bidding process. Talking to the people who are in charge of the tax lien auction is crucial to your success.

Potential Profit

You determine your potential profit on two criteria. The first criterion is your investment strategy. Are you investing for super-high returns? Are you investing for ownership of the property? The second criterion is the bidding system used by the taxing authority.

If you are investing for super-high returns, then communication with the taxing authority is paramount. The return that you get on your tax lien investment may be less than the maximum potential profit allowed by law for that particular state. The actual return you will receive on your tax lien investment will be determined by the tax lien auction process itself. In many areas, if two or more bidders are bidding on a tax lien, these bidders will compete by bidding down the interest rate they are willing to take on the tax lien until only one bidder is left.

Arizona real estate tax liens are always sold for the exact amount of the current delinquent real property taxes, interest, penalties, fees, and expenses at the tax lien sale. If there is more than one bidder bidding on a particular tax lien, then the successful bidder will be the one who "offers to accept the lowest rate of interest upon the amount so paid."

Remember, every tax lien offered for bid in Arizona is offered at an interest rate of 16 percent. If two or more investors are interested in acquiring a particular tax lien, they compete by bidding down the interest rate. It starts at 16 percent annual interest, then 15 percent, then 14 percent, then 13 percent.

By finding out from the taxing authority the history of their tax lien sales, you may discover that the winning bidders accepted interest rates in the 6 percent, 7 percent, or 8 percent range in previous years. This may be well below your projected potential profit range. You may then discover you need to make your investment in less popular bidding areas.

Florida has the same bidding system:

> Each certificate shall be struck off to the person who will pay the taxes, interest, costs, and charges and will demand the lowest rate of interest, not in excess of the maximum rate of interest allowed by this chapter. The tax collector shall accept bids in even increments and in fractional interest rate bids of one-quarter of 1 percent only.

It can become so competitive in Illinois that some investors have bid down the interest rate to the 3 percent and 4 percent range! Are they just caught up in a bidding frenzy? Perhaps there is more to this than meets the eye. These bidders know something that most of the other investors do not know.

They know if a property owner does not pay the real estate property taxes for the next year following the tax sale, then the tax lien holder (the investor) can. This is called subtaxing the tax lien. The amount subtaxed will be approximately equal to the amount paid for the tax lien.

Illinois law states:

> Any person desiring to redeem shall deposit with the county clerk of the county in which the property is situated, in legal money . . . in an amount equal to the total of the following: The total of all taxes, special assessments, accrued interest on those taxes and special assessments and costs charged in connection with the payment of those taxes or special assessments, which have been paid by the tax certificate holder on or after the date those taxes or special assessments become delinquent together with 12 percent penalty on each amount so paid for each year or portion thereof intervening between the date of that payment and the date of redemption.

Have you figured it out? The tax lien investor receives a 12 percent penalty return on any amount subtaxed! By buying the tax lien the first year at an extremely low interest rate, you control the following year.

Let us say the tax lien investor bought a tax lien with a $5,000 face amount for a low interest rate bid of 3 percent for each six-month interval. The property owner redeems the tax lien after two years. The investor pays the second year's property taxes (the subtax).

When the property owner redeems the tax lien, they must pay the investor 6 percent annual interest for the original tax lien amount for two years. They must also pay the investor 12 percent penalty interest for each year on the subtaxed amount! By knowing the history of these extremely competitive tax lien auctions, you can invest in them and still make a profit.

Tax Lien	$5,000
Six-Month Interest	×3%
Six-Month Return	$150
Number of Six-Month Intervals	×4
Two-Year Return	$600
Annual Interest Rate	6%
Subtax	$5,000
12-Month Interest	×12%
One-Year Return	$600

As you can see, the one-year return on the subtax amount equals the two-year return on the original tax lien. So, maybe this investor was not caught up in the frenzy of the bidding process after all!

Rotation Bidding

In several taxing jurisdictions, if two or more bidders bid up the dollar amount of the opening minimum bid it creates a surplus bid amount. The winning bidder would then pay the entire amount bid to receive the tax lien. If the property owner redeems the tax lien, the tax lien investor is repaid just the amount of the opening minimum bid plus interest. The surplus is lost to the investor.

Also, the investor receives no interest on the surplus amount. As a result, if an investor pays a premium for a particular tax lien and the property owner redeemed the tax lien in a short period of time, then the investor could actually lose money on the investment.

Most investors are reluctant to make surplus bids, so taxing authorities use rotation bidding. They conduct the bidding at the tax lien auction by where the bidders are seated or by the order of registration. When your turn comes up you must buy the tax lien offered for sale.

If you refuse to buy the tax lien, it is offered to the next bidder in the rotation. This process continues until the tax lien is purchased or all bidders have declined to buy it. The practical effect is that it reduces surplus or high-bid bidding.

In Maryland if two or more bidders are bidding on a tax lien, the price of the tax lien increases. The amount bid over the opening minimum bid does not have to be paid by the investor. You have to pay that amount if and when you obtain a deed to the real estate.

First Come, First Served

Certain areas use a first-come, first-served method to determine who will be the tax lien investor offered a particular tax lien. Kentucky law states:

> If there is more than one (1) willing purchaser who has made an offer, the one having made the most recent purchase of a tax claim against the same delinquent or the same property shall have preference; if there is no such person, the person being the first, in the judgment of the sheriff, to offer to pay cash in the full amount of the tax claim shall receive priority for the purchase of the tax claim.

In Montana the opening bid at a tax sale is both the minimum bid and the maximum bid! The county treasurers sell tax liens over-the-counter on a first-come, first-served basis. They do this because no one shows up at the county treasurer's office on the date of sale.

In fact, in some of the more populous Montana counties there have never been two or more investors attending the annual tax lien sale! There is no competitive bidding. Real estate tax lien investors just show up on the day of the tax sale to buy the tax liens.

Our favorite bidding system is in Wyoming. Many of the 15 county treasurers conduct their auctions by giving each bidder a bidder's number and each bidder's number is assigned a corresponding bingo ball.

A bingo machine is then used to choose a number for each tax lien being sold. If your number comes up, then bingo! You are given the option to buy the tax lien or pass on buying the tax lien.

A final comment on these first-come, first-served bidding methods: This does not affect the interest rate return that you will receive. This does not affect the security of the investment.

However, these bidding methods do reduce the chances that you will be able to invest a significant amount of dollars. You may find yourself being in a room with 100 other real estate tax lien investors. There may be only 200 real estate tax liens available to buy.

Therefore, you need to research all 200 properties. That way, when you are randomly called to say yes or no on a particular tax lien, you will know if you want to buy the tax lien or pass on buying it.

In the next chapter we will talk about money partners for your tax lien investing. Some of you have plenty of money to begin your real estate tax lien investing. Others of you have a moderate amount of investment cash. There also are those of you who have little or no money to invest.

We have found that if you can find a good deal, finding the money to fund that good deal is easy. So, your ability to study the real estate tax lien market and find a good tax lien investment is worth money to your money partner(s). Are you ready to find some money?

CHAPTER 11

Money Partners

Some of you have gotten to this point in the book and are really excited about investing in real estate tax liens. You are going to make a real estate tax lien investment as soon as you can come up with some investment capital. You know what we mean. If you could just get your hands on some of the green stuff, the cash, the moola you would be ready to start investing.

This chapter is directed toward you. We will accept no excuses. We are going to show you how to use money partners to fund your great tax lien deals. You find a great real estate tax lien investment. You bring it to your money partners. They fund the investment. You split the profit with your money partners.

What Is a Partnership?

A partnership is two or more people putting their money, brains, talents, skills, resources, and economic clout together to achieve a successful investment result. A successful partnership takes more than just money. We say there are six OPs of investment partnerships. OPs stands for *other people's*.

The Six OPs

The six OPs are Other People's Money, Other People's Brains, Other People's Talents, Other People's Skills, Other People's Resources, and Other People's Economic Clout.

1. Other People's Money

We have found that the best money to invest is other people's money. The risk of the investment is born by the people who put up the money. If you find a super-low-risk investment with super-high returns it is easy to find other people to fund the investment. When you help the people with the money make more money, you will make money, too.

Certainly, if you have your own investment capital you will be able to make more money doing the investment yourself. Our experience in real estate investing says the best results are obtained when you spread the risk and spread the wealth. We understand that a piece of the pie is better than no pie at all.

You could be sitting there with plenty of money to invest. Your problem is where are you going to invest it? You need to partner with someone who has the brains, skills, and talents to bring you an investment. Real estate tax lien investing is your investment.

2. Other People's Brains

If you do not have the money to make a real estate tax lien investment, you can have the brains to make a real estate tax lien investment. You could be one of those blessed people who have the money and the brains. However, you may still lack the talents and skills to make a successful tax lien investment.

If you do not feel like you have enough wattage upstairs to be comfortable making a tax lien investment, get a partner for your Brain Trust. In fact, if you need some help, e-mail us at thetrustee@hotmail.com. We will be glad to be your Brain Trust.

3. Other People's Talents

Combining the talents of people to make a successful real estate investment is one of the most satisfying types of partnerships we have put together. Some people are talented at finding a good tax lien investment. Some people are talented at finding money partners. Some people are talented at putting a partnership together. What are your talents?

We recommend you take a blank piece of paper and start writing down what your talents are. Be bold. This is no time to be humble. You know what you are good at. This will also help you determine where you need partnership help. We know some of you are super-talented. Being the lone ranger doing tax lien investing is tough and lonely.

4. Other People's Skills

Using other people's skills can expedite your tax lien investing success. You need someone in your partnership who is a skilled listener. You need someone in your partnership who is a skilled negotiator. You need someone in your partnership who is a skilled leader. What are your skills?

Again, we recommend you take a blank piece of paper and start writing down what your skills are. In today's world skills are sometimes referred to as skill sets.

A useful skill set for tax lien investing is being good with people. This means being friendly, respectful, patient, and honest. Do you have this skill set?

5. Other People's Resources

The biggest resource we have found that contributes to a successful tax lien investing partnership is other people's time. Time, time, time! Do you find that everything today takes too much time? (Try writing a book!) There are many details to take care of and follow up on in real estate tax lien investing.

Having people in your partnership who have the time just to get things done is a godsend. Sometimes these people are called gophers. They go for this. They go for that. We have all heard the expression that time is money. This is certainly the case in any real estate investment.

6. Other People's Economic Clout

Other people's economic clout is the OPEC of real estate investing. Your goal is to have your own tax lien investment cartel! You do not have the cash to invest? No problem. You do not have the economic clout to establish a credit line? No problem.

Just put someone into your partnership who has economic clout. Find someone who has the cash. Find someone who has the credit line. Find someone who has the ability to provide a strong financial statement. Remember, if you have the talent and skill to put the real estate tax lien partnership cartel together, you are going to make a ton of money.

Group Investing: Syndication

Group investing is called syndication. A syndication or partnership has members of the group with matching objectives. The matching objectives in real estate tax lien investing would be super-high returns with super-low risks.

There are five main structures that are used to form a syndicate. These five structures are a corporation, a limited liability company, a general partnership, a real estate investment trust (REIT), and a limited partnership.

1. Corporation

Corporations have been around for more than 100 years. Most big businesses are incorporated. You do not have to be a big business to incorporate. Corporations are usually formed in the state where you are doing business. We recommend you consult with an attorney.

By forming a corporation you have central management. The main reason to form a corporation is to have limited liability. If you are doing business as a corporation and are sued, you have no personal liability. Only the corporate assets can be taken.

Of course there is a caveat. The corporate shield can be pierced by a skilled attorney. The second caveat is the double taxation of a corporation. The corporation profits are taxed at a corporate rate. The shareholders of the corporation are taxed on the dividends they receive from the corporation.

Another type of corporation is called an S corporation. This is used by people who are sole proprietors. You have the corporate liability shield. Any profits are taxed to the owner individually. There is no double taxation.

2. Limited Liability Company

An improvement on the corporation is the limited liability company. This is primarily for two or more people who want to form a partnership. They want the limited liability risk of a corporation. They do not want the double taxation and record keeping headaches of a corporate structure.

Limited liability companies have become quite popular over the last 10 years. A limited liability company may be the ideal partnership structure for some of you to do real estate tax lien investing. We recommend you consult with an attorney.

3. General Partnership

A general partnership is a partnership between equals. There can be two or more general partners. Each general partner has an equal say in the business of the partnership.

Unlike a corporation or a limited liability company, a general partnership has unlimited liability. Each general partner can bind the partnership. If one of the general partners is sued, all the general partners are on the hook. A general partnership has to file a partnership tax return.

We feel that some type of a partnership agreement may be the simplest and easiest way to put together a group for real estate tax lien investing. Again, we recommend you talk to an attorney to help you put any type of partnership agreement together.

4. Real Estate Investment Trust

A real estate investment trust, or REIT for short, is a public investment offering. Ninety percent of the net income is distributed to the shareholders. Unlike a corporation, there is no double taxation. The REIT is not taxed. Only the investors who receive distributions from the REIT are taxed.

We do not recommend REITs. They are too passive an investment for us. What we like about real estate investing is being proactive. We like being in control of our real estate investments as much as possible. This is the basis of this book and all the books in the Win Going In! series.

Some of you may be interested in a REIT that invests in real estate tax liens. As far as we know, no REIT makes tax lien investments. Check for yourself. One may come along.

5. Limited Partnership

A limited partnership can be public or private. A public limited partnership is big. A private limited partnership is small. Public limited partnerships are controlled by federal and state securities regulatory bodies.

The smallest limited partnership consists of two people. There has to be one general partner. There has to be one limited partner. The general partner is responsible for all decision making. The general partner chooses where and when to invest the partnership money.

The limited partner is called a limited partner because they have limited liability. The limited partner can lose no more money than the amount of money they contributed to the partnership. If a limited partner contributed $10,000 to make real estate tax lien investments and the partnership lost $20,000, the limited partner could lose only their $10,000. A limited partner has no say so in when, where, or how the partnership is going to invest.

You may want to put together money partners for real estate tax lien investment purposes using a limited partnership format. You would be the general partner who would actually do all the work. The money you invested would be the partnership's money.

You would be paid a general partnership fee. After all the limited partners had their investment returned and received their profit, you may be entitled to receive additional money for your limited partnership interest.

Say you put together five limited partners who each contributed $20,000 to the partnership. You, as the general partner, contribute your brain, talents, and skills to make real estate tax lien investments. You are paid $10,000 for your services. There is $5,000 available for expenses. This leaves $85,000 to be invested in real estate tax liens.

Limited Partnership

Limited Partners' Contribution	$100,000
General Partner's Fee	$10,000
Partnership Expenses	$5,000
Invested in Tax Liens	$85,000

Say you have the partnership invest in tax liens from the state of Iowa. The tax liens are redeemed by the property owners two years down the line. How would the partnership make out?

Partnership Return

Invested in Tax Liens	$85,000
Interest Rate	×24%
One-Year Return	$20,400
Invested Two Years	×2
Two-Year Return	$40,400

Net Return to Partnership

Invested in Tax Liens	$85,000
Two-Year Return	$40,400
Total Return	$125,400
Limited Partners' Investment	$100,000
Net Return to Partnership	$25,400

According to the partnership agreement, the limited partners will receive their $20,000 investment back first. Then they will receive a 10 percent annual return on their investment. You will receive the next $3,000 as the general partner. After that any remaining money will be split equally between you as the general partner and the five limited partners.

Each limited partner has received their $20,000 investment back. Now each limited partner receives 10 percent annual interest on their $20,000 investment for two years.

Limited Partners' Interest

Limited Partner Investment	$20,000
Annual Interest Rate	×10%
Annual Interest	$2,000
For Two Years	×2
Two Years of Interest	$4,000

A $4,000 return for each limited partner multiplied by five limited partners is $20,000.

Total Limited Partners' Interest

Each Limited Partner	$4,000
Five Limited Partners	×5
Total Interest to Partners	$20,000

We then subtract the $20,000 in total interest to partners from the net return to partnership of $25,400. This leaves an additional $5,400.

Additional Money

Net Return to Partnership	$25,400
Total Interest to Partners	$20,000
Additional Money	$5,400

Now for the fun part. You are entitled to receive the next $3,000 from the additional money per the partnership agreement. This leaves $2,400. You and the five limited partners then will split this $2,400 six ways. Each of you will receive $400. Is being the general partner fun or what?

Additional Money

Additional Money	$5,400
General Partner	$3,000
Six-Way Split	$2,400
Each Receives	$2,400 / 6 = $400

The total return each limited partner receives is $4,400. This is over a two year period and is on an investment of $20,000. This is an 11 percent annual return on the limited partners investment. Do you think you might be able to interest some people in an 11 percent annual return?

The total return you receive as the general partner of the limited partnership is $13,400. This is the $10,000 general partner's fee, the $3,000 in additional money, and the $400 as your share of the six-way split. Do you think you might be able to force yourself to be a general partner of a limited partnership that invests in real estate tax liens?

Your Return as General Partner

General Partner's Fee	$10,000
Additional Money	$3,000
Six-Way Split	$400
General Partner Makes	$13,400

Remember, any expenses you have as the general partner are paid by the partnership. Travel expenses to and from a tax lien sale are paid. Phone, fax, Internet, and office expenses are paid by the partnership.

How-to-Convince-a-Partner Checklist

How do you convince someone to be your money partner? We are going to give you a 14-point checklist that we have found useful in our real estate investing. This checklist is not exhaustive. If you have something to add to it, then by all means do so. This is what you do at the appointment with a potential money partner.

1. Show up to the Appointment on Time

This is number one on our checklist for a reason. Everyone agrees that time is money. Being late to a meeting with a potential money partner sends the wrong signal. Why should they agree to fund your deal if you begin by not valuing their time?

2. Act Professionally

This is number two on our list for a reason. People with money want to feel comfortable with you. This is a business relationship. This is not a social relationship. A fool and their money are soon parted. Potential money partners are not fools. They have their money. Act professionally; you may get some of it.

3. Dress Accordingly

First impressions. You cannot make a first impression a second time. Business attire is appropriate for a business meeting. Dress your part. Your part is as professional real estate tax lien investor.

4. Leave the Kids at Home

We feel this is so obvious that we almost omitted it from this checklist. You would be surprised how many business meetings we attended where the other party showed up with their children in tow. "I couldn't get a baby sitter," just does not make the right impression.

5. Be Honest and Friendly

People who have money can smell a rat. They will ask you questions about your knowledge and experience. Do not lie. If you have never done a real estate tax lien investment and they ask you how many you have done, tell them the truth. It is all right to smile.

6. Listen, Listen, Listen

You have heard the old saying, God gave you two ears and one mouth for a reason. Find out what the money partner wants. They know you want their money.

7. Matching, Mirroring, and Pacing

During the conversation with the potential money partner, try matching and mirroring them. If they cross their arms, you cross your arms. If they stand up, you stand up. If they get excited, you get excited.

Pacing has to do with avoiding giving people a drink out of a fire hydrant. Yes, you want to convey your excitement about real estate tax lien investing. Let the other person get excited and convey their excitement back to you.

8. Use Your Rapport-Building Skills

You should be good with people. If you are not, then you are the wrong person to talk to the potential money partner. Have the partner on your team who is good building rapport with people go the appointment.

People do business with people they like doing business with. If you are cold, distant, and arrogant, you are not going to build rapport. You are not going to get any money, either.

9. Show Expertise and Prove It

This is where you must have done your homework. Even if you are just starting out, you can demonstrate expertise. Have a presentation that you can make. Most people are visual. You will do far better with something to show the potential money partner than just winging it by flapping your lips.

10. Compare Bank Interest Rates

This is a follow-up to showing expertise. This is also a no-brainer. Ask the potential money partner what interest rates they are getting on their money market accounts or certificates of deposit? They will make your case for you.

11. Compare Other Investments

Ask the potential money partner what kind of return they are getting on their stock portfolio? If they are invested in real estate, ask them how they like being a landlord? Use the super-high returns and super-low risk idea to make your case for investing in real estate tax liens.

12. Be Prepared for Surprises and Have a Plan B

People who have money love to pull surprises. They may ask you to provide a name and number of someone you have worked with in tax lien investing. Perhaps another investor. Perhaps another money partner. They may even ask you to call them right then and there. If you tell no stories you will not be caught in any lies.

Plan B is being able to direct the potential money partner to making an investment in something other than a real estate tax lien. They may not be interested in tax liens. However, they are sold on you. They may want you on their team. They may make you an offer you cannot refuse.

13. Ask for the Money

You have to ask for the money from the potential money partner. They are not going to look up and say how much money do you want? As in any business situation you have to ask for the order.

We recommend you ask for the money at the beginning, middle, and end of your appointment. That way you have three chances to get a yes from your money partner.

14. Thank the Person for Their Time

Perhaps you were not successful in your quest to get a money partner. By thanking the person for their time you leave the door open for further conversations. We have actually gotten a call the next day from a money partner who changed their mind.

Creative Ways to Use Partners

There is more than one way to utilize a money partner. While they may not be willing or able to put up the money for you, here are six creative ways to use a money partner.

1. Borrow Their Financial Statement

The money partner may have no available liquid funds to invest in the partnership. The money partner may have a very strong financial statement. Give the money partner a piece of the partnership for the use of their financial statement.

You may be able to borrow money using their financial statement. In effect you are bringing in a cosigner to create investment funds. We suggest you give the money partner the same return using their financial statement as you would if they put up the cash.

2. Borrow Their Cash

The money partner may have the cash to put in the real estate tax lien partnership investment but not the inclination to do so. If real estate tax lien investing is a new endeavor for them, they may not feel comfortable.

They may feel comfortable with you, however. They may loan you the money. Whether the tax lien investment is successful or not, you are on the hook for the return of the money partner's money.

3. Have Them Pledge Their Savings Account

The money partner may have money tied up in long-term certificates of deposit. If they cash in the certificates of deposit early, they may have to pay a substantial penalty.

Suggest they pledge the certificates of deposit for a loan or a line of credit. The certificates of deposit remain in place and act as collateral for the loan. They then have the money to invest in the partnership or loan to you for the partnership.

4. Use Their Line of Credit

If the money partner has a line of credit, you may be set as well. You have the line of credit set up to go. Then it is available to fund any tax lien purchases at the tax lien sale.

The line of credit is also useful if you are trying to make a deal with the property owner before the tax lien sale. Cash always talks in a negotiation with the property owner.

5. Borrow Money on Their Credit Card

You would be surprised how large a credit line some people have on their credit cards. They may also have a relatively low interest rate. You may find a money partner who would be willing to make the spread on what the partnership will pay them in interest and what the interest rate is on the cash advances on their credit card.

6. Give a Promissory Note and Pay Interest

You may have a piece of real estate that has a fairly good-size equity position. Your money partner may want the added security of a promissory note secured by the equity in your property.

Rather than just borrowing the money from the money partner and signing an unsecured note, you give them the protection of real estate. This is the same protection you have when you buy a real estate tax lien. The property becomes the security for your investment.

Partnership Agreements Checklist

In this last section we are going to give our 21-point checklist for what must be included in any partnership agreement. We recommend you have an attorney either put together your partnership agreements or look over any partnership agreements you put together.

1. The Name of the Partnership

While this may seem obvious to some of you, this is an important point. If you are going to get heavily involved in real estate tax lien investing using partnerships, naming the partnerships becomes necessary simply from a logistics point of view.

Also, you want to take advantage of the pride factor for people in the naming of the partnership. Your money partner may want the partnership named after them. Believe it or not this can be a deal closer for you with your money partner. Letting them name the partnership may get you the money!

2. The Term of the Partnership

All agreements must have a beginning date and an ending date. We recommend you have separate partnership agreements for each tax lien investing location and year. This makes tracking your partnership investments much easier.

The 2005 tax lien purchases partnership agreement for the Colorado tax lien investment group will need to have a term that runs through the property owner's redemption period. In Colorado the property owner's redemption period is three years. Add a year to make sure you can dispose of the property. The term of this partnership should be four years or until the partnership is dissolved by partner agreement.

3. The Purpose of the Partnership

The purpose of the partnership is to make money. You want to say something like, the purpose of the partnership is to make money investing in real estate tax liens.

The purpose should be stated in a concise manner. Short and sweet purpose statements are best. A third party (the judge) should be able to know exactly what the purpose of the partnership is if there is a dispute among partners.

4 The Business Goals of the Partners

The business goals of the partners can be similar but also different. The business goals of the partners should be similar in the aspect of everyone wanting to make money. It does not work if one investor is looking for an investment loss to get a tax write-off while the other investors want an investment gain.

However, the business goals of the partners can be different with regard to acceptable rates of return on the investment. Also, some of the partners may have a longer or shorter timeline for receiving their initial investment back. You put the shorter timeline investors into tax lien investments that have a shorter right of redemption period for the property owner.

5. The Cash or Property Contributed to the Partnership

This is a very important enumeration. This is what each partner puts in to start the partnership business. It is the seed money, so to speak. While cash is always nice, other property or resources may be necessary.

One partner may contribute office space. Another partner may contribute office equipment. Another partner may contribute their legal advice both to start the partnership and to handle any legal issues down the road.

6. What Happens if More Cash Is Needed?

This is something that every partnership hopes never is going to happen. It just makes sense to have this handled in writing in the partnership agreement before there are any problems.

The partnership may need extra cash for good reasons as well as bad reasons. You may get to a tax lien sale and find there are some deals too good to pass up. Call the money partner with the credit line and get some more partnership money invested.

7. The Skills the Partners Are Contributing

We have already talked about skills, talents, and brains as being worthwhile partnership contributions. It is important to list each partner's contributions to the partnership in these areas.

It may be especially important for you as the general partner, when you may not be contributing any cash to the partnership. Down the road when the money comes in, your other partners may get greedy. Why should they give you all that money specified in the partnership agreement? Because you earned it and because of the skill sets you contributed.

8. The Distribution of the Profits

This may be the most important part of the partnership agreement. If you leave this part out in the beginning, we promise you that you will have problems in the end.

Who gets what and when they get it is something all the partners need to know and agree on from the get-go. This way a perfectly wonderful partnership that makes money will not be destroyed by greed and ill will.

9. What Happens if There Are Losses?

Equally important to who gets the money is who absorbs the potential losses. While no one wants to throw a wet blanket on the excitement and enthusiasm at the beginning of the partnership, you must talk about losses.

While it seems obvious that the partners who put up the money would absorb the losses, the losses do not have to fall on the money partners alone. It depends on how the partnership agreement decides to handle the losses. You as the general partner could agree to have your general partnership fee reduced.

10. Salaries, Guarantees, or Drawing Accounts

Who gets paid how much, when, and for what? Who is given a guarantee? Who is authorized to take draws on the partnership bank accounts? How many partnership signatures are required on a partnership check?

The general partner typically handles the day in, day out business of the partnership. The general partner typically has access to the bank accounts of the partnership. The partnership may want to put in some safeguards so that the general partner, or for that matter any of the partners, cannot disappear with the partnership money.

11. Withdrawals of Contributed Assets or Capital

The partnership must decide how and when the partners can withdraw their contributed assets and capital. For example, the partner who is the attorney needs to have a cap on the amount of time they do attorney business for the partnership. Once this time is contributed, then the attorney should be compensated monetarily by the partnership for doing partnership business.

Money partners should get their initial capital back before any other partners make a profit. There is no profit to distribute until all investors are paid back their initial partnership investment. The partnership agreement must address this. Otherwise when money comes into the partnership, chaos ensues.

12. General Management Provisions

The partnership must have general management provisions. This allows for the daily functioning of the partnership. Who is in charge? Who reports to whom? When must the general partner go back to the other partners for permission or guidance?

What accounting procedures are going to be used? Is the partnership using accrual or cash basis? Who is going to do the accounting? Is one of the partners an accountant? Who is going to track expenses for tax purposes? Who is responsible for filing the partnership tax return?

13. Expense Accounts

Who gets to have an expense account? Who gets reimbursed for partnership expenses? When do they get reimbursed? Who reimburses them? Is the general partner in charge of tracking partnership expenses?

Expense accounts are the most easily abused partnership account. This is probably true of any business. The point is, you must treat the partnership as a business.

14. Accounting and Check-Signing Rules

All money of the partnership must be tracked. Money that comes into the partnership must be tracked. Money that goes out of the partnership, even if to other partners, must be tracked. We suggest you use ALICE.

ALICE is the acronym for assets, liabilities, income, capital, and expenses. The partnership balance sheet is made up of the partnership assets on one side and the partnership liabilities and capital on the other side. The two sides must balance. Hence the name *balance sheet.* By the way, capital is another name for net worth.

Say you have partnership assets of $100,000. You have partnership liabilities of $15,000. You have partnership capital, or net worth, of $85,000.

Balance Sheet

Assets	$100,000		Liabilities	$15,000
			Capital	$85,000
	$100,000	Totals		$100,000

The partnership profit and loss statement is made up of the partnership income and expenses. All the partnership income is tracked. All the partnership expenses are tracked. When the expenses are subtracted from the income you have a partnership profit or loss. If there is more partnership income than partnership expenses, then the partnership has a profit. If there are more partnership expenses than income, then the partnership has a loss.

15. Handling Disputes

Believe us when we tell you that every partnership will experience disputes. A dispute resolution section in the partnership agreement must be included. We recommend voluntary arbitration first. Then we recommend binding arbitration second.

If there is still an unresolved dispute, then we recommend going to see the judge. All the partners need to be aware, that once you go to see the judge, the partnership business is now open to public scrutiny. Keep the disputes in house, please!

16. Sale or Assignment of a Partnership Interest

There must be a way for each partner to sell or assign their partnership interest. It is far better to allow a disgruntled partner to get out of the partnership than to force them to remain in the partnership. Establish a method to determine the value of the partnership interest in the partnership agreement.

We recommend that the other partners in the partnership have a first right of refusal to buy a departing partner's partnership interest. Again, this will be in all the partners' best interest. Who better knows the partnership than the other partners? Who better knows the value of the partnership interest than the other partners?

17. Admission of New Partners

From time to time it may be necessary or advisable to bring in a new partner or partners to the partnership. Objective criteria must be set out in the partnership agreement as to the when and how to bring aboard new partners.

Obviously, you are looking for new partners who can bring something to the partnership. Are they bringing an infusion of cash? Are they bringing an infusion of brains, skills, or talents? In other words, why are you going to let them be partners?

18. Expulsion of a Partner

This can be a nasty and expensive undertaking, even when the partnership agreement specifies the grounds for taking such an action. We cannot imagine how even more difficult, expensive, and nasty an expulsion of a partner would be without a procedure delineated in the partnership agreement.

Our experience with expelling a partner from a partnership tells us several things. It may be in the partnership's best interest to pay the unwanted partner to go away. This may mean giving that partner more money than the partnership agreement says they are entitled to. It is your call.

19. Continuing Business if a Partner Withdraws or Dies

Unfortunately partners sometimes get sick. Sometimes a partner gets divorced. A partner may file for bankruptcy. A partner could die. You still must be able to carry on the business of the partnership.

By covering these possibilities in the partnership agreement, you can make a bumpy transition smoother. Remember, a partnership interest is willable. You may not want the heirs of one of your partners involved in the partnership business.

20. Determining Value of a Departing Partner's Interest

Determining the value of a departing partner's partnership interest should be spelled out in the partnership agreement. It should really be quite cut and dried. If everyone agrees at the beginning of the partnership how this valuation is going to be done, then you can avoid major problems down the road.

We recommend specifying in the partnership agreement that at least one independent valuation of the partnership interest be done. This lessens the possibility of legal action. E-mail us if you need our help.

21. Dissolution and Termination Procedures

Last but not least is a way to close down, wrap up, and put to bed the partnership. Even a successful partnership needs to have a way to be ended. In fact we prefer partnerships that do have a definite ending date.

Our experience with partnerships has been that when everyone knows when the partnership is going to end, it handles a basic human need for completion. If every one of the partners is happy with the results of the partnership, then close it down and start another one.

Now that you know everything there is to know about partnerships, we are going to turn our attention to making money in real estate tax lien investing tax free! In the next chapter we will show you how to buy real estate tax liens using retirement dollars. There is nothing like making a profit and not having to split it with Uncle Sam.

CHAPTER 12

Buying Real Estate Tax Liens with Retirement Dollars

In Chapter 1 we touched on using your retirement dollars to make real estate tax lien certificate investments. In this chapter we are going to expand that discussion to include using retirement dollars to acquire real estate tax lien deeds.

We are also going to talk about the federal income tax consequences of investing in real estate tax lien certificates if you are investing outside of a tax-deferred or tax-free program. And we will talk about the tax consequences of buying and selling tax lien deeds outside of these retirement programs.

Any time we talk about federal income tax consequences, people seem to pay very close attention to the conversation. Before we turn our attention to the specifics of the federal income tax consequences of investing in real estate tax lien certificates or tax lien deeds, we are going to talk to you about the federal income tax system.

This conversation is not a political conversation. This conversation is an investment conversation. Every investor needs to take into account the federal income tax consequences of whatever investment they are considering.

The Federal Income Tax System

The bottom line for any investment is the after-tax return on that investment. The federal income tax is a system. There is a design to this system. By taking the time to study the design of the federal income tax system, you can decrease the amount of federal income tax you pay. This will increase the amount of return on your investments that you get to keep.

The first thing you need to know about the federal income tax system is that part of the design is to keep people from realizing there is a design to the system. The vast majority of taxpayers are overwhelmed by the federal income tax system. We are going to point out some things to empower you in the face of the federal income tax system.

By the way, we have the answer to every one of your federal income tax questions. Bill has vast knowledge and experience as a certified tax preparer in the state of California and as a tax negotiator negotiating with the Internal Revenue Service (IRS) in the state of Texas. The answer to your tax question is: It all depends!

We are not kidding. We would be glad to help you with any of your federal income tax questions or problems. Just e-mail us at wrcarey@hotmail.com. How much money will you get to keep from the profit on your real estate tax lien investment? It all depends! Let us look at some examples.

Business Start-up Costs

The new tax law says you can deduct up to $5,000 of business start-up costs at the front end. This means if you are starting your real estate tax lien investing business in 2005, you can deduct up to $5,000 in your business start-up costs in the 2005 tax year.

Business start-up costs can be written off for up to $50,000! However, everything over $5,000 in business start-up costs most be amortized over 15 years. In 2004 business start-up costs over $5,000 could be written off over five years.

You may decide to form a corporation or a partnership to conduct your real estate tax lien investing. Organizational costs for your corporation or partnership can be written off based on these rules. You just need to be thinking about this from the get-go as you begin your real estate tax lien investment business.

Say you have $9,500 in business start-up costs in 2005 for your tax lien investment partnership. Say several of the partnership tax liens are redeemed by the property owners in 2005. Say the partnership has $5,300 in profits on these redeemed tax liens.

How would the partnership tax return look based on just this information? We will use the income and expenses format. The partnership has a profit of $5,300. We know we can write off the first $5,000 of the $9,500 in business start-up costs.

We can also amortize the remaining $4,500 of the business start-up costs over 15 years. This gives an additional $300 yearly write-off. The partnership profit of $5,300 would be totally offset by the business start-up costs. Plus there is a $300 write-off for the next 14 years.

Income and Expenses

Income		Expenses
$5,300	Tax Liens Redeemed	
	Business Start-up	$5,000
	Amortized Costs	$300
$5,300	Totals	$5,300

So how much money does the partnership keep untaxed? The total income of $5,300! And, this is just a small example isolating one piece of the system. If you did not know about the start-up costs write-off, the partnership could be paying tax on $5,300 worth of income.

Losses

What happens if your partnership has a loss investing in real estate tax liens? Normally business losses can be carried forward to offset future gains. What about offsetting past gains?

Normally, business losses can be carried back three years to offset gains. By studying the design of the tax system, you may discover added benefits to what everyone seems to know.

Owners of worthless securities have a longer time period to file refund claims. They are allowed seven years to file an amended return and claim a loss. This is much longer than the usual three-year statute of limitations.

Investors in partnerships do not get this benefit. Unfortunately, this was what a tax court told a taxpayer who bought into a partnership that turned out to be a Ponzi scheme. This was the case even though the government indicted the perpetrators for securities fraud. Only the losses from worthless stocks, bonds, or notes get the extra refund time. Worthless partnerships do not qualify.

That does not seem to bode well for a real estate tax lien investment partnership that loses money. What if your real estate tax lien investment partnership loses money? Will you and your partners be able to take advantage of the four extra years to file amended returns? You already know what our answer is. It all depends!

Buying Real Estate Tax Liens with Retirement Dollars

A large number of retirement plan limits are going up for 2005. The 401(k) maximum is rising to $14,000. Employees who were born prior to 1954 can contribute up to $18,000. These contribution limitations apply to 403(b) and 457 plans as well.

The cap for SIMPLE IRAs goes to $10,000. A simple IRA is a salary-reduction retirement plan that qualifying small employers (more than 100 workers) may offer their employees. A self-employed person, like a real estate tax lien investor, may set up a SIMPLE IRA. If you were born before 1954 the cap is $12,000. You can have a salary of up to $210,000. For defined-contribution plans like Keoghs and profit-sharing plans, the pay-in ceiling is $42,000. The benefit limit for pension plans is $170,000 in 2005. Employees making more than $95,000 are treated as high-paids in 2005 for purposes of the nondiscrimination rules for retirement plans.

What types of retirement programs can you use to invest in real estate tax liens? How about a garden variety IRA? How about a Roth IRA? How about a SEP IRA? How about a Keogh?

Retirement Programs

Consider the incredible difference investing in real estate tax liens would make to your retirement program. Open a self-directed Roth IRA, a SEP IRA, or a Keogh at age 45 and invest in tax lien certificates.

At age 70, by investing $3,000 a year with an 18 percent annual return, you will have more than $1 million. This is on a $75,000 total investment. You invested $3,000 a year for 25 years.

Tax Lien Certificate

Roth IRA

Investment	$3,000 Yearly
Interest Rate	18%
Term	25 Years
Return	$1,027,810

What would happen if you opened a Roth IRA at age 35? We will use the same numbers: 3,000 yearly, 18 percent interest rate, but for 35 years. At age 70, how much money do you think you would have accumulated? You will have $5.5 million! This is on a $105,000 total investment!

Tax Lien Certificate

Roth IRA

Investment	$3,000 Yearly
Interest Rate	18%
Term	35 Years
Return	$5,500,000

What would happen if you opened a Roth IRA at age 25? We will use the same numbers: $3,000 yearly, 18 percent interest rate, but for 45 years. You better stand up for this. At age

70, on your $135,000 total investment, you would have $28.5 million!

Tax Lien Certificate

Roth IRA

Investment	$3,000 Yearly
Interest Rate	18%
Term	45 Years
Return	$28,500,000

Rule of 72

It is now time to give you one of the most important rules for any investment or investor: the Rule of 72. The Rule of 72 says to take the annual rate of return you are receiving on your investment and divide it into 72.

The resulting number will tell you how long it will take for your investment amount to double. This assumes you are not reducing your investment return by paying federal income taxes. It also assumes you are reinvesting all your profits back into the investment.

If you have a monetary investment goal, using the Rule of 72 can give you a quick way to calculate the amount of time it will take for you to reach your goal. Say you have $32,000 to invest. Your investment goal is to turn that $32,000 into $1 million. $32,000 is 3.2 percent of $1 million.

You are going to invest in real estate tax liens. Let us assume you are going to receive an 18 percent annual return. Using the Rule of 72, how long will it take for you to reach your goal? You divide 72 by the 18 percent annual return; 18 goes into 72 four times. This means your investment will double in four years. Your $32,000 will double to $64,000.

In another four years your $64,000 will double into $128,000. In another four years your $128,000 will double to $256,000. In another four years your $256,000 will double to $512,000. In the next four years your $512,000 will double to $1,024,000.

Rule Of 72

72 / 18% = 4 Years Investment Doubles
$32,000 to $64,000 4 Years
$64,000 to $128,000 8 Years
$128,000 to $256,000 12 Years
$256,000 to $512,000 16 Years
$512,000 to $1,024,000 20 Years

Acquiring the Deed with Retirement Programs

What happens when the property owner does not redeem your property tax lien during the property owner's redemption period? Even if your investment strategy is to buy real estate tax liens for super-high returns, you still would foreclose on any of your unredeemed tax liens and get the deeds to the properties.

This does not change just because you are buying the tax liens inside a retirement program. You still must foreclose on any unredeemed tax liens and obtain the deeds to the properties. This simply protects your investment. You may also want to do this because obtaining property deeds was your investment strategy to begin with.

Say you foreclose on a tax lien and obtain the deed. Now you own the property. To be more technical, your retirement program owns the property. You want to take tile to the property in the name of your retirement program.

If your Roth IRA bought the tax lien on which you had to foreclose, then the tax deed you receive from the taxing authority needs to be designated with your Roth IRA as the property owner. If you take title to the property outside of your retirement program, then Houston, we have a tax problem.

Now that your retirement program owns the property, what can your retirement program do with the property? How many of you are thinking the answer is: It all depends. Good for you!

In this situation, as in any investment situation, there are two sides to the conversation. The first side to the conversation is the investment conversation. What is the best thing to do to have this investment make money? The second side to the conversation is the taxation conversation. How do we minimize or eliminate any tax consequences on this investment?

You always want to focus on the investment side of the conversation. If the investment is a lousy investment, you will not make any money. You may even have a loss. This makes the tax side of the conversation moot. You will not be taxed on your investment loss.

Two Options

Once your retirement program owns the property, you have the same two options you would have if you owned the property outside your retirement program. You can sell the property for quick cash. You can hold onto the property and rent it for income and appreciation.

If you sell the property for quick cash, what are the tax consequences on your profit? What we just asked is not correct. We should have asked: If your Roth IRA sells the property for quick cash, what are the tax consequences on the profit?

The tax consequences on the profit from selling the property are the same as the tax consequences on the profit from receiving an investment return on the tax lien itself. There is no tax consequence! The retirement program shelters the profit from taxation.

If you rent the property, what are the tax consequences on your rental income? Again, what we just asked is not correct. We should have asked: If your Roth IRA rents the property, what are the tax consequences on the rental income?

It all depends! We are not trying to be cute here. You may not want the property to be in your Roth IRA and be a rental property. The Roth IRA is already tax sheltered. There are wonderful tax benefits to owning rental property, like taking depreciation. These tax benefits will be lost if the rental property is owned by the Roth IRA. You may be better off tax wise owning the rental property outside your Roth IRA!

Buying Real Estate Tax Liens with Investment Dollars

What are the federal income tax consequences of buying real estate tax liens with investment dollars? We are talking here about buying outside your retirement program. Actually, there are no federal income tax consequences when you buy real estate tax liens with investment dollars. The federal income tax consequences occur when you sell your real estate tax liens.

Technically, when one of your tax liens is redeemed by the property owner, you did not sell the tax lien. However, the IRS sees any profit you made when the property owner redeems your tax lien as a taxable event. When the IRS recognizes a gain, then there is a tax consequence to you.

We are focusing here on federal income tax consequences. There also may be state income tax consequences if you live in a state that has a state income tax. However, the bulk of the tax consequences are going to come from the federal government.

Capital Gain or Ordinary Income?

As an investor, after you determine the potential profit you can make on an investment, you look at how to minimize the tax consequences on the profits from that investment. The Internal Revenue Code (IRC) makes a distinction on how profits are taxed.

If the IRC says that your investment is a capital investment, then any profits you make on that capital investment are considered capital gains. Capital gains receive very favorable income tax treatment. Capital gains are taxed at a maximum 15 percent.

Say you had a $100,000 capital gain that was recognized by the IRC for 2005. What would be the maximum capital gains tax you would have to pay on that $100,000 gain?

You would take your $100,000 capital gain and multiply it by 15 percent. The maximum capital gains tax you would pay is $15,000.

Capital Gains Tax

Recognized Capital Gain	$100,000
Capital Gain Tax Rate	×15%
Capital Gains Tax	$15,000

If the IRC says that your investment is not a capital investment or you have not held the investment for a long enough period of time, then any profits you make on that investment are considered ordinary income. Ordinary income receives very unfavorable income tax treatment. Ordinary income can be taxed at a maximum 36 percent tax rate.

Say you had $100,000 in ordinary income that was recognized by the IRC for 2005. What would be the maximum ordinary income tax you would have to pay on that $100,000 ordinary income?

You would take your $100,000 ordinary income and multiply it by 36 percent. The maximum ordinary income tax you would pay is $36,000.

Ordinary Income Tax

Recognized Ordinary Income	$100,000
Ordinary Income Tax Rate	×36%
Ordinary Income Tax	$36,000

As you can see, the difference in the tax consequences is huge. There is a $21,000 tax increase on the same $100,000 profit between the capital gains tax and the ordinary income tax.

Tax Difference

Ordinary Income Tax	$36,000
Capital Gains Tax	$15,000
Tax Difference	$21,000

What becomes truly flabbergasting is when you calculate how much damage to your portfolio growth occurs with the higher taxation of the IRC designation of ordinary income tax treatment. Instead of having $85,000 growing in your portfolio after taxes, you have $64,000 growing in your portfolio after taxes.

If you put the $64,000 in a tax-deferred vehicle for 30 years at a 12 percent annual return, the $64,000 would grow to almost $2 million. If you put the $85,000 in a tax-deferred vehicle for 30 years at a 12 percent annual return, the $85,000 would grow to more than $2.5 million!

$64,000 Grows To

$64,000
12%
30 Years
$1,917,435

$85,000 Grows To

$85,000
12%
30 Years
$2,546,593

Your big question is: How are real estate tax lien investments treated by the IRC? We think you know what our big answer is. It all depends! Remember, this conversation is occurring outside of retirement programs. We are talking about treatment of investment dollars.

You want the answer to be the IRC treats all real estate tax lien investments as capital investments. The IRS wants the answer to be the IRC treats all real estate tax lien investments as ordinary income. We think the answer is somewhere in between. We recommend you consult with your tax professional. If you want to consult with us, email wrcarey@hotmail.com.

Brain Trust

Let us give you a Brain Trust take on this taxation of real estate tax lien investments. Let us assume that you have a real estate tax lien investment strategy of buying tax liens for super-high returns. Let us assume you are content with the IRC interpretation that any profit you make will be taxed as ordinary income.

Unfortunately, the property owner does not redeem your tax lien. You foreclose on your tax lien and acquire the deed to the property. You turn the property into rental real estate. You hold the property for the appropriate amount of time according to the IRC. You then sell the property.

Should your profit be taxed at ordinary income tax rates? Should your profit be taxed at capital gains tax rates? Even though you were prepared to pay tax on the profit at the ordinary income tax rate if your tax lien was redeemed, would it be all right with you to pay tax on your profit at the capital gains tax rate? Are you sure? Do we have to do any arm-twisting? Would you rather have $64,000 after taxes or would you rather have $85,000 after taxes? A no-brainer, right?

In Chapter 13 we are going to tell you what to watch for when you are doing your real estate tax lien investing. You may be surprised what you can encounter out there. Our job is to take away the nasty surprises.

We also will give you some ideas on how to successfully deal with any of those nasty surprises you encounter. What can you do to protect your real estate tax lien investment when the property owner files for bankruptcy? What will you do if the property that is the security for your tax lien investment is destroyed? Has anyone heard of the Environmental Protection Agency? To bring back an old saying: Don't worry. Be happy!

Bankruptcy and Other Problems

W hile there is no pun intended, we are amused that Chapter 13 is about bankruptcy and other problems you may encounter in your real estate tax lien investing adventure. Of course, Chapter 13 also is a type of bankruptcy contained in the Federal Bankruptcy Code!

There are two other problems we will delve into in this chapter. The first of these problems is the destruction of the improvements on the property. The second of these problems is any environmental issues that may affect the value of the property.

Bankruptcy may delay or stop you from foreclosing on your tax lien. The destruction of the property or environmental issues may make the property that is the security for your tax lien worth less than the value of your tax lien. In fact, the environmental issues could make the property just plain worthless.

Bankruptcy

What do you do when the property owner/taxpayer files for bankruptcy? If the property owner files for bankruptcy, all the assets of the property owner are going to be frozen by the bankruptcy court. The property owner will not be redeeming your tax lien any time soon. Even if the redemption period is about to end, you may not be able to foreclose on your tax lien.

Normally, there are two ways that you will discover that the property owner has filed for bankruptcy. You may be notified of the bankruptcy because you are the tax lien holder of record. You may discover that the property owner has filed for bankruptcy at the courthouse as you attempt to foreclose on your tax lien.

Bankruptcy is a legal procedure established by federal law to assist debtors who cannot meet their financial obligations. The founding fathers of this country were so opposed to the traditional British solution of throwing debtors into prison that they created an alternative solution.

Two Categories

Bankruptcies fall into two categories: liquidation and reorganization. Liquidation bankruptcies fall under Chapter 7 of the United State Bankruptcy Code. The debtor who takes this path ends up turning over all their nonexempt assets to the bankruptcy court. A court-appointed trustee then has the responsibility of liquidating (selling) the assets and distributing the proceeds to the existing creditors on a pro rata basis.

Any debts that remain unsatisfied at that time are discharged and legally nullified. The trustee works for both the debtor and the creditors. It is the duty of the trustee to try to preserve the debtor's assets as much as possible to satisfy creditors.

Bankruptcies intended to assist the debtor with financial rehabilitation through reorganization come under the categories of Chapter 13 and Chapter 11. A Chapter 13 bankruptcy is intended for individuals with a regular source of income. A plan is proposed by which the debtor will continue to make payments on the debts and make up back payments with interest. A modified, extended schedule is often used to do this.

A Chapter 11 bankruptcy is used by corporations, partnerships, and those individuals who do not qualify for a Chapter 13 plan. The court procedures can be complex and lengthy. The cost of a Chapter 11 can be surprisingly expensive.

Foreclosure Stops

The moment a property owner in default files a petition for bankruptcy, foreclosure proceedings stop immediately. While this tends to affect mortgage lenders, it also will affect you foreclosing on your tax lien.

This is because a legal moratorium called an automatic stay is imposed by the bankruptcy court. It prevents creditors from pursuing any legal actions to enforce their claims against a debtor. In other words, everything stays put until the bankruptcy court hears the case.

If a foreclosure sale is held after a bankruptcy petition has been filed, the foreclosure will be ruled null and void by the bankruptcy judge. *Null and void* are not good words to hear from a court. From the bankruptcy court's point of view, the foreclosure sale never took place!

A mortgage lender must first seek relief from the automatic stay in order to proceed with its foreclosure. You must do the same in order to proceed with your foreclosure on your tax lien. The Bankruptcy Act says the court must hear a lender's petition for relief from stay within 30 days. If the court fails to do so, the stay is automatically lifted. Once the stay is lifted, the lender and you can proceed with your foreclosures.

The amount of equity found in the property will affect the judge's decision to grant relief from the stay. If there is significant value in the property being foreclosed, the judge will not grant relief from the automatic stay. The hope is that some of that equity can be used to satisfy other creditors. If there is very little equity in the property, the judge will probably grant a relief from the automatic stay and allow the foreclosing lender to proceed.

The situation with a foreclosure on a tax lien when there is no foreclosure going on concurrently with a mortgage lender needs some clarification. You may or may not be able to proceed with your tax lien foreclosure once the property owner files bankruptcy.

This is because the judge may decide that you would be acquiring too much equity in the property beyond what you are owed for the tax lien. It is not that you will not be paid the amount of your tax lien. You also will still be entitled to the interest, penalties, fees, costs, and expenses associated with your tax lien.

In other words, you are not going to lose your tax lien investment to the bankruptcy. Your tax lien is a senior lien. Your tax lien will be paid by the property owner or a buyer at the court-ordered bankruptcy liquidation.

Let us say you are owed $8,000 for you tax lien, interest, penalties, fees, costs, and expenses. The property is worth $75,000. You have an undivided 70 percent interest in the property based on your tax lien bid. The property owner retains an undivided 30 percent interest in the property.

The redemption period closes for the property owner to redeem your tax lien. You file the paperwork to foreclose on your tax lien. Once you foreclose you will receive a tax deed that gives you a 70 percent undivided interest in the property.

Let us see how much equity you would have in the property.

Tax Lien Foreclosure

Property Value	$75,000
Your Percentage Interest	×70%
Your Equity Position	$52,500

You are owed $8,000 for you tax lien. Not too bad, turning your $8,000 investment into a $52,500 return! That is a 656 percent return on your investment!

Tax Deed Return

Your Equity Position	$52,500
Tax Lien Investment	$8,000
Return on Investment	$52,500 / $8,000 = 656%

Unfortunately, the property owner files bankruptcy before you can foreclose. The bankruptcy judge stays your foreclosure. The property owner has an asset worth $75,000. The bankruptcy judge orders a bankruptcy sale of the property. The property owner has three creditors who have claims of

$125,000. What will happen to your tax lien and your tax lien foreclosure?

You will not be allowed to foreclose on your tax lien. You will become the priority creditor at the court ordered bankruptcy sale. The highest bidder at the bankruptcy sale will receive clear title to the property. From the money received by the sale the court will disburse the proceeds to the creditors.

Say the winning bid for the property is $58,000. How will the money be disbursed by the bankruptcy court? The good news is that you will receive the first $8,000 for your tax lien as the priority creditor. The remaining $50,000 will be allotted to the three creditors with the $125,000 in claims.

Bankruptcy Sale

Winning Bid	$58,000
Your Tax Lien	$8,000
Remaining Funds for Creditors	$50,000

As you can easily see, the creditors will not receive all of their claims. The other creditors will not be happy with $50,000 to pay off $125,000. They are going to receive 40 cents on the dollar.

Creditors Receive

Creditors Receive	$50,000
Creditors Owed	$125,000
Percentage Received	$50,000 / $125,000 = 40%

You may not be happy either. You went from foreclosing on your tax lien and obtaining a 70 percent undivided interest in the property worth $52,500 to receiving $8,000 from the bankruptcy court. However, you were the only creditor to receive 100 percent of what you were owed! As we have been saying all along about real estate tax lien investing, you have super-low risks.

Cram Down or Short Sale

We are going to give you another piece of the bankruptcy conversation. If a lender is foreclosing concurrently with you foreclosing on your tax lien, it could affect your ability to acquire the deed to the property. You will still be protected on the amount of your tax lien.

Lenders are most fearful of the court's authority to impose a cram-down or short-sale provision. The court can move to modify the terms of the mortgage or trust deed. This could include modifying the payment schedule to help the debtor or actually reducing the principal amount owed on the mortgage note. The cram-down provision can be used only with reorganization types of bankruptcies (Chapters 11 and 13), where the property plays a key role in the reorganization plan.

Creative Debtors

Debtors have come up with some pretty creative ways to stall foreclosures. Maybe you thought that a person can file a bankruptcy only once every seven years? That is true of Chapter 7 liquidations, but it is not true with Chapters 11 and 13 reorganizations.

The law does not prohibit the act of filing bankruptcy, and it is the filing that brings on the automatic stay. Because of this, a growing number of debtors are using that loophole to further delay the foreclosure process. Many judges are now wise to this trickery and will quickly lift the new stay.

Bankruptcies Filed after a Foreclosure Sale

There have been cases reported where a bankruptcy judge has overturned a foreclosure sale that occurred just prior to the filing of the bankruptcy petition. The judge may rule that the equity in the property could have been used to pay more creditors.

Because the Bankruptcy Code is a federal law, a debtor in any state can file a bankruptcy petition and stop the foreclosure process. If the bankruptcy petition is filed 15 days into the foreclosure, the foreclosure will resume on the 15th day after the automatic stay is lifted. In other words, the lender does not have to go back to the beginning of the foreclosure. They resume the foreclosure from the point where they stopped.

Bankruptcy Summary

Bankruptcy is a serious event that could affect the timing and ultimate outcome of any foreclosure. A property owner's bankruptcy does not mean you will never get paid on your real estate tax lien investment. You will be paid, but the payment may be delayed.

The bankruptcy court takes control and decides how the property owner's assets will be apportioned to pay their debts. Bankruptcy law determines how the debts are paid. Higher-priority liens like tax liens are paid first. This reduces your risk in real estate tax lien investing.

If you become aware of a bankruptcy filed by a property owner that affects your real estate tax lien investment, you will have to file a claim with the bankruptcy court. If you receive a notice of the bankruptcy proceeding, it will give you instructions on how to file your tax lien claim.

If you do not receive instructions from the bankruptcy court on what to do, then call the taxing authority's office in the area where the property is located. They will be able to coach you on what actions you should take.

Finally, it is important to make sure that your tax lien is on record with the bankruptcy court. Also make sure that the bankruptcy court has your contact information. Then you will have to wait on the bankruptcy court to make its decisions.

Destruction of Improvements

Though this is a fairly unlikely occurrence, it is possible. A fire, hurricane, tornado, or natural disaster could destroy the home or the improvements on the property. This could have a negative impact on the security for your tax lien.

This may not be as bad as it sounds. Most property owners carry casualty insurance. This will cover the cost of repairs. In some cases, the casualty insurance will pay off the outstanding liens if there is a total loss.

The amount of money you have invested in the tax lien is relatively small compared to the value of the property. Remember, we recommended the property have a value a minimum of six times the amount of the tax lien.

Sometimes the value of the land is greater than the value of the improvements on the land. Then, even if the improvements on the property are destroyed, the property retains sufficient value for you to have enough security for your tax lien.

For some of you this may be a research consideration. You may want to make sure that the land is worth more than the buildings. You can get a sense of the value of the land and the value of the improvements by looking at the allocation between the land and the improvements given by the taxing authority. This can be found on the property tax bill for the property.

Environmental Issues

This is a fairly rare occurrence. Your initial research will usually turn up any existing environmental issues. If there is an environmental problem in the area, stay away from the properties in the area. Do not buy tax liens on properties near commercial properties that could be contaminated.

There could be a problem with contamination if the site was formerly an auto repair shop, a dry cleaner, a gas station, a chemical plant, or a paint factory. Environmental issues are one of the reasons we recommended avoiding commercial properties.

Two Problems

There are two problems you have as a tax lien investor with environmental issues. The first problem is if your tax lien investment strategy is buying tax liens for super-high returns. You want the property owner to redeem your tax lien. The second problem is if your tax lien investment strategy is buying the tax liens to wind up acquiring the deed to the property. You want the property to have value.

If there is an environmental problem with the property, it is highly unlikely that the property owner will redeem your tax lien. This is because the property owner may have encountered huge expenses associated with cleaning up the property.

The property owner may have no money left to redeem your tax lien. They may decide to abandon the property rather than clean up the property. If the property owner abandons the property, they are certainly not interested in redeeming your tax lien.

If you foreclose on your tax lien and take title to the property, you may be in for a big surprise. If the property is contaminated by toxic waste, hazardous chemicals, mold, radon gas, or lead paint, you may be liable for the cleanup costs as the property owner.

Of course this would be the case only if you foreclosed on your tax lien and acquired the deed to the property. No one says you have to foreclose on your tax lien. You could wait it out and see if the property is eventually cleaned up. Your tax lien is still a lien against the title to the property. Eventually, your tax lien may be paid off.

Other than doing your homework, there is not much more that you can do to avoid environmental problems. The best way to protect yourself from losing your personal assets to pay for environmental cleanup is to never own property in your name.

We have already suggested protecting yourself by incorporating your tax lien investment business. Incorporation provides a shield for your personal assets. The most you will lose is the amount you have in the corporation's name.

You also could form a limited liability company (LLC). You could be a limited partner in a limited partnership. All of these structures provide you with personal asset protection.

The likelihood that any of the three problems we have discussed in this chapter occurring is relatively small. The property owner filing bankruptcy is the most likely occurrence statistically. The destruction of the property improvements is statistically the next most likely occurrence. An environmental problem is the least likely occurrence, statistically.

In the next chapter we will give you important information on the tax lien states. We cover six key topics. These six topics are interest rates, key dates, bidding types, form of payments, redemption periods, and tax deed information. With this information you can begin to formulate your real estate tax lien investing strategy for receiving super-high investment returns.

CHAPTER 14

Tax Lien States

This chapter is designed to give you a synopsis of the basic information you need in order to choose where to make a real estate tax lien investment. We recommend you look to see if your state is a tax lien state. If your state is not a tax lien state we recommend you look for a state nearby.

We list the states alphabetically. Under each state we provide information for six topics. These six topics are interest rates, key dates, bidding types, form of payments, redemption periods, and tax deed information.

Most states have laws regarding real estate tax liens published online. Because state laws do not cover this information uniformly, we recommend you call the local taxing authority to verify the procedures for your area of interest. Chapter 15, "Tax Deed States," contains the information for the non-tax-lien states.

Alabama

1. Interest rate is 12 percent annually.
2. Tax lien sales are held in early May of each year. Publication of available properties usually occurs between early March and the sale date. Property taxes are due in October, but become delinquent on January 1.
3. Bidding is a buyer's bid, with the face amount of the lien being the minimum bid. Any excess funds gener-

ated over the face amount of lien is paid to the owner or placed in the county general fund. If the excess funds are placed in the general fund, the property owner may request these funds from the county.

4. Payment must be made immediately in cash or certified check.

5. Redemption period is three years.

6. Tax deed will be delivered to the purchaser of the tax lien three years after sale if the property is not redeemed. Purchaser of the tax lien certificate must return the certificate to the judge of probate in return for the tax deed.

Arizona

1. Interest rate is 16 percent annually.

2. Tax lien sales are held once a year in February. County treasurers must compile lists of properties with delinquent taxes by December 31 of each year. Properties for which tax liens will be sold are published in the newspaper and on the door of the county courthouse for at least two weeks prior to the sale.

3. Bidding is an interest rate bid. The successful purchaser will be the bidder who pays the face amount of the lien and agrees to accept the lowest interest rate not to exceed 16 percent.

4. Payment must be made on the sale date in cash.

5. Redemption period is three years.

6. Tax deed, also called a treasurer's deed, can be obtained by doing the following: After three-year redemption period, but before 10 years after sale, the purchaser of the tax lien certificate must initiate judicial foreclosure to close off the property owner's right to redeem.

   Between 30 and 180 days prior to initiating this superior court action, the purchaser must send a certified notice of intent to the property owner, to the address of the property, and to the tax bill mailing address. This certified notice must specify the name of the property owner, the parcel number of the property, the legal description of the property, and the number of the certificate of purchase.

Colorado

1. Interest rate is the federal discount rate plus 9 percent.
2. Tax lien sales are held by the second Monday in December at the county treasurer's office. The county treasurer must publish notice of the sale beginning four weeks before the sale date. Publication is usually in a local newspaper or, in the absence of a local newspaper, at the county treasurer's office.
3. Bidding is a buyer's bid. The highest bidder obtains the certificate of purchase, and only the face amount of the lien earns interest.
4. Payment must be made in cash.
5. Redemption period is three years.
6. Tax deed, or treasurer's deed, can be requested from the county treasurer after three years. You must present the certificate of purchase to the treasurer, pay a fee, and request a deed to the property. Any property taxes assessed on the property during that three-year period and not paid must be paid by you before you can obtain the deed.

Florida

1. Interest rate is up to 18 percent.
2. Tax lien sales are typically held annually in early June. Check with the county to verify. Publication occurs in a local publication for the three weeks prior to the sale.
3. Bidding is an interest rate bid. The lowest interest rate bid receives the certificate. Bids are accepted only in quarter-percent increments.

4. Payment must be made within 48 hours. You must also provide a deposit to the tax collector prior to bidding on a certificate.
5. Redemption period is two years following the April 1 of the year the certificate was obtained.
6. Tax deed can be applied for after the redemption period has elapsed and prior to its expiration, which is seven years from the date of issuance. You must pay all unpaid taxes and fees on the property plus a $15 application fee. The county will then accept bids on the tax deed. The first bid will be the amount the applicant has invested in the property. If another bidder outbids the applicant and obtains the deed, the applicant's money will be refunded.

Illinois

1. Interest rate in Illinois is on a staggered schedule. Different rates are applied based on when the property is redeemed. If the property is redeemed within two months of sale date, the interest will be 3 percent per month. If the property is redeemed between two and six months of sale date, the interest will be 12 percent of sale amount. If the property is redeemed between six and 12 months of sale date, the interest will be 24 percent of sale amount. If the property is redeemed between 12 and 18 months from sale date, the interest will be 36 percent of sale amount. If the property is redeemed between 18 and 24 months from sale date, the interest will be 48 percent of sale amount. If the property is redeemed after 24 months from sale date, the interest will be 48 percent of sale amount plus 6 percent per year for each year thereafter. Interest earned on tax liens purchased at a Scavenger Sale is 12 percent per six months for the first four years then 6 percent per year for each year thereafter.
2. Tax lien sales are held annually. The state statutes do not specify in what month the sale is to be held, so

check with the county. Publication of the sale generally occurs in the month prior to the sale. You must preregister and present a deposit 10 days before the sale to participate.

Illinois also has what is called a Scavenger Sale (mentioned in 1 preceding). These are held in odd-numbered years and are for properties with delinquencies in two years that were not sold at the annual sale.

3. Bidding is an interest rate bid, with bidding starting at 18 percent per six months. The lowest interest rate is accepted. Based on that rate, the interest will be calculated in six-month intervals.

   Bidding at Scavenger Sales is a flat amount. You must bid on the amount you are willing to pay for the delinquent taxes and fees.

4. Payment must be made immediately.

5. Redemption period is generally two years. There are two exceptions, however. If the property is vacant farmland, the redemption period is only six months. If the property is improved residential property with at least one but not more than six living units, the redemption period is two years and six months. The purchaser of the tax certificate also has the right to extend the redemption period.

6. Tax deeds can be obtained once the redemption period has expired. The purchaser of the tax certificate must provide a Take Notice to the county clerk within four months and 15 days of sale date. This provides notice to the property owner that the tax certificate on the property has been sold. You must also file another notice between three and five months prior to the expiration of redemption. Both notices must contain the county of the property, the date of the sale of the tax certificate, the tax certificate number, the year of the delinquent taxes, sold for special assessment of whatever taxing authority, the special assessment number, and the warrant number. If the redemption period expires and you have not filed a deed petition, the right to do so expires as well.

Indiana

1. Interest rate is 10 percent of the minimum bid if the property is redeemed within six months of the tax lien sale. The minimum bid is the face amount of the tax lien. The winning bid can be higher than the minimum bid. The interest rate is 15 percent of the minimum bid if the property is redeemed between six months and one year of the tax lien sale. The redeeming property owner is also required to pay the difference between the purchase price and the minimum bid plus 10 percent annual interest on that amount.

   If you paid any additional property taxes after the sale, the redeeming owner must pay that amount also plus 10 percent annual interest on that amount. Any attorney's fees or title search costs also must be paid by the redeeming owner.

2. Tax lien sales are generally held between August 1 and November 1 of each year. The county treasurer must notify the county auditor of all delinquent properties prior to July 1 of each year. The county auditor must then compile a notice detailing all properties eligible for sale. The notice must contain the list of eligible properties; a statement that these properties will be sold at auction to the highest bidder; a statement that the minimum sale amount for each property is equal to the sum of all delinquent taxes and assessments and associated penalties, taxes, and assessments due in the year of the sale, and an additional fee determined by the county auditor to cover postage, publication, and other costs related to the tax sale, as well as any unpaid costs from a prior tax sale; a statement of the interest percentages the owner must pay to redeem the property; a description and location of the property; the owner's name; and the date and other particulars of the sale.

3. Bidding is on the amount you are willing to pay to purchase the taxes and fees associated with the property. The amount you pay is applied to taxes and fees. If there is any surplus, it goes into a tax sale surplus

fund. This is a highest bid scenario. A claim may be filed to obtain thcsc funds by either the property owner whose ownership is forfeited upon issuance of a tax deed or the purchaser of the tax certificate if the property is redeemed. If no one claims the funds after three years, the amount is transferred to the auditor's general fund.

4. Payment must be made immediately.
5. Redemption period is generally one year.
6. Tax deeds can be obtained after the redemption period. You must give notice by certified mail of the tax lien sale to the property owner and any other party with interest in the property within nine months of the sale date. This notice must contain a statement of when the tax deed petition will be filed, a description and location of the property, the date of the tax certificate sale, the name of the purchaser of the tax certificate, a statement detailing the amount of money required for the property redemption, a notification that the purchaser is entitled to reimbursement for amounts noted in the interest rate section, a statement that the property has not yet been redeemed and that purchaser of the tax certificate may receive a tax deed if property is not redeemed, and a statement that the owner may be entitled to tax sale surplus funds if the property is not redeemed.

You must file a petition for a tax deed within six months of the expiration of the redemption period. A granted tax deed entitles you to the property free and clear of liens and encumbrances, except for any federal tax liens that may have priority.

Iowa

1. Interest rate is 2 percent per month, or 24 percent annually.
2. Tax lien sales occur in June of each year. Publication occurs between one and three weeks prior to the sale

and includes a property description, the owner's information, and the amounts due associated with the property. A nonrefundable registration fee may be required to take part in the bidding.

3. Bidding is on interest in the property. The bidder who will pay the lien amounts and accept the smallest percentage of interest in the property obtains the tax certificate.

4. Payment is due immediately.

5. Redemption period is generally two years.

6. Tax deeds are obtainable if you follow the procedure. If no action is taken to pursue the deed, the tax certificate expires three years following the sale date. Three months prior to expiration of the redemption period (this is usually one year and nine months after sale date), you must give notice to the property owner that the right of redemption will expire in 90 days.

Kentucky

1. Interest rate is 12 percent annually, computed monthly. Each portion of a month is considered one month; for example, property redeemed 15.5 months after the sale would earn interest on 16 months.

2. Tax lien sales must be publicized 15 days prior to the sale. State law does not specify when the sale is to be held, so check with the county. Most sales are held at the end of April.

3. Bidding is not specified in state statutes. Check with the county on their method.

4. Payment is due immediately.

5. Redemption period is not a set time period. One year after the tax sale, you may pursue collection from owner or enforcement of the tax lien.

6. Tax deeds are obtainable through judicial foreclosure. You must notify the property owner of the sale and the rate of interest, which will accrue within 50 days of the foreclosure sale date. After one year, you may

pursue formal collection of amounts owed to you or you may wish to enforce the lien through foreclosure.

Louisiana

1. Interest rate is 12 percent per year. There is an automatic 5 percent penalty in the first year added to the 12 percent.
2. Tax lien sale date is not specified in statutes. Check with the parish.
3. Bidding is on property interest. The bidder who will pay the lien amounts and accept the smallest percentage of interest in the property obtains the tax certificate.
4. Payment must be made immediately.
5. Redemption period is three years. In New Orleans, abandoned residential or commercial property or blighted property has a redemption period of only 18 months.
6. Tax deed is issued after purchase at the tax sale. The tax deed must be recorded soon thereafter. The property owner has three years from the date of the recording of the deed to redeem the property.

Maryland

1. Interest rate is set by the county. The interest rate varies from 6 percent to 24 percent.
2. Tax lien sale dates are set by the county. Publication of the event usually occurs between 30 and 60 days prior to the tax sale.
3. Bidding is on the amount you are willing to pay to purchase the taxes and fees associated with the property. The highest bidder wins. The property will not be sold for less than the sum of all delinquent taxes, fees, and penalties. A high-bid premium may be added to

the purchase price. If the highest bid exceeds 40 percent of the property's cash value, then 20 percent of the difference between the bid and the cash value of the property is added to the purchase price. The high-bid amount is calculated differently if the property is located in Baltimore or if the property is under agricultural use assessment. If either of these situations applies, check with the local taxing authority.

4. Payment of all taxes and fees plus the high-bid premium must be made on the day of the sale. Any excess over these amounts may be paid later.

5. Redemption period is not a set time period. To obtain title to the property, you must file foreclosure proceedings to end the redemption period.

6. Tax deed may be obtained by filing a complaint to foreclose the owner's right of redemption. This is a judicial proceeding. You need to file the complaint at least six months after the sale but not longer than two years after the sale. If no filing is made within two years, the tax certificate expires. Your complaint to begin foreclosure proceedings should contain a statement that the tax certificate on the property was sold, a description and location of the property, a statement that the owner has not redeemed the property, a request to serve process on defendant (property owner), a request to notify all parties with an interest in the property, a request that the court foreclose the owner's rights of redemption, and an itemization of the amount required for redemption.

Massachusetts

1. Interest rate is 14 percent.
2. Tax lien sales are scheduled by local officials.
3. Bidding is on the property interest. The bidder who will pay the lien amounts and accept the smallest percentage of interest in the property obtains the tax certificate.

4. Payment must be made immediately.

5. Redemption period is not a set time period. Six months after purchasing the tax certificate, you may pursue foreclosure to close off the redemption period.

6. Tax deed is issued upon purchase of the tax certificate. This deed must be recorded within 60 days of sale date. To obtain actual title to the property, you must initiate a judicial foreclosure proceeding.

Mississippi

1. Interest rate is 1.5 percent per month, or 18 percent annually.

2. Tax lien sales are held annually at the end of August. The tax collector is required to publish the properties and the scheduled place and time of the tax sale during the month of August. This is done in the local newspaper and at the county courthouse.

3. Bidding is a buyer's bid. Only the face amount of the lien earns interest.

4. Payment must be made immediately with cash, check, money order, or cashier's check.

5. Redemption period is two years.

6. Tax deeds may be requested once the redemption period expires and you receive notification from the county clerk that the property is being forfeited. You will then have a period of time to respond, pay any fees, and request the deed.

Missouri

1. Interest rate is 10 percent annually, with 8 percent interest earned on any subsequent taxes paid by the purchaser.

2. Tax lien sales are held annually on the fourth Monday of August. Publication usually occurs two to three weeks prior to the sale.

3. Bidding is on the property interest. The bidder willing to pay the face amount of the lien for the least interest in the property obtains the certificate. Nonresidents of Missouri may not bid.
4. Payment must be made immediately with cash, check, or cashier's check to avoid being assessed a penalty.
5. Redemption period is two years.
6. Tax deed must be applied for within six months after the expiration of the redemption period.

Montana

1. Interest rate is five-sixths of 1 percent per month, or 10 percent annually.
2. Tax lien sales are held annually in June or July. Publication must be made in a newspaper or public place for three weeks, beginning no later than the last Monday in June. The sale is conducted at the county courthouse.
3. Bidding is a highest bid scenario. Interest accrues on the amount for which the tax lien certificate was purchased.
4. Payment must be made on the day of the sale in cash.
5. Redemption period is three years.
6. Tax deed will be granted to the purchaser of the tax lien certificate if the property is not redeemed in the three-year period. The tax deed must then be recorded.

Nebraska

1. Interest rate is 14 percent. When you purchase a tax lien in Nebraska, you are responsible for paying subsequent taxes when they become delinquent. You will have a perpetual tax lien; as you pay subsequent taxes, they are added to the amount of the lien.

2. Tax lien sales dates can be set by the county but typically occur on the first Monday in March of each year. The county treasurer must compile a list of properties with delinquent taxes between four and six weeks prior to the first Monday in March. This list must be published weekly for the three weeks preceding the sale.

3. Bidding is a property interest bid. The bidder willing to accept the least amount of interest in the property and pay the amount of the lien obtains the certificate.

4. Payment must be made on the day of the sale. Counties determine the forms of acceptable payment.

5. Redemption period is three years.

6. Tax deed is available after expiration of redemption period. Three months prior to application for the deed, you must serve a notice to the property owner detailing the property and its legal description, the name of the owner or person responsible for assessment, and the year of the delinquent taxes.

New Hampshire

1. Interest rate is 18 percent. After you purchase the tax lien, you are responsible for subsequent taxes as they become due.

2. Tax lien sales must be published in two public places at least 25 days before the sale.

3. Bidding is on property interest. The bidder willing to pay the face amount of the lien and to accept the smallest amount of undivided interest in the property obtains the certificate.

4. Payment must be made immediately in a form acceptable by the county.

5. Redemption period is two years.

6. Tax deed is issued by the treasurer. If the purchaser of the certificate complies with filing requirements, they receive the deed after the two-year filing period. As purchaser, you must give notice to any mortgagee (lender) with a security interest in the

property within 45 days of tax sale. The notice must provide a description of the property, the property owner's name, and the amount of the lien. If you pay any subsequent taxes, you must notify the lender of this as well within 30 days of your payment.

New Jersey

1. Interest rate is a maximum of 18 percent. The purchaser of the certificate is not required to pay subsequent taxes; if these become delinquent, separate certificates will be auctioned for the property. When the property is redeemed, you as the purchaser of the certificate, may be entitled to charge the property owner additional amounts for expenses.
2. Tax lien sales are held annually, usually in the spring. However, each county can set its own date. Publication is made in newspapers for four weeks prior to the sale.
3. Bidding is an interest rate bid. The bidder willing to accept the lowest rate of interest and pays the entire face amount of the lien plus expenses obtains the certificate. Expenses include the cost of publication prior to the sale.
4. Payment must be made immediately in a form acceptable by the county.
5. Redemption period is two years.
6. You must record the certificate of purchase within three months of tax sale for it to remain valid as a lien against the property. Following the expiration of the redemption period, you must initiate judicial foreclosure on the property.

Rhode Island

1. Interest rate is 12 percent. One year after sale date, the purchaser of the tax lien certificate is considered

jointly and severally liable for the property. This means the county can pursue collection of subsequent taxes from you.

2. Tax lien sales are scheduled by the county. Publication is required in the newspaper and at least two public places for three weeks prior to the sale.

3. Bidding is on the property interest. The bidder willing to pay the face amount of the lien and to accept the smallest portion of undivided interest in the property obtains the certificate.

4. Payment must be made immediately in a form acceptable to the county.

5. Redemption period is one year.

6. Tax deed is issued immediately to the purchaser of the tax lien certificate. The deed must be recorded within 60 days of the sale date to remain valid and is subject to the owner's right of redemption. As a tax deed title holder, you are responsible for notifying the county of your address if it changes. One year from the sale date, you must petition to the superior court to foreclose the owner's right of redemption in order to obtain clear title to the property.

South Carolina

1. Interest rate earned depends on when the property is redeemed. If the property is redeemed within three months of the sale, the tax lien purchaser earns a flat 3 percent on the amount paid for the lien; this is 12 percent annually. If the property is redeemed four, five, or six months after the sale, the purchaser earns a flat 6 percent on the amount paid for the lien. If the property is redeemed seven, eight, or nine months after the sale, the purchaser earns a flat 9 percent on the amount paid for the lien. If the property is redeemed during the last three months prior to expiration of redemption, the purchaser earns a flat 12 percent on the amount paid for the lien.

2. Tax lien sales are held annually in December of each year. Publication usually occurs in the four weeks preceding the sale.
3. Bidding is a highest bid scenario. The amount paid for the tax lien accrues interest.
4. Payment is due immediately in a form acceptable by the county.
5. Redemption period is one year.
6. If the property is not redeemed, a quitclaim deed will be provided to the tax lien purchaser within 30 days. The county and state make no warranties pertaining to the quality of the title.

South Dakota

1. Interest rate is a maximum of 10 percent. You, as the purchaser of the certificate, have the option of paying subsequent taxes and earning the same rate of interest. These taxes begin to accrue interest on the day they would have become delinquent, not on the day you pay them.
2. Tax lien sales are held annually in December. Publication of the sale and the properties eligible for sale must be made once during the week before the sale date in the newspaper and in a public place.
3. Bidding is an interest rate bid. The bidder willing to pay the face amount of the lien and accept the lowest interest rate obtains the certificate.
4. Payment must be made immediately in a form acceptable to the county.
5. Redemption period is three years for properties located within a municipality and four years for properties located outside a municipality.
6. Tax deed issuance can be initiated after expiration of the redemption period and within six years of tax sale date. You must provide a notice of intention to the property owner of record. The notice must state the

sale date, the property description, the name of the purchaser, the date the redemption right will expire, and your intention to obtain the deed for the property in 60 days. The county will issue a deed 60 days after this notice.

Tennessee

1. Interest rate is 10 percent per year.
2. Tax lien sales are held annually on dates set by the county.
3. Bidding is a highest bid scenario. The entire amount of your bid earns interest.
4. Payment is due within 24 hours of sale in a form acceptable to the county. Failure to pay bid amount could result in legal action.
5. Redemption period is one year.
6. Tax deed can be requested after sale is confirmed. This typically occurs within 30 days following the sale.

Vermont

1. Interest rate is 1 percent per month.
2. Tax lien sales are scheduled by the county. Publication must be made in a public place and local newspaper for three weeks prior to the sale.
3. Bidding is a property interest bid. The bidder who pays the face amount of the lien and is willing to accept the smallest portion of interest in the property obtains the lien.
4. Payment must be made in terms acceptable to the county.
5. Redemption period is one year.
6. Tax deed will be issued by the tax collector after the one-year redemption period has expired.

West Virginia

1. Interest rate is 1 percent per month, or 12 percent annualized. As the tax lien purchaser, you will receive interest on the amount of lien, any subsequent taxes paid, and certain expenses incurred by you to make the purchase. You have the option to pay subsequent taxes in order to protect your interest in the property.
2. Tax lien sales are scheduled by the county, but usually occur in October or November. Publication is made in local newspapers three to six weeks prior to the sale.
3. Bidding is a buyer's bid. The face amount of the lien earns interest.
4. Payment must be made immediately in a form acceptable to the county.
5. Redemption period is 18 months.
6. Tax deed can be obtained by following certain filing requirements. Between October 31 and December 31 of the year following the tax sale, you must make a list of those parties who have an interest in the property. You must then ask the county clerk to serve notice to these parties. You may also give the clerk an itemization of reasonable expenses, including legal expenses, you have incurred to examine the title of the property and prepare the list. The clerk will request a deposit for the expenses of servicing such notice. You must also at this time turn over your original certificate of purchase that documents your ownership of the lien. The deed will be issued after the notice has been sent to all interested parties.

Wyoming

1. Interest rate is 18 percent.
2. Tax lien sales are scheduled by the county. State law specifies that the sale must be held between May and

September. Publication must be made three weeks prior to the sale.

3. Bidding in Wyoming is unique. The county assigns each bidder a number and then calls numbers at random. The called bidder may purchase liens on five properties.

4. Payment must be made immediately in a form acceptable to the county.

5. Redemption period is four years.

6. Tax deed can be obtained by applying for the tax deed between four and six years after the tax sale. You must also serve written notice to anyone currently in possession of the property and the owner of record according to the assessment office. If the property is abandoned or otherwise unoccupied, you must publish the notice in the newspaper for three consecutive weeks. The notice also must be sent to any lenders with recorded liens on the property. The notice must provide the date of the tax sale, the name of the property owner responsible for the delinquent taxes, a property description, the year of the assessment, the date the redemption period will expire, the date you will apply for the tax deed (which must be within three months of the notice), and the amount of special assessments, if any, on the property. After complying with these notice requirements, you can apply at the treasurer's office for a deed. You will be required to turn over your certificate of purchase and sign a statement that you have followed the procedures.

District of Columbia

1. Interest rate is 1.5 percent per month, or 18 percent annually.

2. Tax lien sales are held annually in July. Publication is made several weeks prior to the sale.

3. Bidding is a buyer's bid. The face amount of the lien earns interest.
4. Payment must be made within five days of the sale with cash, certified check, cashier's check, money order, or bank check.
5. Redemption period is six months.
6. Tax deed can be obtained by filing a court action between six months and one year following the tax sale.

In the next chapter we give you the information you need to pursue tax deeds in the non-tax-lien states, or tax deed states.

CHAPTER 15

Tax Deed States

C hapter 15 is designed to give you a synopsis of the basic information you need in order to choose where to make a real estate tax deed investment. This chapter complements Chapter 14, "Tax Lien States."

This chapter is for those of you who, like us, live in a tax deed state (in our case Texas). You may find you are very happy investing in tax deeds rather than tax liens. The material presented is not exhaustive because of the constraints of space.

Most states have laws regarding real estate tax deeds published online. Because state laws do not cover this information uniformly, we recommend you call the local taxing authority to verify the procedures for your area of interest. We list the states alphabetically.

Alaska

If a property owner does not pay real property taxes, then the property eventually will be foreclosed. Foreclosed property that is located in any area of the borough (the Alaskan term for *county*) outside of any cities is deeded to and becomes the property of the borough.

Foreclosed property located in a city is deeded to and becomes the property of the city. However, the city must pay to the borough any unpaid property taxes and costs of foreclosure levied against the property before the foreclosure.

Property-tax-foreclosed property conveyed to any borough or city by tax foreclosure and not required for a public purpose may be sold. The governing body of a borough or city must by ordinance establish a formal procedure for disposal of land owned by that entity.

These ordinances are sometimes very restrictive. Others, however, are much less restrictive. Whatever the entity selling the tax-foreclosed properties at public auction, the opening bid is the same. The opening bid is the delinquent borough or city taxes accrued through the date of sale, together with all applicable penalties, interest, and costs, including the costs of sale.

From the standpoint of tax sale investors, the sales procedures found in the Anchorage Municipal Charter Code and Regulations of the Municipality of Anchorage (being a unified home rule municipality—i.e., a home rule borough in which no cities may exist) are extremely restrictive. The procedures provide that all sales of municipal land to private parties "shall be for the fair market value of the interest disposed of" and that the department of property and facility management may select any of a number of sales methods. The auction method is most frequently used.

Anchorage

The Department of Property and Facility Management may enter direct negotiations with interested parties who seek to acquire municipal land. The department may invite sealed bids for municipal land, specifying the time and place for receiving bids and the minimum acceptable bid.

The Department of Property and Facility Management may offer municipal land for sale at public auction, specifying a minimum acceptable bid or specifying that if no higher price is offered the land shall be sold pursuant to a preexisting contract for sale for the minimum bid amount.

The Department of Property and Facility Management may invitc proposals to purchase municipal land for a fixed price. The invitation shall specify the basis upon which proposals shall be evaluated, which may include but need not be limited to the quality of proposed development of the land and its benefit to the community, the qualifications and organization of the proposers, the value of the proposed improvements to the land and the rents or resale prices to be charged by the proposer.

Fairbanks

The Code of Ordinances is not nearly as restrictive, providing simply that: "The city shall have and may exercise all rights and powers in the sale and disposal of real property as if the city were a private person. The city may sell or dispose of any real property, including property acquired or held for or devoted to a public use, when in the judgment of the city council it is no longer required for municipal purposes."

Kenai Peninsula

The Code of Ordinances states that the borough assembly, by ordinance, shall designate tax-foreclosed lands acquired as either foreclosed lands retained for a public purpose or foreclosed lands for sale. Foreclosed properties not retained for public purpose must be disposed of in accordance with state law and the following procedure:

1. A copy of the notice of sale shall be sent by certified mail to the record owner at the time of the tax foreclosure. The mailed notice shall include advice to the record owner of his right to repurchase the property.
2. The notice of sale shall be published in a newspaper(s) of general circulation in the borough no less than 30 days before the date of the sale and posted within that time in at least three public places in the borough.
3. Disposal shall be at public outcry auction conducted by the director of finance, or his designee, unless the assembly has provided otherwise in the ordinance authorizing the sale.

Upon satisfactory identification, the record owner at the time of tax foreclosure, or his assigns, may at any time before the sale, or contract for sale, of tax-foreclosed property repurchase that property for the full amount due to the borough and any city under the judgment and decree of foreclosure plus accrued interest and associated costs, delinquent taxes assessed and levied as though it had continued in private ownership, and any recording fees.

Any person asserting to be an assignee of the record owner shall provide an abstract of title, title opinion, or title report, at no cost to the borough, establishing his right to repurchase. The borough shall retain from the proceeds of the sale of each parcel of tax-foreclosed land only that amount attributable to delinquent borough taxes accrued through the date of sale, together with all applicable penalties, interests, and costs, including the costs of sale.

All proceeds received by the borough from the sale of each parcel of tax-foreclosed land, which are in excess of the amounts of real property taxes, penalties, interest, and applicable costs accruing through the date of sale, shall be held by the borough on behalf of the former record owner for six months from the date of sale.

The former record owner of tax-foreclosed real property that has been held by the borough for less than 10 years after the close of the redemption period, that has never been designated for retention of public purpose, and that is sold by the borough at a tax foreclosure sale shall be entitled to that portion of the proceeds of the sale that exceeds all sums due to the borough and city. If the proceeds of the sale of the tax-foreclosed property sold by the borough exceeds the sums due to the borough and city, the borough shall provide the former record owner of the property with written notice advising him of the amount of the excess and the manner in which a claim for the balance of the proceeds may be submitted.

This notice shall be mailed to the former owner at his or her last address of record. Upon presentation of a proper claim, the borough shall remit the excess proceeds to the former record owner. Any claim for the excess proceeds filed after six months from the date of sale of the property is forever barred, and the amount of excess proceeds shall be transferred to the general fund of the borough.

Seward

The Code of Ordinances states simply: "After the city has held any tax delinquent real property for one year, it may hold the same for public use or sell at public sale."

Arkansas

Arkansas tax sales are called tax-delinquent sales. These sales are public oral-bid foreclosure auctions of the real estate that is security for the delinquent taxes. They are conducted throughout the calendar year for all 75 Arkansas counties by an Arkansas state agency. This agency is the Commissioner of State Lands.

California

California tax sales are called tax-defaulted land sales. These sales are public oral-bid foreclosure auction sales of the real estate that is security for the delinquent taxes. They are conducted throughout the calendar year by each of the 58 county tax collectors.

Connecticut

Connecticut is divided into eight geographic regions called counties. These counties do not have functioning governments nor do they collect real property taxes. The tax collectors for the various towns, cities, boroughs, fire districts, or other municipalities collect real property taxes.

Each tax collector may sell the real property that is security for delinquent taxes at "public auction to the highest bidder all of said real property, to pay the taxes with the interest, fees and other charges allowed by law. Within two weeks after such sale, the collector shall execute a deed thereof to the purchaser and shall lodge the same in the office of the town clerk of such town, where it shall remain unrecorded one year from the date of such sale."

However, the collector's deed operates more as a tax lien certificate than an actual deed conveying title to the real property. There is a statutory right of redemption:

> If the delinquent taxpayer, mortgagee, lienholder or other record encumbrancer whose interest in the property will be affected by such sale, within one year from the date of such sale, pays or tenders to the collector, the amount of taxes, interest and charges which were due and owing at the time of the sale together with interest on the total purchase price paid by the purchaser at the rate of eighteen per cent per annum from the date of such sale, such deed . . . shall be delivered to the collector by the town clerk for cancellation.

Delaware

Delaware tax sales are conducted at the county level by each of the three counties: Kent, New Castle, and Sussex. Kent and Sussex counties conduct tax sales in the same manner. New Castle County conducts their tax sales differently.

However, both types of tax sales are public oral-bid foreclosure sales of the real property. The high bidder in New Castle County receives a certificate that acts more like a conveyance. The high bidder in Kent and Sussex Counties receives a deed that acts more like a tax certificate than a conveyance. In all three counties there is a one-year right of redemption.

Florida

Florida is a chameleon state. On one hand, Florida is a tax certificate tax-sale state, hence its inclusion in Chapter 14. Tax certificates with an 18 percent annual interest rate are offered for sale annually on or before June 1 or the 60 days after the date of delinquency, whichever is later. Each tax collector of the 67 Florida counties sells tax lien certificates. On the other hand, Florida is a public oral bid-foreclosure auction tax-sale state as far as the acquisition of real estate is concerned, hence its inclusion in Chapter 15.

If a tax lien certificate held either by an investor or by the county is not redeemed by the property owner, a normal tax lien foreclosure does not take place. The real estate itself must be sold at a public oral-bid foreclosure auction tax sale. This is called a tax deed sale. This sale is conducted by the clerk of the circuit court.

Tax Certificate Sales

The Florida tax certificate tax sale for unpaid taxes is a public oral-bid auction sale of the right to pay delinquent taxes, interest, and costs. This right is given to the person who will pay the taxes, interest, costs, and charges and will demand the lowest rate of interest, not in excess of the maximum 18 percent rate of interest allowed by law. The winning bidder is that person willing to receive the lowest interest rate on the tax lien certificate. The winning bidder gets a document called a certificate of sale. Tax sales are conducted annually by each of Florida's 67 county tax collectors during the months of April, May, or June.

Over-the-Counter Sales

Those tax certificates not sold at the annual tax sale are given to the county. Florida law states:

> Any person may...purchase a county held certificate at any time after the certificate is issued and before a tax deed is issued or the property is placed on the list of lands available for sale.

Public Oral-Bid Foreclosure Auction Sales (Tax Deed Sales)

Florida law states:

> The holder of any tax certificate, other than the county, at any time after two years have elapsed since April 1 of

the year of issuance of the tax certificate and before the expiration of 7 years from the date of issuance, may file the certificate and an application for a tax deed with the tax collector of the county where the lands described in the certificate are located.

The county shall make application for a deed on all certificates two years after April 1 of the year of issuance of the certificates. The clerk of the circuit court is charged with the responsibility of notifying all appropriate parties and advertising the real property that is security for the tax certificate for sale.

The lands advertised for sale to the highest bidder as a result of an application...shall be sold at public auction by the clerk of the circuit court, or his deputy, of the county where the lands are located on the date, at the time, and at the location as set forth in the published notice, which shall be during the regular hours his office is open. At the time and place, the clerk shall read the notice of sale and shall offer the lands described in the notice for sale to the highest bidder for cash at public outcry.

The amount required to redeem the tax certificate, plus the amounts paid by the holder to the clerk of the circuit court in charges for costs of sale, redemption of other tax certificates on the same lands, and all other costs to the applicant for tax deed, plus interest thereon at the rate of 1.5 percent per month for the period running from the month after the date of application for the deed through the month of sale and costs incurred for the service of notice...shall be considered the bid of the certificate holder for the property.

However, if the land to be sold is assessed on the latest tax roll as homestead property, the bid of the certificate holder shall be increased to include an amount equal to one-half of the assessed value of the homestead property as required by Law.

If there are no higher bids, the land shall be sold to the certificate holder. If there are no other bids, the certificate holder shall have the right to bid as others present may bid, and the property shall be sold to the highest bidder.

Georgia

Georgia tax sales are public oral-bid auctions of the property that is security for the delinquent real property taxes. The property is sold to the highest bidder for cash. The county sheriff or the county tax commissioner conducts the sales.

The sales are held on the first Tuesday of each month on the courthouse steps. The opening bid is the amount of delinquent taxes plus interest, penalties, fees, and costs. After payment of the amount bid by the high bidder, the county sheriff or the tax commissioner executes and records a tax deed.

The tax deed does not immediately convey full right, title, and interest in and to the property, including the right to immediate possession. The original property owner or any persons having a right, title, interest in, or lien upon the property may redeem the property at any time within 12 months from the date of the purchase at tax sale.

They must pay the amount paid by the high bidder for the property at the tax sale plus 20 percent of that amount for each year, or fraction of a year, between the sale date and the date the redemption is made. They must also pay any property tax paid on the property by the high bidder after the sale.

After the expiration of the 12-month redemption period, the high bidder "may terminate, foreclose, divest, and forever bar the right to redeem the property from the sale" through an administrative nonjudicial process. However, the "title under a tax deed properly executed on or after July 1, 1996, at a valid and legal sale shall ripen by prescription after a period of four years from the recordation of that deed in the land records in the county in which said land is located."

Transfer of Execution

Under Georgia law, the county tax commissioner or municipal tax collector can make a transfer of execution to third parties other than the delinquent taxpayer. If such a transfer is properly made, the "person to whom the execution is transferred shall have the same rights as to enforcing the execution and priority of payment as might have been exercised or claimed before the transfer" by the county or municipality.

This means that third-party investors—you—can obtain a real estate tax lien with an interest rate of 1 percent per month or fraction thereof. The investor can then collect the delinquent taxes plus interest. The investor could also cause the sale of the property that is security for the tax lien at a county sheriff's tax sale as just described.

Judicial Tax Foreclosures

In addition to any other rights and remedies provided under state law for the enforcement of tax liens by the State of Georgia and its counties and municipalities, a second tax sale method is available solely to the governmental entities authorized by law to collect ad valorem taxes and shall not extend to any transferee of tax executions or tax liens.

Hawaii

In Hawaii tax sales are public oral-bid foreclosure auction sales of the real property that is security for the delinquent real property taxes. The opening bid is the lien together with all interest, penalties, costs, expenses, and charges.

> The tax collector or the tax collector's assistant shall, on payment of the purchase price, make, execute, and deliver all proper conveyances necessary in the premises and the delivery of the conveyances shall vest in the purchaser the title to the property sold; provided that the deed to the premises shall be recorded within sixty days after the sale; provided further that the taxpayer may redeem the property sold by payment to the purchaser at the sale, within one year from the date thereof, or if the deed shall not have been recorded within sixty days after the sale, then within one year

from the date of recording of the deed, of the amount paid by the purchaser, together with all costs and expenses which the purchaser was required to pay, including the fee for recording the deed, and in addition thereto, interest on such amount at the rate of twelve per cent a year, but in a case of redemption more than one year after the date of sale by reason of extension of the redemption period on account of late recording of the tax deed, interest shall not be added for the extended redemption period.

Idaho

All properties with delinquent real property taxes in Idaho that are not paid are eventually foreclosed and acquired by one of the 44 counties in which the property is situated. Then the board of county commissioners shall have the power and authority to sell or offer for sale at public auction any real or personal property belonging to the county not necessary for its use. If the county decides to sell county tax-deeded real estate at public auction, then the property shall be sold to the highest bidder.

The board of county commissioners may reserve the right to reject any and all bids and shall have discretionary authority to reject or accept any bid which may be made for an amount less than the total amount of all delinquent taxes, late charges, costs and interest which may have accrued against any property so offered for sale, including the amount specified in the tax deed to the county.

Kansas

Kansas is a public oral-bid foreclosure auction tax-sale state. The high bidder gets a deed to the real estate being sold.

Louisiana

In Louisiana, parishes and those municipalities for which property taxes are not collected by the parish conduct tax sales. They sell the property upon which delinquent taxes are due on or before the first day of May of the year following the year in which the taxes were assessed, or as soon thereafter as possible.

According to the Louisiana Constitution: "On the day of sale, the collector shall sell the portion of the property which the debtor points out. If the debtor does not point out sufficient property, the collector shall sell immediately the least quantity of property which any bidder will buy for the amount of the taxes, interest, and costs."

Louisiana law states:

If the property is divisible in kind and a part of the whole is sufficient to satisfy such aggregate charges, the collector shall require the bid or bids to be for such lesser portion of the whole property as will satisfy such charges and shall not entertain a bid in excess thereof.

In determining if the property is divisible in kind the description of the property on the assessment rolls shall be binding on the tax collector. The tax collector shall not be required and shall be prohibited from dividing the property into smaller quantities than that contained in the description of the property contained on the assessment rolls.

If the tax collector determines from the description of the property contained on the assessment rolls that it is not divisible in kind he shall then proceed to sell such lesser undivided interest of the whole property as will satisfy such charges and shall not entertain a bid in excess thereof.

The tax collector shall execute and sign in person or by deputy a deed of sale to purchasers of any real estate sold for taxes. The deed conveys the right to possession of the property.

Louisiana law then states: "Upon the presentation of a certified copy of a tax deed to any judge of competent jurisdiction the judge shall in chambers grant an order of seizure and possession, commanding the sheriff to seize such property and place the purchaser in actual possession thereof; but the purchaser may take actual possession without such order, with the consent or acquiescence of the tax debtor or otherwise, provided no force or violence shall be used."

However, according to the Louisiana Constitution, "The property sold shall be redeemable for three years after the date of recordation of the tax sale, by paying the price given, including costs, five percent penalty thereon, and interest at the rate of one percent per month until redemption."

Maine

In Maine properties with delinquent real property taxes that are not paid are foreclosed and acquired by the city or town in which the property is located. Then the cities or towns can sell the tax titles through tax lien foreclosure or sewer lien foreclosure.

Michigan

Beginning on the third Tuesday in July, the county treasurer of each of Michigan's 83 counties or the Department of Natural Resources of the State of Michigan, if a county has so elected, may hold one or more property sales.

These are properties that have been foreclosed by a court judgment. They are sold by public auction to the person bidding the highest amount above the minimum bid. The high bidder must pay by cash, certified check, or money order at the close of each day's bidding.

Then beginning on the third Tuesday in September, all property not previously sold by the county or the Department of Natural Resources shall be reoffered for sale, subject to the same requirements as the prior sale. Finally, beginning on the third Tuesday in November immediately following the September sale, all property not previously sold shall again be reoffered for sale, subject to the same requirements as the prior sale except that the minimum bid shall not be required.

Minnesota

In Minnesota properties with delinquent real property taxes that are not paid are foreclosed and acquired by one of the 87 counties in which the property is located. After being processed by the county, one of four actions will occur. There will be a public auction of the property. The property will be sold to an adjacent property owner if the property cannot be built on. The county will transfer ownership to a city for an authorized public use. A temporary hold will be placed on the property to allow for further review by environmental agencies.

The former property owners lose all their property rights as of the date of forfeiture. They can make an application to repurchase the forfeited parcel. The county can agree or forbid to allow the former owner to buy back the property.

If there is a public auction the county auditor will offer the properties in the order of how they appear in the notice of sale. The property will be sold to the highest bidder. However, the sales price must be at least for the appraised value!

The appraised value is the market value. Minnesota law states: "Market value means the usual selling price at the place where the property to which the term is applied shall be at the time of assessment; being the price which could be maintained at a private sale or an auction sale, if it is determined by the assessor that the price from the auction sale represents an arms length transaction. The price obtained at a forced sale shall not be considered."

Minnesota, we have a problem! If the properties sold at tax sales have to be sold at the appraised value, then why would you as a tax sale investor buy real estate at such sales?

We recommend you approach the property owner. Buy the property from them before the county takes title.

Nevada

Nevada tax sales are public oral-bid foreclosure auction tax sales. The property that is security for the delinquent real property taxes is sold to the highest bidder.

New York

After acquiring title through the judicial foreclosure process, New York law allows the taxing authority to sell the foreclosed real estate. The real estate that is security for the delinquent tax liens that are foreclosed becomes the property of the tax district.

> Whenever any tax district shall become vested with the title to real property by virtue of a foreclosure proceeding brought pursuant to the provisions of this article such tax district is hereby authorized to sell and convey the real property so acquired, either with or without advertising for bids, notwithstanding the provisions of any general, special or local law.
>
> No such sale shall be effective unless and until such sale shall have been approved and confirmed by a majority vote of the governing body of the tax district, except that no such approval shall be required when the property is sold at public auction to the highest bidder.

New York City

New York City sells tax liens to collect delinquent property taxes. For further information, contact the New York City Department of Finance.

North Carolina

North Carolina tax sales are public oral-bid foreclosure auction tax sales. The property is sold to the highest bidder. The tax sales are conducted by a court-appointed commissioner. The sales are held at the courthouse.

The commissioner must report the results of the foreclosure sale to the court within three days following the sale. At any time within 10 days after the commissioner files his report of the foreclosure sale with the court, any person having an interest in the real property may file exceptions to the report and any person wishing to do so may file an increased bid.

This is called an upset bid. The upset bid must be for an amount exceeding the reported sale price by 10 percent of the first $1,000 plus 5 percent of any excess above $1,000. The minimum increase must be $25.00.

At any time after the expiration of 10 days from the time the commissioner files their report, if no exception or increased bid has been filed, the commissioner may apply for judgment of confirmation for the sale. This can happen only after the court has passed upon exceptions filed or if an upset bid has been made.

North Dakota

All properties with delinquent real property taxes that are not paid are eventually foreclosed and acquired by one of the 53 counties, depending on where the property is located. Those counties then resell the properties at tax sales.

These sales must be held on the third Tuesday of November of each calendar year at the county auditor's office or the usual place where the county holds district court. Prior to sale, the county board of commissioners must appraise all properties acquired by the county by tax deed.

If the fair market value of the property is more than the total amount due against the property, the minimum sale price of the property must be at least equal to the total amount due against the property. If the fair market value of the property is less than the total amount due against the property, the board must fix a fair minimum sale price for the property.

Each property must be sold at the annual auction to the highest bidder for no less than the amount of the minimum sale price as fixed before the sale. The sale can be made for cash or for 25 percent of the purchase price in cash, and the balance, evidenced by a contract for deed, may be paid in equal annual installments over a period of not more than 10 years.

Ohio

The county auditor is required to compile a list of all delinquent lands in the county and deliver a duplicate of that list to the county treasurer. If the property taxes charged against any particular parcel of real property are not paid within 60 days after the delivery of the delinquent land list duplicate by the auditor to the treasurer, "the county treasurer shall enforce the lien for such taxes by civil action in the treasurer's official capacity as treasurer, for the sale of such premises, in the court of common pleas of the county in the same way mortgage liens are enforced."

The tax sale is conducted by the county sheriff. It is called a sheriff's sale, sheriff's sale of tax delinquent property, tax delinquent sale, or foreclosure sale. The tax sale is held along with the sheriff's mortgage foreclosure sales. Such sales are public oral-bid auction sales of the tax-delinquent real property to the highest bidder. Court confirmation is required.

Oregon

All properties with delinquent real property taxes that are not paid are foreclosed and acquired by one of the 36 counties where the property is located. By law the "county governing body may, whenever it deems it to the best interest of the county so to do, sell and convey any real estate owned and not in use for county purposes."

The sale of such property is done by public auction. This may be called a county sale of tax-foreclosed property or land.

Pennsylvania

Pennsylvania is a public oral-bid foreclosure action tax-sale state. The real estate itself is sold at public auction to the highest bidder. Each County Tax Claim Bureau is able to sell parcels in one of four ways:

Upset Sale

The County Tax Claim Bureau shall schedule the date of the upset sale no earlier than the second Monday of September and before October 1, and the sale may be adjourned, readjourned, or continued. At least 30 days prior to any scheduled sale, the bureau shall "give notice thereof, not less than once in two newspapers of general circulation in the county, if so many are published therein, and once in the legal journal, if any, designated by the court for the publication of legal notices." The notice will include the purpose, the time, the place, and the terms of the sale, including the approximate upset price, the descriptions of the properties to be sold, and the name of the owner.

No additional notice of sale is required when the sale is adjourned, readjourned, or continued if the sale is held by the end of the calendar year. The bureau may, for convenience and because of the number of properties involved, schedule sales of property in various taxing districts or wards on different dates. Generally, the bureau is required to hold all sales by the end of the calendar year. A property cannot be sold at an upset tax sale for less than its upset price.

The total of the tax lien is the amount of the absolute claim. This is the delinquent real property taxes plus penalties, interests and costs, the amount of any other tax claim or tax judgment due on such property, the amount of all accrued taxes including taxes levied for the current year, the amount of the municipal claims against the property, and the record costs and costs of sale, including pro rata costs of the publication of notice and costs of mail and posted notices in connection with the return of the claim and mail and posted notices of sale.

The purchaser of any property at an upset sale shall pay to the bureau the entire purchase money on the date of the sale, no later than one hour before the close of business or at such other time on said date as designated by the bureau. If the money is not paid, the sale shall be voided and the property shall be put up again at the same sale, if possible, or at any adjournment, readjournment or continuation of the sale.

After the court of common pleas has confirmed the sale and the purchaser has paid the amount of his bid, it shall be the duty of the bureau to make to the said purchaser, their heirs or assigns a deed in fee simple for the property sold. Each such deed shall be in the name of the bureau as trustee grantor and shall be executed and duly acknowledged before the principal clerk of court by the director of the bureau and a notation of such deed and acknowledgement shall be duly entered on the proper records.

The deed shall, before delivery, be recorded in the office for the recording of deeds at the cost of the purchaser. Every such sale shall convey title to the property under and subject to the lien of every recorded obligation, claim, lien, estate, mortgage, ground rent and Commonwealth tax lien not included in the upset price with which said property may have or shall become charged or for which it may become liable.

Private Sale

If a property has been exposed to a public upset bid tax sale and such property was not sold, because no bid was made equal to the upset price, the tax claim bureau may agree to sell the property at private sale. This can be at any price approved by the bureau. Notice of the proposed sale, stating the price and the property proposed to be sold, shall be given to each such taxing district and to the owner of the property.

Notice shall also be given by publication at least two times, with approximately 10 days intervening between each publication, in at least one newspaper of general circulation published in the county where the property is located and in the official legal journal of that county.

The notice by publication shall set forth the location of the property, the date and place of sale, the price and terms of sale, and the provision that the property will be sold free and clear of all tax claims and tax judgments.

The corporate authorities of any taxing district having any tax claims or tax judgments against the property that is to be sold, the owner, an interested party, or a person interested in purchasing the property may, if not satisfied that the sale price approved by the bureau is sufficient, within 45 days after notice of the proposed sale, petition the court of common pleas of the county to disapprove the sale.

The court shall, in such case, after notice to each such taxing district, the owner, the bureau, the purchaser and any other person who have joined in the petition, hear all parties. After such hearing, the court may either confirm or disapprove the sale as to it appears just and proper.

If the sale is disapproved, the court shall at the same time fix a price below which such property shall not be sold and order that, if no private sale can be arranged, the property be sold at a public judicial sale under this act. If more than one party agrees to pay the minimum price set by the court, the bureau shall sell the property to that party without the necessity of an auction.

When an offer to purchase any such property has been received, and the bureau has disapproved the price, the bureau shall, on the written instructions of any interested taxing district, submit by petition the proposed sale to the court of common pleas of the county for approval. The court shall, after affording the owner and each taxing district having any tax claims or tax judgments against the property an opportunity to be heard on the sale.

If the court approves the sale, it shall be completed as though it had been approved by the bureau and by all taxing districts having any interest in the property. When the price for the private sale of any property has been finally approved or confirmed, the bureau shall "upon payment over of the purchase price make to the purchaser, their heirs or assigns, a deed in fee simple for the property sold.

Each deed shall be in the name of the bureau, as trustee grantor and shall be executed and duly acknowledged before the principal clerk of the court by the director. The deed shall convey title to the purchaser "free, clear and discharged of all tax claims and tax judgments, whether or not returned, filed or entered, as provided by this or any other act."

Judicial Sale

If within 10 months after the date of the scheduled upset sale, the tax claim bureau has not filed a petition for a judicial sale or the property has not been sold at private sale, the bureau "shall, within the next immediately following two months, file a petition for judicial sale of the property."

In cases where the upset price shall not be bid at any sale, the sale "shall be continued, but not beyond the end of the calendar year, without further advertising, and the bureau may, at any time during or after the continuance, and shall, immediately at the written direction of a taxing district, file its petition in the court of common pleas of the county to sell the property at a mandatory judicial sale."

The bureau "shall set forth on the petition the tax claim upon which the property was exposed for sale, that neither the owner, his heirs or legal representatives or any lien creditor, his heirs, assigns or legal representatives or other person interested has caused stay of sale, discharge of tax claim or removal from sale, that the property was exposed to public sale and the date of such sale, that before exposing the property to public sale the bureau fixed an upset price and that it was unable to obtain a bid sufficient to pay said upset price."

Upon the presentation of the petition, accompanied with searches, showing the state of the record and the ownership of the property and all tax and municipal claims, liens, mortgages, ground rents, charges, and estates against the same, the court "shall grant a rule upon all parties thus shown to be interested to appear and show cause why a decree should not be made that said property be sold, freed and cleared of their respective tax and municipal claims, liens, mortgages, charges and estates, except separately taxed ground rents."

The rule "shall be made returnable in not more than thirty days from the date the petition was presented or as otherwise determined by the court. If upon hearing the court is satisfied that service of the rule was done in a proper manner and that the facts stated in the petition are true, it shall order and decree that the property be sold at a subsequent day."

The property freed and cleared of all tax and municipal claims, mortgages, liens, charges, and estates, except separately taxed ground rents, will be sold to the highest bidder. The purchaser at such sale "shall take and thereafter have an absolute title to the property free and clear of all tax and municipal claims, mortgages, liens, charges and estates of whatever kind, except ground rents, separately taxed." The court order may specify that no sale shall be made except to the county unless a bid equal to such costs is offered.

Repository Sale

Whenever any property is put up for public judicial sale upon order of the court, the county commissioners are authorized to bid up to and including one dollar over and above all costs for the property at the sale. If the property is sold to them, the county shall take and have an absolute fee simple interest in the property free and clear of all tax and municipal claims, mortgages, liens, charges, and estates of whatever kind, except ground rents. This property may then be sold by the county in any manner as provided by law.

Tennessee

Tennessee tax sales are public oral-bid foreclosure sales of the real property that is security for the delinquent real property taxes. After a one-year redemption period, the high bidder gets a tax deed of conveyance generally called a clerk and master deed.

The Tennessee tax sale system operates similarly to a typical tax lien certificate system. One exception is that the property itself is bid up and, after the expiration of the one-year period of redemption, the high bidder automatically receives a deed to the property.

Properties not bid on at the tax sale are bid in the name of the county unless the county legislative body determines that the environmental risks are such that it is not in the best interests of the county to offer a minimum bid at the tax sale.

> After the period of redemption has elapsed, it shall be the duty of the county executive to arrange to sell every tract of such land as expeditiously and advantageously as possible. In no event shall any tract of land be sold for an amount less than the total amount of the taxes, penalty, cost and interest.

If it appears that it is impossible to sell any tract of land for this amount, upon application the county legislative body in session may grant permission to offer the land for sale at some amount to be fixed by the county legislative body.

> Whenever the sale of a tract of land is arranged by the county executive, the deed shall not be executed and the same shall not become final until ten days after the publication in a newspaper published in the county of a notice of the proposed sale. If anyone, during such ten days, increases the offer made for the land by ten percent or more, the party making the first offer shall be notified and a day fixed when both parties shall appear and make offers. The tract of land shall be sold to the party making the highest and best offer.

Texas

At any time after its tax on property becomes delinquent, a taxing unit, including the county or any other taxing unit such as a city or independent school district that collects its own taxes, may file suit to foreclose the real property tax lien securing payment of the tax. The governing body of a taxing unit may contract with any competent attorney to represent the unit to enforce the collection of delinquent taxes.

If judgment in a suit to collect a delinquent tax is for foreclosure of a tax lien, the court shall order the property sold in satisfaction of the amount of the judgment. Property ordered sold "pursuant to foreclosure of a tax lien shall be sold in the manner similar property is sold under execution, i.e., at a public oral bid foreclosure auction sale conducted by the county sheriff or precinct constable, as the case might be, on the courthouse steps on the first Tuesday of the month."

The property is sold to the highest bidder for cash or cash equivalent. The high bidder receives a sheriff's deed or constable's deed, depending upon who conducted the sale. However, the ownership is encumbered by either a 180-day or a two-year right of redemption held by the former property owner at the time of sale.

The redemption period is measured from the date the deed is recorded at the county clerk's office. The right of redemption lasts for 180 days from that date for all real property other than homesteaded property and property appraised by the county appraisal district as agriculture use, in which case it is two years. If the property is not redeemed, the right of redemption terminates automatically by operation of law.

Those properties not receiving any bids at a Texas tax sale are given to the taxing unit that initiated the suit to foreclose the lien. They are held in trust for all taxing units owed delinquent property taxes secured by the property. These properties are frequently called trust or trustee properties.

Utah

Utah is a public oral-bid foreclosure auction tax-sale state. The real property that is security for the delinquent real property taxes is sold to the highest bidder. The opening minimum bid is taxes, penalties, interest, and administrative costs. Each of Utah's 29 counties must conduct its annual final tax sale on the last Wednesday in May.

Vermont

Vermont tax sales are public oral-bid foreclosure sales of the real property that is security for the delinquent real property taxes. After a one-year redemption period, the high bidder gets a collector's deed. The Vermont tax sale system operates similarly to a typical tax lien certificate system except that the property itself is bid up.

Virginia

Virginia is a public oral-bid foreclosure auction tax-sale state where the real property that is security for the delinquent real property taxes is sold to the highest bidder. The opening bid at a Virginia public oral-bid foreclosure auction tax sale is the real property back taxes, penalties, interest, reasonable attorneys' fees, costs, and any liens chargeable.

Virginia law states: "The court shall allow as part of the costs, to be paid into the treasury of the county, city or town, a reasonable sum to defray the cost of its attorneys and the expenses of publication and appraisal necessary for the purpose of instituting such suit and such fees and commissions, including fees for preparing and executing deeds, as would be allowed if the suit were an ordinary lien creditor's suit."

These sales are to be conducted as a creditor's bill in equity and are subject to court confirmation. However, Virginia law states: "the sale price achieved at a public auction shall be prima facie, but rebutable [sic], evidence of the value of the property for purposes of the approval of the sale."

Washington

Washington tax sales are public oral-bid foreclosure auction sales of the real estate that is security for the delinquent taxes. They are conducted throughout each calendar year by each of the 39 county treasurers. There is no redemption period after the sale except in cases where the owner on the day of the sale was either a minor child or a person adjudicated to be legally incompetent. In those cases, there is a three-year redemption period.

Wisconsin

All properties with delinquent real property taxes that are not paid are foreclosed and acquired by one of the 72 counties where the property is located. Those counties then resell the properties at tax sales called sales of tax delinquent real estate.

Except for Milwaukee County, however, "no tax delinquent real estate acquired by a county may be sold unless the sale and appraised value of such real estate has first been advertised by publication. Any county may accept the bid most advantageous to it but every bid less than the appraised value of the property shall be rejected. Any county is authorized to sell for an amount equal to or above the appraised value, without having to advertise again, any land previously advertised for sale."

CONCLUSION

ongratulations on completing *Make Money in Real Estate Tax Liens: How to Guarantee Returns Up to 50%.* We know you have a lot of material to digest. Our hope is that we have stimulated your interest in making money in real estate tax liens.

Our recommendation is for you to go back to the areas that are of the most interest for you. Please reread them. Are you a super-high return investor? Do you want to purchase real estate tax liens so you can acquire property deeds? Then get started. Look at property. Contact a property owner who is scheduled for a tax lien sale. Make them an offer for their property.

Have an offer accepted. Flip the property or the contract. Assign something. Go to a foreclosure sale. Go to a tax lien sale. Find a money partner. Our point is: Do something! Get on the road to making some money!

We are always coming up with more creative possibilities for investments and problem solving. So, as we bid you adieu, we have this to say to you: Get creative! Pull a group of people together and contact us for a seminar.

Are you a lone ranger right now? You will not be for long when you start investing in real estate tax liens. If you like, you can e-mail us for fee-based consulting. We are always open to new possibilities, so let us know if you need a partner. Get out there and do something *now!*

Let us know what did or did not work for you. We want to hear about your experiences in the real estate tax lien investing arena. You can contact us through our publisher, e-mail us at thetrustee@hotmail.com, or write to us at P.O. Box 274, Bedford TX 76095-0274.

Remember to watch for more of the Win Going In! series. The first book in the series was *The New Path to Real Estate Wealth: Earning without Owning. Quick Cash in Foreclosures* was the second book in the series. This is the third book in the Win Going In! series. God bless y'all!

Chantal & Bill Carey

Deeds Chart

G = Grant deed is a deed using the word grant in the clause that awards ownership. This written document is used by the grantor (seller) to transfer title to the grantee (buyer). Grant deeds have two implied warranties. One is that the grantor has not previously transferred the title. The other is that the title is free from encumbrances that are not visible to the grantee. This deed also transfers any title acquired by the grantor after delivery of the deed.

W = Warranty deed is a deed in which the grantor (usually the seller) guarantees the title to be in the condition indicated in the deed. The grantor agrees to protect the grantee (usually the buyer) against all claimants to the property.

*= Special deed.

STATE	DEEDS	STATE	DEEDS
Alabama	W	Hawaii	W
Alaska	W	Idaho	W
Arizona	G	Illinois	G, W
Arkansas	G	Indiana	W
California	G	Iowa	W
Colorado	W	Kansas	W
Connecticut	W	Kentucky	W
Delaware	G	Louisiana	W
Washington, D.C.	G	Maine	W
Florida	W	Maryland	W
Georgia	W	Massachusetts	W

233

STATE	DEEDS	STATE	DEEDS
Michigan	W	Oregon	W
Minnesota	W	Pennsylvania	G
Mississippi	W	Puerto Rico	*
Missouri	W	Rhode Island	W
Montana	G	South Carolina	G,W
Nebraska	W	South Dakota	W
Nevada	G	Tennessee	W
New Hampshire	W	Texas	G
New Jersey	G,W	Utah	W
New Mexico	W	Vermont	W
New York	G	Virginia	G
North Carolina	W	Washington	W
North Dakota	G,W	West Virginia	G
Ohio	W	Wisconsin	W
Oklahoma	G	Wyoming	W

APPENDIX B

Loans Chart

M = Mortgage, a contract by which you promise your property without giving up possession of the property to secure a loan. You also retain title to the property.

TD = Trust deed, a contract used as a security device for a loan on your property, by which you transfer bare (naked) legal title with the power of sale to a trustee. This transfer is in effect until you have totally paid off the loan. In the meantime you have possession of the property.

*Mortgage preferred; trust deed also valid.

**Trust deed preferred; mortgage also valid.

***Use note to secure debt.

STATE	DEEDS	STATE	DEEDS
Alabama	M, TD	Hawaii	M
Alaska	M, TD	Idaho	M, TD
Arizona	M, TD	Illinois	M, TD
Arkansas	M	Indiana	M, TD
California	TD	Iowa	M, TD
Colorado	TD	Kansas	M
Connecticut	M	Kentucky	M, TD*
Delaware	M	Louisiana	M
Washington, D.C.	TD	Maine	M
Florida	M, TD	Maryland	M, TD
Georgia	***	Massachusetts	M

STATE	DEEDS	STATE	DEEDS
Michigan	M	Oregon	M,TD
Minnesota	M	Pennsylvania	M
Mississippi	M,TD**	Puerto Rico	M
Missouri	TD	Rhode Island	M
Montana	M,TD*	South Carolina	M,TD
Nebraska	M,TD	South Dakota	M
Nevada	M,TD	Tennessee	TD
New Hampshire	M	Texas	TD
New Jersey	M	Utah	M,TD
New Mexico	M,TD	Vermont	M
New York	M	Virginia	M,TD*
North Carolina	M,TD	Washington	M,TD
North Dakota	M,TD	West Virginia	TD
Ohio	M	Wisconsin	M
Oklahoma	M,TD	Wyoming	M,TD

APPENDIX C

Contracts and Paperwork

PURCHASE CONTRACT FOR REAL ESTATE AND DEPOSIT RECEIPT
This is meant to be a legally binding agreement. Read it carefully.

City:_____ State:_____ Date:_____

Received from _____, the buyer, the sum of $_____

shown by ☐ cash, ☐ cashier's check, ☐ personal check, or ☐ _____

payable to _____

to be held uncashed until this offer is accepted as deposit toward the purchase price of

_____ dollars ($_____)

for the purchase of property located in the state of _____,

county of _____, city of _____,

and known as _____.

CAPTIONS: The headings and captions in this document are to make reference easy and are not intended as a part of this agreement.

1. **FIXTURES:** All permanently installed fixtures, fittings, and plantings that are attached to the property or for which special openings were made, as well as their controls, if any, are included in the purchase price, including _____

_____

    except _____.

2. **PERSONAL PROPERTY:** The following items of personal property, free of liens and without warranty, are included: _____

_____

3. **PROPERTY CONDITION:** Seller guarantees, that through the date seller makes possession available to buyer

    A.   The property and improvements, including grounds and landscaping, shall be maintained in the same condition as on the date of acceptance of the offer;

    B.   The roof is free of all known leaks;

    C.   All permanently installed fixtures and fittings, as well as their controls, if any, are operative;

    D.   Seller shall replace any cracked or broken glass;

    E.   And _____

    F.   Except _____
_____

4. **SELLER REPRESENTATION:** Seller guarantees that until the date escrow closes that seller knows of no violation notices of codes, laws, or other regulations issued or filed against the property.

5. **SUPPLEMENTS:** The attached documents are incorporated in this document:

    ☐ _____

    ☐ _____

    ☐ _____

    ☐ _____
                                                              (continued)

Buyer and seller acknowledge receiving a duplicate of this page, which is page 1 of ____ pages.

Buyers' initials (_____) (_____)   Sellers' initials (_____) (_____)

PURCHASE CONTRACT FOR REAL ESTATE AND DEPOSIT RECEIPT

Property known as _____

6. **ESCROW:** Buyer and seller shall deliver signed instructions to _____
   _____ , the escrow holder, within _____ calendar days of
   acceptance of the offer. The offer shall provide for closing within _____ calendar days of acceptance.
   Escrow fees to be paid as follows: _____
   _____

7. **OCCUPANCY:** Buyer ☐ does ☐ does not intend to occupy property as buyer's primary
   residence.

8. **POSSESSION:** Possession and occupancy shall be delivered to buyer ☐ on the close of escrow,
   ☐ no later than _____ days after the close of escrow, or ☐ _____

9. **KEYS:** Seller shall provide keys and/or other means to operate all property locks and alarms, if any,
   when possession is available to the buyer.

10. **FINANCING:**   This agreement depends on the buyer obtaining financing.
    A. DILIGENCE AND GOOD FAITH - Buyer agrees to act with diligence and
        good faith to obtain all appropriate financing.
    B. DEPOSIT is due on acceptance and is to be deposited into _____
        _____ in the amount of $_____
    C. INCREASED DEPOSIT is due within _____ days of acceptance and is to be
        deposited into _____ in the amount of $_____
    D. DOWN PAYMENT BALANCE is to be deposited into _____
        _____ on or before _____ in the amount of $_____
    E. NEW FIRST LOAN - Buyer to apply for, qualify for, and obtain new first loan
        in the amount of .... $_____
        payable monthly at approximately $_____
        including interest at origination not to exceed _____ %
        ☐ fixed rate ☐ other _____
        all due _____ years from the date of origination.
        Loan fee at origination not to exceed $_____ .
        Seller agrees to pay a maximum of _____ FHA/VA discount points.
        Additional terms:_____
        _____
        _____

    F. EXISTING FIRST LOAN - Buyer to ☐ assume ☐ take title subject to
        an existing first loan with an approximate balance of .... $_____
        payable monthly at $_____ including interest at _____ %
        ☐ fixed rate ☐ other _____
        Fees not to exceed $_____ . Disposition of impound account ___
        _____
        Additional terms: _____
        _____
        _____

                                                                          (continued)

Buyer and seller acknowledge receiving a duplicate of this page, which is page 2 of ____ pages.
          Buyers' initials (_____) (_____)   Sellers' initials (_____) (_____)

PURCHASE CONTRACT FOR REAL ESTATE AND DEPOSIT RECEIPT

Property known as _____

10. FINANCING:

G. NOTE SECURED BY TRUST DEED - Buyer to sign a note secured by a
☐ first, ☐ second, ☐ third trust deed in the amount of .... $_____
in favor of seller, payable monthly at $_____ or more
including interest at _____ %
☐ fixed rate ☐ other _____
all due ☐ _____ years from date of origination or ☐ upon sale or
transfer of the property.
A late charge of $_____ shall be due on any installment not paid
within _____ days of the date due.
Additional terms: _____
_____ .

H. NEW SECOND LOAN - Buyer to apply for, qualify for, and obtain new
second loan in the amount of .... $_____
payable monthly at approximately $_____
including interest at origination not to exceed _____ %
☐ fixed rate ☐ other _____
all due _____ years from date of origination.
Buyer's loan fees not to exceed $_____ .
Seller agrees to pay a maximum of _____ FHA/VA discount points.
Additional terms: _____
_____ .

I. EXISTING SECOND LOAN - Buyer to ☐ assume ☐ take title subject
to an existing second loan with an approximate balance of .... $_____
payable monthly at $_____ including interest at _____ %
☐ fixed rate ☐ other _____
Buyers loan fees not to exceed $_____ .
Additional terms: _____
_____ .

J. OTHER PROVISIONS - If buyer assumes or takes title "subject to" an existing
loan, seller shall provide buyer with copies of applicable notes and trust deeds.
Buyer is allowed _____ calendar days after receipt of such copies to
examine the copies for the features that affect the loan and to notify seller in
writing of disapproval. Buyer shall not unreasonably withhold approval.
Failure to notify seller in writing shall conclusively be considered approval.

K. ADDITIONAL FINANCING TERMS: _____
_____
_____

L. TOTAL PURCHASE PRICE... $_____
(continued)

Buyer and seller acknowledge receiving a duplicate of this page, which is page 3 of ____ pages.
Buyers' initials (_____) (_____)   Sellers' initials (_____) (_____)

PURCHASE CONTRACT FOR REAL ESTATE AND DEPOSIT RECEIPT

Property known as _____

11. TITLE: Title is to be free of conditions, easements, encumbrances, liens, restrictions, and rights of
record other than the following:
  A. Current property taxes;
  B. Covenants, conditions, restrictions, and public utility easements of record, if any, if the items do not
       adversely affect the continuing use of the property for the purposes for which it is currently used,
       unless the buyer reasonably disapproves in writing within _____ calendar days of receipt of a
       current preliminary report furnished at _____ expense; and
  C. Seller shall furnish buyer at _____ expense, a _____
       policy issued by _____ company,
       showing title vested in buyer subject only to the above. If seller is unwilling or unable to eliminate
       any title matter disapproved by buyer as indicated above, the buyer may end this agreement. If
       seller fails to deliver title as indicated above, buyer may end this agreement. In either case, deposit
       shall be returned to the buyer.

12. VESTING: The title shall vest as follows: _____
_____ unless noted otherwise in the buyer's escrow instructions.

13. PRORATIONS: Association dues, interest, payments on assessments and bonds assumed by the
buyer, premiums on insurance acceptable to the buyer, property taxes, rents, and _____
_____ shall be paid current and prorated as of
☐ the day the deed records; or ☐ _____.
Bonds or assessments that are now a lien shall be paid current by seller; payments not yet due to be
☐ assumed by the buyer, ☐ paid in full by the seller, including payments not yet due; or
☐ _____.
County transfer tax, if applicable, shall be paid by _____ . The _____
transfer tax or transfer fee shall be paid by _____ . Reassessment of the property when
ownership changes affects taxes to be paid. A supplemental tax bill may be issued, which shall be
paid by the seller for periods before escrow closes and by the buyer for periods after escrow
closes. Buyer and seller shall handle between themselves tax bills issued after escrow closes.

14. TAX WITHHOLDING: Under the Foreign Investment in Real Property Tax Act (FIRPTA), buyers of
U.S. real property *must* deduct and withhold from the seller's proceeds 10% of the gross sales price
unless an exemption applies. States may require that additional money be withheld.

15. OTHER TERMS AND CONDITIONS:
_____
_____
_____
_____
_____
_____
_____

16. ATTORNEY'S FEES: In any action, arbitration, or proceeding arising out of this agreement, the
prevailing party shall be entitled to reasonable attorney's fees and costs.

(continued)

Buyer and seller acknowledge receiving a duplicate of this page, which is page 4 of ____ pages.
        Buyers' initials (_____) (_____)   Sellers' initials (_____) (_____)

PURCHASE CONTRACT FOR REAL ESTATE AND DEPOSIT RECEIPT

Property known as _____

17. ENTIRE CONTRACT:
- A. Time is important.
- B. All earlier agreements between buyer and seller are made a part of this agreement, which makes up the whole contract. The terms of this contract are intended by buyer and seller as their final agreement about the terms that are included in this contract. The terms of this contract may not be contradicted by evidence of any earlier agreement or any oral contract made at the same time as this written contract.
- C. The buyer and seller agree that this contract makes up the complete and exclusive statement of the contract's terms and that no extraneous evidence of any kind may be introduced in any judicial or arbitration proceeding, if any, about this contract.

18. AMENDMENTS:
The buyer and seller may not alter, amend, change, or modify this contract except by further agreement in writing signed by both buyer and seller.

19. OFFER:
- A. This makes up an offer to purchase the property described.
- B. Unless acceptance is signed by seller and a signed copy is delivered in person, by mail, or facsimile and received by the buyer at the address indicated below within _____ calendar days of the date of this contract, this offer will be considered revoked and the deposit shall be returned.
- C. Buyer has read and acknowledges receipt of a copy of this offer.
- D. This agreement and any addition or modification relating to this agreement including any photocopy or facsimile of this contract may be signed in two or more counterparts, all of which shall make up one and the same writing.

BUYER:_____   BUYER:_____

Address:_____   Address:_____

_____   _____

Telephone:_____   Telephone:_____

ACCEPTANCE

The seller who signed below accepts and agrees to sell the property in the manner indicated below.

☐ On the above terms and conditions.   ☐ Subject to the attached counteroffer.

SELLER:_____   SELLER:_____

Address:_____   Address:_____

_____   _____

Telephone:_____   Telephone:_____

Buyer and Seller acknowledge receiving a duplicate of this page, which is page 5 of ____ pages.

Buyers' initials (_____) (_____)   Sellers' initials (_____) (_____)

PURCHASE CONTRACT FOR REAL ESTATE
ADDITIONAL TERMS AND CONDITIONS
This is meant to be a legally binding agreement. Read it carefully.

This document contains additional terms and conditions to the Purchase Contract for Real Estate and Deposit Receipt for the purchase of the property located in the state of_____,
county of _____, city of _____,
and known as _____.
This document, when used, is meant to be an addition to the Purchase Contract for Real Estate and Deposit Receipt.

CAPTIONS: The headings and captions in this document are to make reference easy and are not intended as a part of this agreement.

To be included in the agreement, items *must* be initialed by both *buyer(s)* and *seller(s)*.

1. **PHYSICAL AND GEOLOGICAL INSPECTIONS:**
   A. Buyer has the right, at buyer's expense, to select a licensed contractor and /or other qualified professional(s) to make inspections of the property for possible environmental hazards.
      - These inspections can include inspections, investigations, tests, and other studies.
      - The inspections can include but are not limited to the fixtures and fittings of the property and controls for the fixtures and fittings, if any; geological conditions; and possible environmental hazards including substances, products, and other conditions.
   B. Buyer shall keep the property free and clear of any liens. Buyer shall indemnify and hold seller harmless from all liability, claims, demands, damages, or costs and shall repair all damages to the property arising from the inspections.
   C. Buyer shall make all claims about defects in the condition of the property that adversely affect continuing use of the property for the purposes for which it is currently being used or as
      _____ in writing, supported by written reports, if any. The buyer shall cause these documents to be delivered to the seller, within the number of calendar days specified below of the acceptance of the offer. For all types of physical inspections, except geological inspections, the documents shall be delivered within _____ calendar days. For geological inspections the documents shall be delivered within _____ calendar days.
   D. Buyer shall provide seller with copies, at no cost to the seller, of all reports about the property obtained by the buyer.
   E. Buyer may cancel this agreement if any of these reports disclose conditions or information unacceptable to the buyer, which the seller is unable or unwilling to correct.
   F. Seller shall make the property available for all inspections.
   G. *Buyer's failure to notify seller in writing regarding the above shall conclusively be considered approval.*

   Initials: Buyers: _____ _____   Sellers: _____ _____

   (continued)

Buyer and seller acknowledge receiving a duplicate of this page, which is page 1 of ____ pages.
   Buyers' initials (_____) (_____)   Sellers' initials (_____) (_____)

PURCHASE CONTRACT FOR REAL ESTATE
ADDITIONAL TERMS AND CONDITIONS

Property known as _____

2. PEST CONTROL

A. Within _____ calendar days of acceptance of the offer, seller shall furnish buyer, at the expense of ☐ buyer, ☐ seller, a current written report of an inspection by _____ _____, a licensed pest control operator. This inspection shall be of one or more of the following areas: ☐ the main building, ☐ detached garage(s) or carport(s), if any, and ☐ the following other structure(s) on the property: _____ _____.

B. If either Buyer or Seller request it, the report shall separately identify each recommendation for corrective action as follows:

Type 1: Infestation or infection that is evident.

Type 2: Conditions present that are considered likely to lead to infestation or infection.

C. If no infestation or infection by wood-destroying pests or organisms is found, the report shall include a written certification that on the inspection date no evidence of active infestation or infection was found.

D. All work recommended to correct conditions described as type 1 shall be at the expense of the ☐ seller. ☐ buyer.

E. All work recommended to correct conditions described as type 2, if requested by the buyer, shall be at the expense of the ☐ seller. ☐ buyer.

F. The repairs shall be done with good workmanship and materials of comparable quality to the originals. These repairs shall include repairs and the replacement of materials removed for repairs. Buyer and seller understand that exact restoration of appearance or cosmetic items following all such repairs is not included.

G. Funds for work agreed to be performed after escrow closes shall be held in escrow and paid on receipt of written certification that the inspected property is now free of active infestation or infection.

H. If the report recommends inspection of inaccessible areas, buyer has the option to accept and approve the report, or within _____ calendar days from receipt of the report to request in writing that a further inspection be made. *Buyer's failure to notify seller in writing of such request shall conclusively be considered approval of the report.*

If additional inspection recommends type 1 or 2 corrective measures, such work shall be done at the expense of whoever is designated in section 2D and/or 2E above. If no infestation is found, the cost of inspection, entry, and closing of inaccessible areas shall be at buyer's expense.

I. Other _____
_____
_____
_____
_____

Initials: Buyers: _____   _____   Sellers: _____   _____

(continued)

Buyer and seller acknowledge receiving a duplicate of this page, which is page 2 of ____ pages.
Buyers' initials (_____) (_____)   Sellers' initials (_____) (_____)

PURCHASE CONTRACT FOR REAL ESTATE
ADDITIONAL TERMS AND CONDITIONS

Property known as _____

3. ENERGY CONSERVATION RETROFIT:

If applicable, governmental laws require that the property be made to conform to minimum energy conservation standards as a condition of sale or transfer; ☐ buyer, ☐ seller shall comply with and pay for the work necessary to meet these requirements. If the seller must bring the property into compliance, the seller may, where the law permits, authorize escrow to credit the buyer with enough funds to cover the cost of the retrofit.

Initials: Buyers: _____ _____   Sellers: _____ _____

4. FLOOD HAZARD AREA DISCLOSURE:

The buyer is informed that the property is located in a "Special Flood Hazard Area" as set forth on a Federal Emergency Management Agency (FEMA) "Flood Insurance Rate Map" (FIRM) or "Flood Hazard Boundary Map" (FHBM).

A. The law requires that, to obtain financing on most structures located in a "Special Flood Hazard Area," lenders require flood insurance where the property or its attachments are security for a loan.

B. No representation is made by the seller as to the legal or economic effects of the National Flood Insurance Program and related legislation.

Initials: Buyers: _____ _____   Sellers: _____ _____

5. HOME PROTECTION PLAN:

Home protection plans may provide additional protection and benefit to seller and buyer. The buyer and seller agree to include a home protection plan to be issued by _____

_____

at a cost not to exceed $_____ to be paid for by ☐ Buyer, ☐ Seller.

Initials: Buyers: _____ _____   Sellers: _____ _____

6. CONDOMINIUM/PLANNED UNIT DEVELOPMENT (PUD):

A. The property is a ☐ condominium ☐ planned unit development (PUD) designated as unit _____ and _____ parking spaces, and an undivided interest in community areas, and

_____

The current monthly assessment charge, fees, or dues by the homeowner's association or other governing body is $_____.

B. As soon as practical, seller shall provide buyer with copies of any documents required by law including the articles of incorporation; claims; covenants, conditions, and restrictions; current rules and regulations; litigations; most current financial statement; and pending special assessments.

C. Buyer is allowed _____ calendar days from receipt to review these documents. If documents disclose conditions or information unacceptable to buyer, buyer may cancel this agreement.

D. *Buyer's failure to notify seller in writing shall conclusively be considered approval.*

Initials: Buyers: _____ _____   Sellers: _____ _____

(continued)

Buyer and seller acknowledge receiving a duplicate of this page, which is page 3 of ____ pages.

Buyers' initials (_____) (_____)   Sellers' initials (_____) (_____)

PURCHASE CONTRACT FOR REAL ESTATE
ADDITIONAL TERMS AND CONDITIONS

Property known as _____

7. **LIQUIDATED DAMAGES:** If buyer fails to complete purchase of the property because of any default of the buyer, seller is released from obligation to sell the property to buyer. Seller may then proceed against buyer on any claim or remedy that seller may have in equity or law. By initialing this paragraph, buyer and seller agree that seller shall retain the deposit as liquidated damages. **NOTICE:** Funds deposited in trust accounts or in escrow are not released automatically in the event of a dispute. Release of funds requires written agreement of the parties, judicial decision, or arbitration.

          Initials: Buyers: _____ _____   Sellers: _____ _____

8. **DISPUTE ARBITRATION:** Any dispute or claim in law or equity arising out of this contract or any resulting transaction shall be decided by neutral binding arbitration in accordance with the rules of the American Arbitration Association and not by state law except as the law provides for judicial review of arbitration proceedings. Judgment upon the award rendered by the arbitrator shall be entered in any court having jurisdiction over the case. The parties shall have the right of discovery.
   The following matters are excluded from arbitration:
   A. A judicial or nonjudicial foreclosure or other action or proceeding to enforce a deed of trust, mortgage, or a real property sales contract.
   B. An unlawful detainer action.
   C. The filing or enforcement of a mechanic's lien.
   D. Any matter that is within the jurisdiction of a probate court, and/or
   E. Bodily injury, wrongful death, hidden or evident defects, and actions to which civil codes apply. The filing of a judicial action to enable the recording of a notice of pending action, for order of attachment, receivership, injunction, or other temporary remedies, shall not be a waiver of the right to arbitrate under this provision.
   NOTICE: Agreement to this provision is voluntary. If you refuse to submit to arbitration after agreeing to this provision, you may be forced to arbitrate. By initialing below you are
   A. Agreeing to have any dispute arising out of the matters included in this "Dispute Arbitration" provision decided by neutral arbitration as provided by your state law.
   B. Giving up any rights you may possess to have the dispute litigated in a court or jury trial.
   C. Giving up your judicial rights to discovery and appeal, unless those rights are specifically included in the "Dispute Arbitration" provision.
   We have read and understood this provision to arbitrate a dispute, and we agree to this provision.

          Initials: Buyers: _____ _____   Sellers: _____ _____

Receipt of this document is acknowledged:
Date:_____   Seller: _____
Date:_____   Seller: _____
Date:_____   Buyer: _____
Date:_____   Buyer: _____

     Buyer and seller acknowledge receiving a duplicate of this page, which is page 4 of ____ pages.
         Buyers' initials (_____) (_____)   Sellers' initials (_____) (_____)

CONTRACT CHANGES AND ADDITIONS
This is meant to be a legally binding agreement. Read it carefully.

The following changes and additions are united with and made a part of the Purchase Contract for Real Estate and Deposit Receipt that is dated _____

between _____, the seller, and

_____, the buyer, on the property

known as _____.

The changes and additions are as follows:

_____

_____

_____

_____

_____

_____

_____

_____

_____

_____

_____

_____

_____

_____

_____

_____

_____

_____

_____

_____

_____

_____

_____

_____

_____

Receipt of this notice is acknowledged:

Date:_____   Seller:_____

Date:_____   Seller:_____

Date:_____   Buyer:_____

Date:_____   Buyer:_____

Buyer and seller acknowledge receiving a duplicate of this page, which is page ____ of ____ pages.

Buyers' initials (_____) (_____)   Sellers' initials (_____) (_____)

COUNTEROFFER

This is meant to be a legally binding agreement. Read it carefully.

This counteroffer to the Purchase Contract for Real Estate and Deposit Receipt on the property known as _____ is dated _____. In this contract _____ is referred to as the buyer and _____ is referred to as the seller.

Seller accepts all of the conditions and terms in the agreement noted above with the following changes:

_____
_____
_____
_____
_____
_____
_____
_____
_____
_____
_____
_____
_____
_____
_____
_____
_____
_____
_____

The seller retains the right to continue to offer the property described for sale. The seller also retains the right to agree to any offer acceptable to seller at any time before the personal acceptance by seller of a copy of this counteroffer, properly accepted and signed by the buyer. *Accept* as used in this document, includes delivery in person, by mail, or by facsimile.

If this counteroffer is not accepted on or before the date of _____ at _____ A.M./P.M., the counteroffer shall be considered canceled and the deposit shall be returned to the buyer. The seller's agreement to another offer shall cancel this counteroffer. This counteroffer and any addition or modification relating to it, including any photocopy or facsimile of it, may be signed in two or more duplicates, all of which will make up the same writing. Acceptance of a copy is acknowledged.

Date:_____   Seller:_____

Time:_____   Seller:_____

(continued)

Buyer and seller acknowledge receiving a duplicate of this page, which is page 1 of ____ pages.

Buyers' initials (_____) (_____)   Sellers' initials (_____) (_____)

COUNTEROFFER
This is meant to be a legally binding agreement. Read it carefully.

Property known as_____

☐ The undersigned buyer accepts the above counteroffer without addition or modification, **OR**
☐ The undersigned buyer accepts the above counteroffer with the following additions or modifications:

If the following additions or modifications are not accepted and a copy properly accepted and signed is not personally delivered to the buyer or _____, the agent obtaining the offer, on or before _____ at _____A.M./P.M., the counteroffer shall be considered canceled and the deposit shall be returned to the buyer. Acceptance of a copy is acknowledged.

_____
_____
_____
_____
_____
_____
_____
_____
_____

Date:_____   Buyer:_____
Time:_____   Buyer:_____

Acceptance of a signed copy on_____ at _____ A.M./P.M. by seller is acknowledged.

IF BUYER MADE ADDITIONS OR MODIFICATIONS ABOVE, THE FOLLOWING IS REQUIRED:
Seller accepts buyer's additions or modifications to seller's counteroffer. The seller agrees to sell on the above terms and conditions. Seller acknowledges receipt of a copy.

Date:_____   Seller:_____
Time:_____   Seller:_____

Buyer and seller acknowledge receiving a duplicate of this page, which is page 2 of ____ pages.
          Buyers' initials (_____) (_____)   Sellers' initials (_____) (_____)

CONDITION(S) RELEASE
This is meant to be a legally binding agreement. Read it carefully.

This addition is a part of the Purchase Contract for Real Estate and Deposit Receipt that is dated
_____between _____(seller)
and _____(buyer) on the property known as
_____ .

Seller has the right to continue to offer subject property for sale.

If the seller accepts a later written offer, in accordance with the named buyer's rights, the buyer shall
have _____hours _____days following receiving notice to remove and renounce in writing the
following condition(s): _____

_____

_____

_____

_____

_____

_____

In the event buyer shall fail to remove the condition(s) within the above time limit, the Purchase Contract
for Real Estate and Deposit Receipt and this agreement shall end and become voidable and the buyer's
deposit shall be returned to the buyer.

This Condition(s) Release shall be considered to have been received by buyer when buyer, or buyer's
agent, has received notice by delivery in person or by certified mail addressed to _____
_____ .

If notice is given by mail, the buyer has until 6:00 P.M. of the third day following the date of mailing
(unless the notice provides another time), to deliver to the seller the buyer's written agreement to remove
and void the condition(s).

The person or persons signing below acknowledge receiving a copy of this document.

RECEIPT FOR DELIVERY IN PERSON

Date:_____   Seller:_____
Date:_____   Seller:_____

Date:_____   Buyer: _____
Date:_____   Buyer: _____

Buyer and seller acknowledge receiving a duplicate of this page, which is page 1 of ____ pages.
   Buyers' initials (_____) (_____)   Sellers' initials (_____) (_____)

ASSIGNMENT OF CONTRACT

Date: _____

Owner: _____   Original Buyer: _____
Address: _____   Address: _____
_____   _____

Telephone: _____   Telephone: _____
Fax Line: _____   Fax Line: _____
Cell Line: _____   Cell Line: _____
E-Mail: _____   E-Mail: _____

New Buyer: _____
Address: _____
_____

Telephone: _____
Fax line: _____
Cell Line: _____
E-mail: _____

Contract Date: _____
Property Address: _____
_____

_____ (Original Buyer) hereby exercises their unqualified right to assign all their rights, obligations, and responsibilities in the above noted Contract dated _____, with _____ (Owner) to _____ (New Buyer). The new buyer of this property hereby agrees to fulfill all of the same terms and conditions of the above referenced Contract, including all closing requirements as originally stated.

The total consideration for this Assignment payable from the New Buyer to the Original Buyer shall be: _____ dollars ($), payable at _____ in the form of a Cashier's check as of the date of the execution of this Assignment of Contract.

Original Buyer: _____   New Buyer: _____
_____   _____
Date: _____   Date: _____

PROMISSORY NOTES

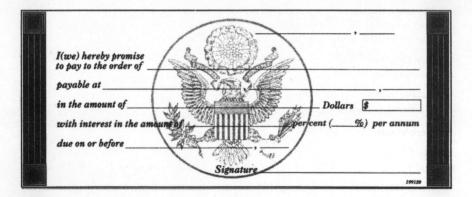

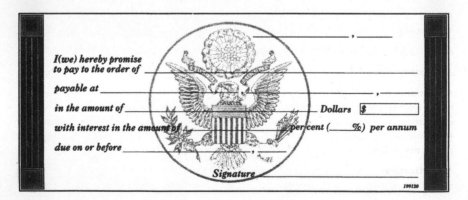

GLOSSARY

Abatement notice A notice to decrease or cease an illegal or unreasonable irritant that hurts, hinders, or damages others or creates a repeated or persisting interference with another's right.

Abstract of title A summary of the history of ownership of a property from public records. This history includes all changes of ownership and claims against the property.

Acceleration clause A provision in a loan document that makes the balance owed on a loan due and payable immediately after a specified event occurs. The event may be missing a payment or violating another provision of the loan.

Acknowledgment A formal declaration before a public official that one has signed a specific document.

Adjustable rate loan Adjustable rate mortgage, ARM; a loan that allows adjustments in the interest rate at specified times based on a named index.

Adjustable rate mortgage *See* Adjustable rate loan.

Adjusted basis The original cost plus capital improvements minus depreciation. Use adjusted basis to compute taxable gain or loss on the sale of a home.

Adjusted sales price As a seller, the price for which you sell your home minus closing costs and commission, if applicable.

Agent A person authorized by another, the principal, to act for him or her in dealing with third parties.

AITD *See* All-inclusive trust deed.

Alienation clause *See* Due-on-sale clause.

All-inclusive trust deed Wraparound mortgage, AITD; a junior (second, third, and so forth) loan (mortgage or trust deed) at one overall interest rate used to wrap the existing loans into a package. The amount is sufficient to cover the existing loans and provide additional funds for the sellers. Sellers pay on existing loans from buyers' payments. Sellers remain primarily responsible for the original loans.

Amortization Gradual paying off of the principal on a loan by payment of regular installments of principal and interest.

Annual percentage rate APR; an interest rate that includes interest, discount points, origination fees, and loan broker's commission.

Appraisal An examination of a property by a qualified professional to estimate the property's market value as of a specific date.

APR *See* Annual percentage rate.

Arbitration Taking of a controversy to an unbiased third person. This person holds a hearing at which both parties may speak and then issues an opinion.

ARM *See* Adjustable rate loan.

Assessment Tax or charge by a governmental body for a specific public improvement covering the property owner's portion of costs. Assessments are in addition to normal property taxes.

Assign Transfer.

Assignee The person to whom interest is transferred.

Assignment Transfer of any property to another. Delegation of duties and rights to another.

Assignor The person from whom interest is transferred.

Assume Buyers taking over primary responsibility for payment of existing loan. Sellers then become secondarily liable for the loan and for any deficiency judgment.

Assumption fee Transfer fee; the fee a lender may charge for work involved in allowing buyers to assume primary liability for payment on an existing loan.

Attorney A person licensed to practice law by giving legal advice or assistance, as well as prosecuting and defending cases in courts.

Authorization to sell A listing contract allowing a real estate professional to act as an agent in the sale of property. (*See also* Listings.)

Bankruptcy Relief by a court of an obligation to pay money owed after turning over all property to a court-appointed trustee.

Basis The cost of a home when purchased, including down payment, loans, and closing costs.

Beneficiary The lender of money on a property used in a trust deed type of loan.

Beneficiary statement A statement provided by a lender using a trust deed type of loan that usually lists claims that do not appear on loan documents.

Bill of lading A contract for the transportation of your goods with a commercial moving company.

Binder An informal contract listing an agreement's main points, later replaced by a formal, detailed written contract.

Breach of contract Failure to perform as promised without a legal excuse (a good reason).

Bridge loan A short-term loan to buyers who are simultaneously selling one house and trying to buy another.

Broker *See* Real estate broker.

Building codes   Regulations by governments giving requirements and standards for structures built in their jurisdictions.

Building permits   County-issued documents that permit you to build after your plans have been approved by the necessary city and county agencies.

Buyer's agent   Selling agent; a real estate broker or sales associate who represents the buyer in a transaction.

Buyer's broker   A real estate broker who represents the buyer. (*See also* Real estate broker.)

Buyer's fees   Charges that are paid for by the buyers.

Buyer's market   A condition in which there are more sellers than buyers; prices generally decrease.

Call   Demand payment of a debt.

Capital asset   Property, both real and personal, held by a taxpayer and not excluded by tax laws.

Capital gain   Profit from selling or exchanging a capital asset in excess of the cost.

Capital improvements   Additions to property that are permanent, increase property value, and have a useful life of more than one year.

Capitalization rate   The rate of return an investment receives.

Capital loss   Loss from selling or exchanging property other than a personal residence at less than its cost.

Cashier's check   A bank's own check guaranteed to be good by the bank at which it is drawn.

Casualty   Loss of or damage to structures or personal property.

Casualty insurance   *See* Hazard insurance.

CC&Rs   Covenants, conditions, and restrictions; a document listing private restrictions on property. Often used when buyers have an interest in common areas.

Certificate of title   A report, produced by a party providing abstracts of titles, stating that based on an examination of public records, the title is properly vested in the present owner.

Classified advertisements   Advertisements that are separated by type and listed accordingly.

Closing   Closing escrow, settlement; the final phase of a real estate transaction that involves signing loan documents, paying closing costs, and delivering the deed. (*See also* Escrow.)

Closing costs   Costs of sale; the additional expenses over and above the purchase price of buying and selling real estate.

Closing escrow   *See* Closing.

Closing fee   *See* Closing.

Closing statement   A written, itemized account given to both seller and buyers at closing by the escrow holder and detailing receipts, disbursements, charges, credits, and prorations.

Commission   Payments to an agent, such as a real estate broker, for services in the selling or buying of a home.

Commitment   An oral or written agreement to make a loan made by a lender to a potential buyer.

Competent person   A person who meets certain criteria set by a state for competency. These laws often include being a natural person who is an adult or an emancipated minor, mentally competent, and not a felon deprived of civil rights; an artificial person may also meet the requirements.

Completion bond   A bond ensuring that if a contractor does not complete a project, an insurance company will pay for the remaining work to be done.

Completion notice   Copy of the document you file and record with your county when work on your home is complete; it places time limits for mechanics' liens.

Condemnation   The act of taking private property for public use after payment of a fair price (compensation).

Conditions   Requirements that must precede the performance or effectiveness of something else. Provisions or qualifications in a deed that if violated or not performed nullify the deed.

Condominium   An undivided ownership in common in a portion of a piece of real property plus a separate interest in space in a building.

Consideration   Anything of value that influences a person to enter into a contract including money, a deed, an item of personal property, an act (including the payment of money), a service, or a promise (such as to pay on a loan). Acts or services must be performed after you and the buyers enter into the contract.

Contingency   A condition on which a valid contract depends.

Contingency release   Wipe-out clause, kick-out provision; provisions providing that you will continue to market your home until you receive another offer to purchase your home that does not contain the contingencies you indicated or buyers remove those contingencies you specified. After you receive a contract without the detailed contingencies, the original buyers have the specified time you agreed on to remove the contingencies or you may sell your home to the buyers who offered you a contract without the contingencies.

Contract for deed   *See* Land sales contract.

Controller's deed   *See* Tax deed.

Conventional loan   A loan that is not guaranteed or insured by a government agency.

Convey   Transfer.

Costs of sale   *See* Closing costs.

Counteroffer   A statement by a person to whom an offer is made proposing a new offer to the original offeror.

Counterparts Two documents considered as one.

Covenants Agreements or promises contained in and conveyed by a deed that are inseparable from the property. Pledges for the performance or nonperformance of certain acts or the use or nonuse of property.

Cram-down provision *See* Short-sale provision.

Credit report A detailed report of a person's credit history and rating.

Dedication A giving of land by a property owner to the public for public use.

Deed A document containing a detailed written description of the property that transfers property ownership.

Deed of trust *See* Trust deed.

Default Failure of a person to fulfill an obligation or perform a duty; failure to make a loan payment when it is due.

Default insurance *See* Mortgage default insurance.

Deficiency judgment A court decision making an individual personally liable for payoff of a remaining amount due because the full amount was not obtained by foreclosure.

Delinquent payment A payment that was not paid when it was due.

Demand fee Demand for payoff charge; a fee for a written request to a lender for lender's demand for payment of the loan in full and the supporting documents necessary for release of the lien against the property.

Demand for payoff charge *See* Demand fee.

Deposit Money that buyers submit with a purchase offer as evidence of their intention and ability to buy.

Depreciation Loss in value from any cause.

Disclosure Making known things that were previously unknown.

Discount points *See* Points.

Discovery Disclosure of things previously unknown.

Discrimination Giving or withholding particular advantages to or from certain types of persons arbitrarily selected from a larger group. Treating other persons unfairly or denying them normal privileges.

Display advertisements Large advertisements that often contain illustrations.

Divided agency Agent's action in representing both parties in a transaction without the knowledge and consent of both.

Documentary transfer tax *See* Transfer tax.

Down payment Money that you and buyers agree on, or that a lender requires, that buyers pay toward the purchase price before escrow can close.

Drawing deed fee A fee for the preparation of a deed.

Dual agent   A broker acting either directly, or through an associate licensee, as agent for both seller and buyer.

Due-on-sale clause   Alienation clause; an acceleration clause in a loan giving the lender the right to demand all sums owed due at once and payable if the property owner transfers title.

Earnest money   *See* Deposit.

Easement   The right a property owner has to use the land of another for a special purpose. It may be valid even if unidentified, unlocated, unmentioned, and unrecorded.

Emancipated minor   A person who is under the age to legally be an adult in the state in which they live but who has some other criteria that allow them to function as adults. The criteria may include being lawfully married or divorced, on duty in the armed forces, or emancipated by court order.

Eminent domain   Governments' power that allows them to take private property for public use after paying what they feel to be a fair price.

Encumbrance   A charge, claim, or lien against a property or personal right or interest in a property that affects or limits the title but does not prevent transfer.

Equity   The part of a property's current value that is owned and on which no money is owed; the property's value minus the liens owed against the property.

Escrow   A process in the transfer of real property in which buyers and sellers deposit documents or money with a neutral third party (the escrow holder). Buyers and sellers give instructions to the escrow holder to hold and deliver documents and money if certain conditions are met.

Escrow instructions   A written agreement between seller and buyer that extrapolates the purchase contract into a form used as directions on how to conduct and close the escrow.

Exclusive agency listing   A listing with only one agency that provides that if the real estate professional obtains the buyer, you must pay the broker the commission. If you sell your home yourself, you are not liable for the commission.

Exclusive right to sell listing   A listing providing that, during the time listed, only that broker has the right to sell your home and earn the commission no matter who makes the sale.

Extended coverage title insurance   This coverage protects against numerous risks that are not a matter of record.

FHA   Federal Housing Administration; a federal governmental agency that manages FHA-insured loans to protect lenders in case of default by buyers.

FHA loan   Financing by having a conventional loan made by a lender and insured by the Federal Housing Administration.

Fiduciary   A person who is in a position of trust who must act in the best interest of clients.

Fire insurance   *See* Hazard insurance.

Fixed-rate loan   A loan on which the percentage of interest remains at the same rate over the life of the loan. The payments of principal remain equal during the entire period.

Fixture   Items permanently attached to or for which special openings were made in a home and its associated structures.

Fix-up costs   The expenses of improvements, repairs, and attractiveness items.

Flood Hazard Area Disclosure   A federally required disclosure to inform buyers that the property is located in a region designated as a special flood hazard area.

Flyers   Leaflets for mass distribution.

Foreclosure   The process by which a property on which a borrower has not paid is sold to satisfy a loan against the property.

Fraud   Willfully concealing or misrepresenting a material fact in order to influence another person to take action. The action results in the person's loss of property or legal rights.

FSBO   For sale by owner; a phrase describing a homeowner selling property without using a real estate broker.

Geological inspection   Inspection for potential or actual geological problems, as well as examination of records to determine whether property falls within any special zones.

Gift deed   A deed given for love and affection.

GI loan   *See* VA loan.

Grant deed   A deed using the word *grant* in the clause that transfers ownership.

Grantee   Buyer; receiver of a title to a property.

Grantor   Seller; holder of a title to a property.

Gross income   Total income it is possible to receive before operating expenses.

Guarantee of title   A warranty that title is vested in the party shown on the deed.

Hazard insurance   Casualty insurance, fire insurance; insurance protection against stated specific hazards such as fire, hail, windstorms, earthquakes, floods, civil disturbances, explosions, riots, theft, and vandalism.

Home equity line of credit   Credit given by a lender based on the amount of one's equity in a property. The line of credit becomes a loan secured by a mortgage or trust deed when the borrower uses some or all of the credit.

Home inspection   *See* Physical inspection.

Home inspector   A qualified person who examines and reports on the general condition of a home's site and structures.

Homeowner's association dues Monthly fees owners of homes pay to their homeowner's association for the items it provides.

Homeowner's insurance   A policy protecting a homeowner from liability and casualty hazards listed in the policy. (*See also* Hazard insurance.)

Home protection plan   *See* Home warranty.

Home warranty   Home protection plan; insurance that items listed are in working order for the specified length of time.

Impounds   Reserve fund; funds held by the lender to assure payment in the future of recurring expenses. These expenses can include insurance premiums and taxes.

Improper delivery   Delivery of a deed that has not passed out of seller's control and/or was not delivered to buyers during the seller's lifetime.

Improvement costs   Expenses for permanent additions.

Improvement notices   Documents sent by governments giving notice of one-time charges for planned improvements (e.g., sidewalks).

Imputed interest rate   The minimum rate the IRS requires for a seller-financed loan. If you charge less than the minimum rate the IRS taxes you on the minimum.

Index   A measurement of interest rates on which changes in interest charges on adjustable rate loans are based.

Inspection records   Notices indicating that inspections have been conducted by the proper local authorities at certain specified points in the building process.

Inspection reports   Reports by inspectors about the condition of various aspects of your property, including defects and repairs considered necessary.

Installment note   A loan paid back in at least two payments of principal on different dates.

Installment sale   A sale that allows the seller to receive payments in more than one tax year.

Interest   A charge or rate paid in arrears (after incurred) to a lender for borrowing money.

Interest-only loan   A loan for which only the interest is paid and no principal is repaid until the final installment.

Interpleader action   Request by a closing agent or escrow holder that a court take custody of the deposited funds and make a judgment as to their distribution.

Jointly and severally liable   Liable along with other parties and personally liable.

Joint tenancy   Vesting wherein two or more parties acquire title at the same time. Each party has an equal, undivided interest and equal right to possess the property, including automatic right of survivorship.

Judgment   Final determination by a court of a matter presented to it. A general monetary obligation on all property of the person who owes the money. This obligation applies in each county where an abstract of the court judgment was recorded.

Kick-out provision   *See* Contingency release.

Lack of capacity   Inability to enter into a contract because one is not a competent person by his or her state's criteria.

Landfill   Soil moved onto the site from another location.

Landlord   The owner or lessor of real property.

Land sales contract   Contract for deed, real property sales contract; an agreement in which the seller retains title to property until the buyer performs all contract conditions.

Lease   A contract that transfers possession and use of designated property for a limited, stated time under specified conditions.

Lease option   A contract that stipulates that potential buyers are leasing a property for an agreed-on rental payment. These buyers have the right to purchase the property before the specified future date for the amount listed in the contract. Part of the lease payment is considered option money toward the purchase price.

Lease purchase   A contract that states that buyers are leasing the property for the agreed-on amount and conditions. The buyers agree to purchase the property at the agreed-on time for the agreed-on amount.

Legal description   A formal description giving a property's location, size, and boundaries in written and/or map form.

Lessee   The tenant or person who leases property from the landlord in order to use it.

Lessor   The landlord or owner of property who leases the property to the tenant for the tenant's use.

Liability   Responsibility for damages to other people or property; what you owe against an asset.

Lien   A claim against a property making the property security for debts such as loans, mechanic's liens, and taxes.

Lien releases   Documents releasing one from monetary liability to the party listed after fully paying that party.

Liquidated damages   The amount of money you may keep if the buyers default or breach the contact.

Lis pendens   An official recorded notice that legal action is pending against the title to the property.

Listing   Authorization to sell; a contract allowing a real estate broker to act as an agent to buy, lease, or sell property for another.

Litigation   Lawsuits.

Loan disclosure statement   A lender's account summary required by the Federal Truth in Lending Act.

Loan discount fee   *See* Points.

Loan fees   One-time charges by the lender for initiating a loan, including points, appraisal, and credit report on buyers.

Loan origination fee   Lender's charge for arranging and processing a loan, usually based on a percentage of the loan.

Loan tie-in fee   A fee charged by whoever handles closing for their work and liability in conforming to the lender's criteria for the buyers' new loan.

Market value   The amount buyers are willing to pay and sellers are willing to accept within a reasonable time.

Marshal's deed   *See* Sheriff's deed.

Material facts   Any facts that if known would influence a person's decision.

Mechanic's lien   A claim filed against property by a contractor, service provider, or supplier for work done or materials provided for which full payment has not been received.

Median price   The price at which half the properties are more expensive and half the properties are less expensive.

MLS   *See* Multiple Listing Service.

Mortgage   A contract to secure a loan by which you promise your property without giving up possession or title.

Mortgage default insurance   Default insurance; insurance coverage enabling the lender to receive a part of the outstanding balance in the event you default.

Mortgage disability insurance   Insurance coverage enabling you to pay monthly mortgage charges in the event you are totally and permanently disabled.

Mortgagee   Lender of money on property using a mortgage.

Mortgage life insurance   Insurance coverage enabling whomever you designate to pay the loan balance if you die.

Mortgagor   Property owner who borrows money using a mortgage.

Multiple Listing Service   MLS; an agency to which real estate brokers belong in order to pool their listings with other real estate brokers. If a sale is made, the listing and selling brokers share the commission.

Negative amortization   Process in which payments on a loan do not cover interest payments and the difference between the payment and interest due are added to the loan balance.

Net listing   A listing providing that the broker retain all money received in excess of the price set by the seller.

Net operating income (NOI)   Gross income minus operating expenses.

Nominal interest rate   Interest rate stated in a promissory note.

Nonconforming uses   Preexisting uses of land allowed to continue even though a current ordinance excluding that use has been enacted for that area.

Notary fee   A charge paid to a notary public to witness signatures on some of the legal documents in a transaction.

Notice of default   Warning sent to a borrower on a loan cautioning the borrower that the payment is delinquent.

Offset statement   A statement regarding a loan provided by the seller when a beneficiary statement is not available.

Open listing   A nonexclusive right-to-sell agreement one can make with one or more real estate professionals. It provides that if you sell your home yourself, you are not liable to the broker for a commission. If, however, a real estate professional obtains the buyers for the property, you must pay the broker the commission you have negotiated.

Operating expenses Property taxes, insurance, maintanance and utilities.

Option A contract to keep an offer to buy, sell, or lease property open for a period and under the agreed-on terms.

Optionee The person who gets the option on a property.

Optionor The owner of a title who gives an option.

Option to buy *See* Purchase option.

Payment records Checks, receipts, and written ledgers.

Payment statements Monthly stubs showing your payment date, amounts applied to principal and interest, and remaining balance due, as well as annual summary statements.

Permission-to-show listing A listing contract that allows a real estate professional to show your property only to the person or persons named in that contract. You pay the commission only if someone on the list purchases your home.

Personal property Items that are not permanently attached to your home or other structures on your property.

Pest control inspection Structural pest control inspection, termite inspection; inspection for infestation or infection by wood-destroying pests or organisms.

Physical inspection Home inspection; examination of the general physical condition of a property's site and structures.

Planned unit development PUD; a subdivision in which the lots are separately owned but other areas are owned in common.

Points Discount points, loan discount fee; a one-time charge by the lender to adjust the yield on the loan to current market conditions or to adjust the rate on the loan to market rate. Each point is equal to 1 percent of the loan balance.

Power of attorney A document that gives one person the power to sign documents for another person.

Power of sale clause A provision in a loan allowing the lender to foreclose and sell borrower's property publicly without a court procedure.

Preliminary title report Report summarizing the title search performed by a title company or lawyer for a property.

Prepayment penalty A fine imposed on a borrower by a lender for the early payoff of a loan or any substantial part of a loan.

Principal One of the parties in a real estate transaction, either the sellers or the buyers.

Principal residence An IRS term denoting the residence wherein you spend the most time during the tax year.

Probate court A court that handles wills and the administration of estates of people who have died.

Promissory note   The written contract you sign promising to pay a definite amount of money by a definite future date.

Property taxes   Taxes; taxes assessed on property at a uniform rate so that the amount of the tax depends on the value.

Property tax statements   Documents that the county assessor's office mails to homeowners itemizing the semiannual or annual tax bill on a home and indicating the payment due dates.

Prorations   Proportional distributions of responsibility for the payment of the expenses of homeownership. This distribution is based on the percentage of an assessment or billing period during which the seller and buyers own the property.

PUD   *See* Planned unit development.

Purchase contract   The contract containing terms and conditions to which you and the buyers agree when you accept the buyers' offer to purchase your home.

Purchase option   Option to buy; the type of contract in which buyers agree to purchase the property for the amount listed in the contract, if they decide to buy your home and make the purchase within the listed period of time, and agree that you keep the option fee if they do not buy the property.

Quitclaim deed   A deed using the word *quitclaim* in the clause granting ownership and thus releasing the grantor from any claim to that property. A quitclaim deed has no warranties.

Real estate   *See* Real property.

Real estate broker   A real estate agent who represents another person in dealing with third parties. This person must take required courses, pass a broker's exam, and be state licensed. A broker may employ other qualified individuals and is responsible for their actions.

Real estate professional   A real estate broker or sales associate.

Real estate sales agent   A person who is licensed by a state and who represents a real estate broker in transactions.

Real Estate Settlement Procedures Act   *See* RESPA.

Real property   Real estate; land and whatever is built on, growing on, or attached to the land.

Real property sales contract   *See* Land sales contract.

Reconveyance deed   A deed that records full satisfaction of a trust deed secured debt on your property and transfers bare legal title from the trustee to you.

Recording   Official entry of liens, reconveyances, and transactions into the permanent records of a county.

Release of contract   An agreement that all responsibilities and rights occurring as a result of a contract are invalid.

Repair costs   Expenses for work maintaining a home's condition, including replacement and restoration.

Request for notice of default   A recorded notice allowing a county recorder to notify lenders of foreclosure on a property in which the lender has an interest.

Rescind   To cancel a contract and restore the parties to the state they would have been in had the contract never been made.

Reserve fund   *See* Impounds.

RESPA   Real Estate Settlement Procedures Act; a federal law that requires that buyers be given, in advance of closing, information regarding their loan.

Restrictions   Encumbrances that limit the use of real estate by specifying actions the owner must take or cannot take on or with his or her property.

Revocation   Involuntary cancellation that occurs when the time limit has expired and one or both parties do not perform in accordance with the terms of the contract.

Sale leaseback   An agreement in which the seller sells the property to buyers who agree to lease the property back to the seller.

Sales associate   A real estate professional with either a broker's or sales license who acts as an agent for a broker.

Satisfaction of mortgage   A document indicating that you have paid your mortgage off in full.

Seller buy-down loan   A loan in which the effective interest rate is bought down (reduced) during the beginning years of the loan by contributions a seller makes.

Seller carry-back loan   A loan for which the seller acts as a lender to carry back or hold mortgage notes from buyers. These notes may be first, second, or even third loans.

Seller's agent   *See* Listing.

Seller's market   A condition in which there are more buyers than sellers; prices generally increase.

Selling agent   *See* Buyer's agent.

Setback   Laws prohibiting the erection of a building within a certain distance of the curb.

Settlement   *See* Closing.

Settling   Sinking and then coming to rest in one place.

Severalty   Vesting of title in which you hold title by yourself.

Sheriff's deed   Marshal's deed; a deed used by courts in foreclosure or in carrying out a judgment. This deed transfers a debtor's title to a buyer.

Short-sale provision   A lender reducing the amount of the loan payoff.

Single agent   An agent representing only one party in a real estate transaction.

Sliding   The large downward movement of a soil mass out of its previous position.

Slippage   The small downward movement of a soil mass out of its previous position.

Special endorsements   Specific endorsements that modify, expand, or delete the coverage of any insurance policy.

Special Studies Zone Disclosure   A form used to inform buyers that a property is in an area specified as a Special Studies Zone by California law. These zones primarily affect areas where there was or may be serious earthquake destruction.

Specific performance   Law that allows one party to sue another to perform as specified under the terms of their contract.

Standard coverage title insurance   The regular investigation for this insurance generally reveals only matters of record and location of the improvements with respect to the lot line.

Straight note   A promise to pay a loan in which the principal is paid as one lump sum, although the interest may be paid in one lump sum or in installments.

Structural pest control inspection   *See* Pest control inspection.

Subescrow fee   A fee charged by some escrow holders for their costs when they handle money.

Subject-to loan   An existing loan for which buyers take over responsibility for the payments, and seller remains primarily liable in the event of a deficiency judgment.

Survey fee   A fee charged for a survey showing the exact location and boundaries of a property.

Syndication   A form of limited partnership used to make real estate investments.

Take sheet   A form used to collect information necessary to prepare the escrow instructions.

Tax deed   Controller's deed; a deed used by a state to transfer title to the buyers.

Taxes   *See* Property taxes.

Tax parcel number   The number assigned to a piece of property by the local taxing authority.

Tax preparers   Persons who prepare tax returns.

Tax stamps   A method of denoting that a transfer tax has been paid in which stamps are affixed to a deed before the deed may be recorded.

Telephone register   A listing of information regarding telephone calls you receive.

Termination of agency   Ending of an agency agreement.

Termite inspection   *See* Pest control inspection.

Time is of the essence   A statement that one party in a contract must perform certain acts within the stated period before the other party can perform.

Title   Evidence of one's right to a property and the extent of that right.

Title insurance   The policy issued to you by the title company on completion of the final title search protecting against claims in the future based on circumstances in the past.

Title insurance companies   Companies issuing title insurance policies.

Title search An examination of information recorded on your property at the county recorder's office. This examination verifies that the property has no outstanding claims or liens against it to adversely affect the buyer or lender and that you can transfer clear legal title to the property.

Transfer fee *See* Assumption fee.

Transfer tax Documentary transfer tax; a tax that some states allow individual counties or cities to place on the transferring of real property.

Trust deed A document, used as a security device for the loan on your property, by which you transfer bare (naked) legal title with the power of sale to a trustee. This transfer is in effect until you have totally paid off the loan.

Trustee A person who holds bare legal title to a property without being the actual owner of the property. The trustee has the power of sale for the lender's benefit.

Trustee's deed A deed used by a trustee in a foreclosure handled outside of court to transfer the debtor's title to buyers.

Trust funds Funds held by a closing agent or escrow holder for the benefit of the buyers or seller.

Truth in lending A federal law that requires disclosure of loan terms to a borrower who is using his or her principal residence as security for a loan.

Unconditional lien release Waiver of liens; a release, usually signed by a contractor, after a job is complete and you made the final payments waiving and releasing all rights and claims against your home.

Unenforceable Not able to be enforced; void.

Unlawful detainer The unjustifiable keeping of possession of real property by someone who originally had the right to possession but no longer has that right.

Unmarketability of title Inability to sell property because of unacceptable encumbrances and liens on the title.

Usury Interest charged in excess of what state law permits.

VA Veterans Administration; the federal government agency that manages VA loans.

VA loan GI loan; financing made by having a conventional loan made by a lender guaranteed by the Veterans Administration.

Variance An approved release from current zoning regulations regarding the use or alteration of property.

Vendee Purchaser or buyer.

Vendor Owner or seller.

Vesting Interest that cannot be revoked.

Veterans Administration *See* VA.

Void To have no effect; unenforceable at law.

Voidable   Able to be set aside.

Waive   Unilateral voluntary relinquishment of a right of which one is aware.

Waiver of liens   *See* Unconditional lien release.

Walk-through inspection   Buyers' physical examination of a property within a few days before closing verifying that systems, appliances, and the house itself are in the agreed-on condition.

Warranties   Printed or written documents guaranteeing the condition of property or its components.

Warranty deed   A deed in which the grantor explicitly guarantees the title to be as indicated in the deed. The grantor agrees to protect buyers against all claimants to the property.

Wipe-out clause   *See* Contingency release.

Work stoppage clause   A clause in a contract giving a contractor the right to stop work if you do not make the required payments.

Wraparound mortgage   *See* All-inclusive trust deed.

Yield   The return on investment including interest and principal expressed annually.

Zoning   Governmental laws establishing building codes and governing the specific uses of land and buildings.

INDEX